MW00974695

Bad Kids...
or Bad Behavior?

Understanding and Managing
Oppositional Defiant, ADHD, Bi-Polar,
and Other Behavior Problems
in the Classroom

By Steven T. Olivas, PhD, HSP

© 2008 by Dr. Steven T. Olivas
All Rights Reserved.

No portion of this book may be reproduced in any fashion, either mechanically or electronically, without the express written permission of the author. Short excerpts may be used with permission of the author or the publisher for media reviews.

First Edition, July 2008

Printed in the United States of America on acid-free paper

ISBN 978-0-9820313-2-2

Prepress by Author's Corner, LLC; books@authors-corner.com

Cover Design and Typography by Joyce Dierschke

Published by:

Author's Corner

AUTHOR'S CORNER, LLC
7978A Coley Davis Road
Nashville, TN 37221
books@authors-corner.com • www.authors-corner.com

Table of Contents

Part III: Positive Reinforcement as a Proactive Strategy

Part IV: Ideas for the Classroom Teacher

Chapter 1

Introduction to the Real Issues

The Truth on Why You Need This Book

Sometimes the Divine Hand of Creativity will, with an audible *THUNK!* flick the top of my head and command true brilliance to fly forth from my fingertips like magma from Mt. Vesuvius. Other times (and I fear this is one of them), I sit here, staring dumbly at the blank computer screen and flashing cursor, until my hands are moved to put forth all the ideas springing from my mind.

First, thank you for picking up this book. I will do my best to impart pearls of wisdom gleaned from my years of clinical and professional experience. I have spent a number of years as a Psychologist in private practice, as a public speaker around the country, as a college professor, and even a couple of stints as an improvisational comedian. Through it all, I think I have learned a thing or two.

The reason for writing this book is really twofold: One, as a part of my seminar work with teachers and administrators around the United States, I have been asked over and over if I have a book based on the materials I teach. The answer has to this point always been a reluctant "no." I wanted to produce a book that speaks *with* you, and not *at* you. While this book will not add anything ground-breaking to the seminar, it will put the material in a format you can return to and reflect upon many times.

Second, I want to put a product out there that changes the pace and tone of most books on this topic. While troubled students bring certain seriousness into our schools and classrooms, many are truly bright, creative, and remarkable kids to deal with. Some of the most interesting and entertaining kids I have seen in therapy have been terrors in the classroom! But rather than come from a position of dire seriousness or dry data regurgitation, I want to assist in building long-term relationships with these children – while simultaneously offering some skills toward short-term classroom management.

If you will allow me a third rationale for this book, it is to offer you a different point of view. Often, books and seminars on this topic are taught by individuals who come from a straight educational background – teachers and administrators teaching teachers and administrators. Their language and nomenclature may be more in line with what you are accustomed to in your career, but they also lack some of the knowledge that may be useful and interesting to you. Hence, I will put my Psychologist stink on these pages, and give you perhaps another dimension as a different way to look at the same situations.

The book will be divided into three main sections. These follow the basic paths of *Positive Behavioral Supports (PBS)*, as I see them. In my view, PBS is founded on two basic principals: first – and perhaps most important – is the relationship you form with the student. Military experts and football coaches may disagree, but for my money, when you deal with children (big or small), a strong relationship will pay dividends that strict behaviorism will not. Relationships are built through understanding... so the first set of chapters will guide you through some of the issues these students bring to the table, and how those issues may have gotten there in the first place.

Part I will also begin to offer ideas for relationship and behavior management with the children. This keeps in line with the second PBS principal of *Proactive Positive Reinforcement*.

Part II of this book will focus briefly on *you*. My Psychologist hat may be showing itself a bit here, but I also believe what *you* bring to the classroom can have a direct effect on the behaviors you are trying to manage. Your leadership and management style will either work to quell bad behaviors before they begin, or hold a magnifying glass to them. And *nobody* wants to see *that* up close!

If you don't know what I mean by that, think back to a grouchy, grumpy, or lousy mood day you've had recently. Do the kids feel it when you are stressed out? Of course they do! Even the good kids will spin out a bit, because your style that day acts to stress out your entire class. Helping you manage and contain some of the stresses and strains of a very difficult job can pay dividends when it comes to behavior management.

And lastly, Part IV of this book will focus entirely on the Positive Reinforcement and Behavioral aspects of PBS. I know you have been taught and over-taught the PBS system, so I don't know if I can offer strokes of insight never before thought of. Still, I am going to give some basic ideas of classroom management tactics I have taught over the years, and throw in some of the great ideas I have heard from educators like you I have met in doing my seminars.

Let's tee it up and kick this seminar off. Killer instinct is required... helmets and shoulder pads optional.

Part I: Understanding the Students in Your Classroom

Chapter 2

A Brief History of Behaviorism

If Skinner Had a Greek Dog

To begin our discussion of dealing with classroom behavior through Positive Behavior Supports, we should at least get an understanding of the basic principals of behaviorism. To begin our discussion, we have to go *way* back… to ancient Greece… old school style to the teachings of a fellow named Aristotle.

Not to say that he started the ball rolling toward behaviorism per se, but he did come up with an important concept pertaining to *motivation*. And let's face it; motivation is truly the underpinning of behaviorism that we employ most in the creation of management strategies in the classroom. In other words, *"What makes these students do what they do… and more importantly, can I help them achieve their goals in more acceptable ways?"*

Enter Aristotle. He came up with a concept that was so simple, it was actually rather profound. He spoke of motivation for ALL human behavior as boiling down to the same prime mover.

He taught that, should he ask *why* you chose to do a certain behavior, you would give him an answer. Then, he would question *why* that answer is important… and you would give another answer.

He would then question *why* that answer is important, and you would give another answer. He would ask *why* again, you would answer again, and so on and so forth down the line. The place you would eventually arrive – that place where Aristotle could no longer question *why* – would be that prime mover.

And that place, according to Aristotle, is *happiness* (Aristotle, from "The Nichomachian Ethics," pp 195-196; Morgan (Ed), 2001). Aristotle philosophized that happiness was the motivator lurking behind our decision to conduct ALL behavior. Let's make this more practical to your life.

If I were to ask you *why* you are reading this book, you would probably answer something along the lines that you wanted to learn some things about classroom management. If I were to ask *why* that is important to you, you would say something about wanting to become a more effective teacher. Again, I would ask *why* that is important. We would follow this chain down to its logical conclusion, and eventually we would arrive at the place Aristotle said was the starting point for decision-making. Eventually, you would come to the conclusion that you did it *to be happy*.

Actually, today we still utilize Aristotle's idea in psychology, but we attribute it more to Carl Rogers and Abraham Maslow than Aristotle himself. You see, Aristotle's thoughts pervaded for a l-o-n-g time, but there stepped onto the scene in the early 1900's a fellow named Sigmund Freud, and all seemed to go batty for a little while. Freud was a bit dark when it came to his theories about human nature and motivation (to say the least!). In simple terms, while Aristotle felt that happiness motivates all human behavior, Freud felt that the two motivators were; 1) sex and 2) aggression (Freud, 1949).

Freud felt that each of us has a bubbling cauldron of sex and aggression in our unconscious mind, and that this cauldron is called the *id* (Freud, 1949). The id is big, and hairy, and has giant teeth that hang out of its mouth, one eye in the middle of its sloping forehead, and drags its knuckles behind it when it walks. Freud was not all that happy of a fellow, if you know what I'm saying. But, while he was vastly important in shaping the way we think about the unconscious, people tended to *poo-poo* his ideas about the role of sex and aggression in motivating behavior.

So, about twenty years later, onto the scene stepped Rogers and Maslow. (Shameless aside; I would make a wonderful joke here about how Rogers and Maslow-stein wrote Broadway Musicals, but you would probably take a minute to hold the book at arm's length and give it a puzzled look before reading on). You all remember Maslow's hierarchy, right? You memorized it for the final exam in your Intro Psych class, and then immediately forgot it because you didn't think you would ever have to use it again.

Oh, just try to tell me I'm wrong!

Anyway, if you recall, on the tippy top of Maslow's Hierarchy sat the pinnacle he felt we all strive to hit: *Self-Actualization* (Maslow, 1943). Bearing in mind that Psychologists like to use big words to mean simple concepts because it makes us feel smart when people don't know what the heck we're talking about, "Self-Actualization" just means *happiness.* Maslow got us back to basics... back to Aristotle. He and Rogers taught that we are all pushed to climb up that hierarchy... that we are all motivated to become all that we can be, and achieve the ultimate prize: happiness.

Happiness motivates all human behavior. Now, apply that same principle to some of the difficult (or angry, or tough) students in your classroom. They too are motivated by happiness, Aristotle would say. But, the world may have dealt a very different hand to them than what we have been dealt. So the way they attempt to achieve happiness may be profoundly skewed from what we consider to be "appropriate behavior." These kids may never achieve a state of joy – rather, for them "happiness" may be defined internally as *coping* or merely *surviving* the world they live in. For these kids, they may have learned to adapt to their lives in ways that are very functional where they come from, but are causing all kinds of problems in a school setting.

For example, let's examine the student from a very chaotic household. He has learned that, in order to get his needs met, he has to act out. His "Voice" has to be louder (metaphorically speaking) than the din that surrounds him. So, he throws wild temper tantrums to achieve an end for himself. At home, this is very functional behavior. He tantrums, parents give in, he gets his needs met. But now, this same child enters school. Same scenario arises, but rather than being functional in the school setting, it is remarkably disruptive.

What is the task of teaching with this student? To re-teach methods for getting needs met, but in a way that is adaptive to this setting; or any setting outside of the chaotic home. The nice thing about behavior is that it can be taught, untaught, and retaught... these processes take a lot of time and energy on the part of those who step into the role of teacher!

So let's leave Aristotle behind and fast forward about 2,000 years... to the birth of psychology as a discipline.

Around the turn of the century, there was a fellow named Pavlov who was hard at work in the former Soviet Union. All of you probably remember him, as this is what you were taught early in the semester in your Introduction to Psychology classes. He was, as you may have already surmised, the guy who became famous by working with dogs. In actuality, Pavlov was not a psychologist. He was, in fact, an investigator of natural sciences, and was interested in studying the salivation patterns of dogs (Pavlov, 1927).

Pavlov had quite an impressive laboratory, with rows of dogs in cages all along tiled aisles. Also working in the lab were assistants who were in charge of caring for and feeding the dogs. To accomplish this, they would, of course, walk up and down the aisles doling out food and well wishes. And all that time, their heels and soles would make *click-click-click* sounds along the tiled floor.

After some time, Pavlov noted something of interest starting to happen. He noticed that the dogs began to salivate when they heard the shoes *click-clicking* along the tile. Thus was the origin of behaviorism; Classical Conditioning! (Pavlov, 1927)

But there was a fundamental issue with Classical Conditioning that made it difficult to translate into anything useful for the classroom teacher reading this book today. Classical Conditioning deals only with behaviors we have absolutely no control over! Pavlov's theory only had to do with reflexes, which are behaviors that occur unbeknownst to us. Pavlov's theory comes into play more when we see some scrumptious food advertised on TV or on a poster, and our mouths begin to water. Yup, just like the dogs in the lab. When it comes to much of the advertising out there today, Madison Avenue loves to go all Pavlovian on us, the consumers, because it works.

Let's fast forward to the United States. Here, we shall get the train rolling on the behavioral theory that works to change behaviors that we *do* have conscious control over. And the fellow who opened the door to this line of thinking was actually one of the very first Psychologists in America, E. L. Thorndike.

Thorndike was looking over Pavlov's work one day, and it occurred to him that we needed something more … he wasn't too sure what that something more was, but as with most advances in science, he had to start somewhere. So, he developed another concept which, like Aristotle's 'happiness' theory, was profound in its simplicity – *The Law of Effect* (Thorndike, 1898).

What is this strange *Law of Effect*?

Thorndike postulated that if we do something, and something good occurs… we are more likely to do it again!

You can guess the other side of the coin; if we do something, and something bad occurs, we are less likely to do it again!

Pure genius! Well actually looking back, it isn't all that profound. But consider the historical context.

Thorndike's Law of Effect was important from a historical perspective because it opened the door for a guy whose work was extraordinarily pivotal when it comes to the world of classroom behavior management. A fellow whose theory you have studied and over studied as teachers; B.F. Skinner.

Even if you don't recognize the name, you will immediately recognize the framework of his theory (Holland & Skinner, 1961).

Positive Reinforcement – Positive Punishment
Negative Reinforcement – Negative Punishment

These concepts may seem very simple at face value. Or they may make you cringe, as they can be somewhat confusing – thus making them favorite exam questions of college professors everywhere. In either case, I will take a moment to define these terms, as we will be using them throughout this book.

Positive Reinforcement is probably the easiest of the four concepts, as the words all seem to make sense together. Plus, it is the one that teachers get encouraged to use most often, so I am guessing most of us are familiar with this one. Positive reinforcement means to give something good in order to increase the incidence of a particular behavior.

The student acts well, you give something he or she likes, the good behavior increases. Not too tough conceptually. Examples of positive re-enforcers are as vast as the children we use them on. Tootsie Rolls®, words of praise, good grades, smiley faces, and free time are all good examples.

And let me say a word about *time*, as this reinforcer is an oft-used go-to term for teachers everywhere. Depending on the developmental level of the students you teach, you may manipulate lunch time, recess time, computer time, free time, lab time, face time … Time! We like to use *time* because it holds two critical elements; a) it tends to work and b) we don't have to mess with huge chunks of time to make our point understood.

For example, let's say you teach third grade. If you make an 8-year-old problem child sit at your side for ten minutes during recess while his buddies are out playing kickball, he is driven bonkers and you have made your point. Of course, with some of the issues the students bring to the table (chronicled in Chapters 4 and 5), it may take multiple repetitions of the reminder or more advanced methods of behavior modification to drive the point. But the ten minutes will have an impact on most kids in a typical classroom.

Even if you are a parent, the element of time as leverage works well with kids. If you send your child to bed ten minutes early, it makes an impact – particularly if he or she has brothers or sisters who are going to *give 'em the razz*. Time is very important to kids, *especially at school*. School is where they are in their element. It is where they are on stage to impress their buddies, or the girls across the hall, or this is where the kids forge their 'rep' and fight to maintain it. Heck, time is even important to kids who are too young to tell time! Use it, and behold the wonder!

And it all takes time.

Okay, time alone will not make a big enough dent with some of your atypical students to make a notable difference. But with these children (and any advanced plan you need to incorporate), you still need to deal with the reinforcement of good and punishment of bad in smaller, day-to-day issues … it takes time and patience.

Oh, and let's not forget the biggie. The positive re-enforcer that brought all of you to education as a profession, *money!* I am quite certain that most of you got into teaching because you wanted a job that would allow you to retire at forty-five with a yacht, private jet, or second home in The South of France…

Let's cover the other three aspects of Skinner's theory (Holland & Skinner, 1961). We first covered Positive Reinforcement. Second, we have a concept that, honestly, most teachers use incorrectly. I will tell you the correct usage of *Negative Reinforcement*, and then you are free to go forth and use it any way you choose.

To begin, if I was to ask you the definition of Negative Reinforcement, you would most likely come back with some version of, "Well, if a student is acting out and I scold him, his bad behavior may actually escalate. That seems like negative reinforcement." In other words, most would agree that negative reinforcement boils down to inadvertently reinforcing a negative behavior.

At face value, this makes a good deal of intuitive sense. Acting out is negative, scolding is negative, and obviously what you are doing is reinforcing, so Negative Reinforcement seems to have all bases covered.

This is a pretty common misperception. In fact, in my seminar aimed at helping teachers learn to cope with acting out behaviors in the classroom, I used to ask teachers to define Negative Reinforcement. Overwhelmingly, the answers would come back in the direction I would predict. Today, I don't even ask, because the misuse of Negative Reinforcement is so widespread. Instead, I just jump to the punch line.

Negative Reinforcement messes with our heads a bit because it sounds like an oxymoron (i.e., how can reinforcement be negative?). Well, as is the case with reinforcement and punishment, *positive* and *negative,* do not pertain to good or bad per se. Rather, they refer to *giving* or *taking away.* When we use the word positive, it means to give. Remember that Positive Reinforcement means to *give* something good in an effort to increase good behavior? Same deal with Negative Reinforcement.

Negative Reinforcement means to *take away* something *bad* in an effort to increase good behavior.

Example: did you, or perhaps someone you knew, have a mom who would nag at you when you were a kid? I can see a few of you nodding vehemently – some with anger, some with abject sadness – as you reckon back on your childhood or teen years. As an aside, I also know the secret many of you are carrying forth from these formative experiences; now *you* have become a parent who nags! But no matter… the circle of life makes human beings somewhat predictable, if not at least a little fun to mess with from time to time.

Back to mom! What did she nag about? Nine times out of ten, the answer people shoot back is, "Clean your room!" Ah, yes… you can almost hear mom's voice echoing through the corridors of your mind as you are lost in the nerve-grating reverie that filled the soundtrack of your high school home life. What would happen to Mom's nagging behavior once that room got cleaned?

Well, presumably, mom would withdraw the nagging once she met her goal of having you clean your room. That is Negative Reinforcement… *taking away something bad in an effort to increase good behavior.*

But here is the rub; if you have a mom who nags, are you really motivated to make her happy? No, probably not. Nagging tends to bring out anger in kids. Therefore, Negative Reinforcement is never as powerful a tool as Positive Reinforcement.

Now to Punishment – again, Positive Punishment is, again, a bit of a brain twister, as those two words do not seem to fit well together in the same phrase. Following the ideology laid out in an earlier paragraph, *positive* must mean to give something; and that is exactly what we have here. Positive Punishment is *giving* something *bad* in an effort to decrease a particular behavior. And the clearest example of this is a good old fashioned spanking.

While typically frowned upon by a number of mental health professionals these days, many of us grew up with a mom or a dad (or both!) who would give a good spank once in a while. I grew up in Wisconsin, and we called it a *lickin'* in my neck of the woods. Furthermore, the worst type of lickin' was a *talkin' lickin'*. That was where your Dad would explain to you exactly why you were the recipient of said lickin' while he was perpetrating the act. From the perspective of most of my friends, we just wanted to get the lickin' over with and could really have done without the explanation.

The final piece to this puzzle is Negative Punishment, and that is the tactic all of you use in the teaching profession. Negative Reinforcement is *taking away* something *good* in order to decrease a behavior. Here again, time can be a wonderful motivator for most kids. Time, privilege, stuff, grades… all of these can be used effectively as leverage in Negative Re-enforcers.

That wraps up the history and terms of behaviorism we will be using throughout this book. Also, this supplies the "nurture" part of the nature/nurture dyad that shapes "normal" into the well-functioning human beings we are today. Look around you the next time you are roaming the hallways. Marvel at the "normal" people that surround you. In Chapter 3, we will offer explanations for abnormal behavior. Buckle up and be sure to stretch before proceeding. It is going to be a wild ride!

Chapter 3

Roots of Abnormal
Classroom Behavior

Is it Just Me, or Am I the Only Normal One in Here?

As we begin the discussion of what may cause negative, or abnormal, behavior, I will structure it a bit for you. We are going to examine a few possibilities. These include some genetic influences, some gender differences, some neurological/neurochemical possibilities, and in Chapter 4 will cover different diagnoses which can contribute to the behavior that makes you drive past the Home Depot® every day and stare lovingly whilst thinking about how nice it would be to work there instead of in your classroom…

Let's talk the "nature" part of the nature/nurture equation. Chapter 2 was all about the shaping that takes place once we are up and walking around… written, right onto the hard drive in our head when we are delivered to mom's front porch in that little kerchief tied around the stork's beak?

The answer is yes. I know this thought may be a bit unsettling to a few of you. You feel it especially strong when you go home for Thanksgiving, and spend a lot of time looking around the table trying to convince yourself that you had to have been adopted.

But there is a genetic influence to the part of personality that remains relatively stable throughout the lifespan. This part of the personality is called *temperament* (Thomas & Chess, 1977), and is even robust to changing life circumstances. In other words, you know folks in your life who are wrapped just a little tighter than most, right... whether they are having a good day or a bad day. On the flip side, you know folks around you who are pretty laid back, right? Good day or bad day, they are still going to remain more laid back than most. Unchanging across time and situation – that is *temperament*.

There was a huge study launched in the late 1950's that tried to examine if there is a static piece of personality. It ended up defining categories for folks based upon their temperaments. This study went on for decades and followed the subjects well into adulthood. It was called the New York Longitudinal Study (NYLS: Chess, Birch & Hertzig, 1960), and ended up creating four categories of temperaments.

① The first temperament category held about 40% of the folks examined, and was called "Easy." This is truly good news that came out of the study, as it was also the largest of the four categories. People with an Easy temperament tended to fall into a routine pretty easily; they tended to adapt to change well, and did not mind structure. These would be kids who, when they are babies, tend to eat at the same time, sleep at the same time, and poop at the same time... pretty easy, you know? And for school, this works well. When these kids hit school age, it hits their strength. They adapt well to the change, and do not mind the routine and structure that school imposes.

② That is the good news. There is, as you can imagine, a dark side to the force... and it is the second category called "Difficult." Some of you may know a student or two who would fall into this category. The Difficult category accounted for only 10% of the participants in the NYLS, but can certainly account for a disproportionate number of classroom issues! These are kids who do not fall into a routine very easily, who do not adapt to change very well, and who struggle against structure. These are children who drive their parents crazy when they are babies, as they will nap at noon some days, at 1:10 some days, at 2:15 some days, not at all other days... no rhyme or reason. And as you can predict, school is going to be totally against the grain for them as students. The routine, change, and structure which is no big deal to the Easy kids seems to be like brushing a dog the wrong way to the difficult ones. They fight it, as school takes them out of their comfort zone.

Before addressing the third category, I will say that the fourth and final category is sort of mishmash, as 35% of the participants in the NYLS could *not* cleanly fit into any of the first three categories. They showed signs of two or all three.

③ The third category is called "Slow-To-Warm-Up." These are kids who are genetically predisposed to being shy. And actually, the same mechanism at work behind the shy kids is also at work in grown-ups who tend to be procrastinators. I'll explain the link to shyness, and then spend a little time bailing out those of you who have worn the "Procrastinator" label for your whole life.

The mechanism behind shyness or gregariousness lies in the part of us called the *sympathetic nervous system*. What the sympathetic nervous system does (and kudos to those of you who already know this) is it activates the *fight-or-flight* response in us. The fight-or-flight response, of course, gets us amped up and ready to rock and roll when we need a burst of energy to either flee or put 'em up.

For the sake of simplicity, follow me on this next metaphor. The fight-or-flight response is triggered in each of us by a little switch in our brain. When the switch gets flipped, we get ready to rock. Our hearts beat faster, our palms sweat a little, our hands shake, our adrenaline flows, and our breath gets rapid. Have you ever been cut off in traffic and get that little sympathetic *"Charge"* shoot through your body? Most of us have had that experience. But let me ask you this; does your body like that feeling? Probably not! In some cases, it can actually *hurt*. It may feel like electricity moving through you, or a tingling in your legs and arms, or it may force you to catch your breath… but whatever the case may be, it tends to be uncomfortable. Tension is created during the sympathetic response, and the majority of us experience this as anxiety.

All of us have that little switch, but we differ in the amount of arousal it takes to flip the switch. For some, it takes very little arousal to activate the fight-or-flight response. For those folks, when they are kids, they begin to approach a new situation or a new group of kids, and their body activates. Their heart pounds, their hands sweat... they get *tense*. Of course, these kids do not like this experience, so they learn to back away to reduce the tension. And over time, they learn to not approach in the first place because of the stress it creates.

On the other hand, I am sure you all know kids who are little thrill seekers. They are the kids (or grown-ups!) who will dive into a situation first, then ask questions only after they are neck-deep in some sort of mess they can no longer get out of. Well, these folks also have a sympathetic nervous response, but it takes a *lot* of arousal to flip that switch in their brain. As a result, they do not feel the anxiety or tension that the shy kids do. They are freed up to approach and experience without anxiety.

Now a word about procrastinators... you all operate under basically the same rules as the shy and gregarious kids. And as all procrastinators will tell you, they do their best work when they feel as though their backs are against the wall. If it is not the night before the project is due, they are not sufficiently motivated to sit down and focus on the problem at hand. The 'motivation' they talk about has to do with flipping that switch. In procrastinators, it takes a lot of arousal to flip the switch in their brain that activates a sympathetic reaction that will shove them headlong into the *action* phase.

For folks who need to get the project done three months before it is actually due (procrastinators typically want to strangle these folks because they make them look bad), they operate with the same principle. It takes a lot less arousal to flip that switch, so they feel the anxiety much earlier in the process.

So procrastinators, you can tell your moms, dads, bosses and spouses that you are not lazy or bored or disinterested... you were born this way! And tell them Doctor Steve said so!

Moving on, let's talk about how gender may play a role in behavior – and specifically, bad behavior – in the classroom. Now technically, the correct term is *sex* rather than *gender*, as *sex* refers to your being physically a boy or a girl and *gender* refers to the emotional or psychological level of masculinity or femininity to which you identify. However, after the whole Freud discussion, I think it may be less confusing if we lean more away from sex as the noun, and more towards gender.

To kick off this segment, ask yourself if boys are the same as girls. Or how about this one: are men the same as women? Please remember, though, throughout this book I will be speaking in *generalities*. All of us can think of exceptions to the rules, but the rules are there for a reason: they tend to work in most instances.

We currently live in a world that is trying to force feed us political correctness, whereby everyone is supposedly the same, bearing the exact same strengths and exact same weaknesses. Unfortunately, the data just does not shake out that way. Boys and men, girls and women, do have relative strengths and weaknesses. Some of these are more evident earlier in life, some later; some of these are nature based, and others nurture; and some of these are horribly offensive to speak of in polite company, (e.g., Do men really parallel park better than women? Do women really multi-task better than men? Does either sex have any *clue* why a lousy 34-cent bag of peanuts is no longer included with a standard coach-fare ticket?).

There are indeed *brain* based differences in boys and girls, men and women. And before we even get into how this impacts your classroom, I have medical images from Harvard University that attempt to distinguish between some of the subtle differences between a man's brain and a woman's brain. These are a bit technical, but please see if you can absorb any of the relevant information before we move into a less complicated direction.

Figure 1

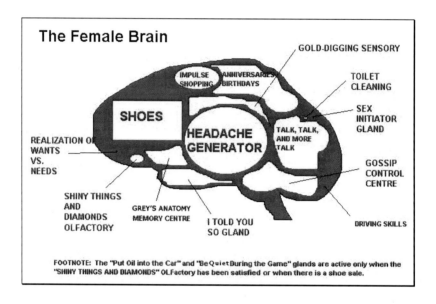

Figure 2

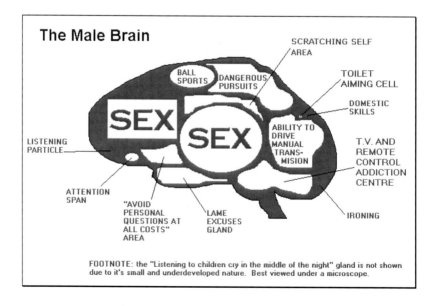

Sorry to blow your mind, but I strive to be as medically up-to-date, balanced, and politically correct as possible. Actually, I'd like to thank the awesome website www.extremefunnyhumor.com for supplying a version of those pictures.

Let's back it down a step, and talk on a more neurological level (hard science for the layman) about how boys and girls may be different in their strengths and weaknesses in the classroom.

I'll start by giving you an easy one. From a physiological perspective, girls have an advantage in the classroom when it comes to the way their ears and eyes take in a situation. In a nutshell, girls view situations more globally than boys. Boys' sensory apparatuses are built more to focus on one thing at a time (Cahill, 2005). For the classroom, the implication is pretty straight forward. If you've got a girl in the back of the room that is into something, and you are at the front of the room teaching, she is more than likely able to take in what she is looking at *and* what you are saying. But, if you've got a boy in the back of the room that is into something, and you are in the front of the room trying to teach, you might as well be on another planet – he's into what he's into… and it will be very difficult for him to follow what you are saying. With our boys in particular, having their eyes on you is of paramount importance; what he is looking at has the best shot of being what he is concentrating on! – *Have boys in front Looking @ you!*

You hear all the time that boys and men are more visual than girls and women. There is some credence to that aspersion, as what a boy is looking at is where his attention has the best shot of landing.

But rather than celebrating our differences, we are goaded into trying to ignore or deny them. Look at it this way: which babies tend to talk first, boys or girls? Who tends to read first? Write first? …Girls, girls, and girls. And that is not to say that boys do not have relative strengths when they are little tykes. Which babies tend to walk first, boys or girls? Who tends to crawl first? Run and jump first? …Boys, boys, and boys. In a nutshell, girls' brains are developing in a direction geared toward communication and boys' brains are developing more toward action. These differences are nature based, as they take place before we even have a chance to intervene and influence. I'll address our external influence later.

When it comes to applying this concept to school, think about who is going to have an easier time when they hit school age. If you said "girls," give yourself a gold star! Girls are going to have a bit of an edge when it comes to school stuff, particularly at an early age. They are going to be better at reading and writing because these activities belong to a skill set they have had more time to practice. Plus, their brains are developing more rapidly and in a more complex manner with regard to these areas than are boys (Maccoby & Jacklin, 1974).

As a result, girls score better on standardized reading and writing tests than boys (Viadero, 1998). This difference begins to even out between fourth and sixth grades, but remnants persist throughout life. Women tend to be better in areas of language application – particularly as it pertains to emotional material. I will discuss more on this later.

When it comes to nature, boys are a bit behind the 8-ball in a couple of other areas that will make school more of a challenge for them. One is ADHD (see Chapter 4 for a full description). While numbers are a bit fluid due to changes in children over time, and different methods of collecting and analyzing data are employed, the ratio of boys to girls who are diagnosed with ADHD is about 4:1 (APA, 2002). Furthermore, the ratio of boys to girls who are sent for an ADHD referral is about 6:1.

I will round out this anecdote by noting that the ratio of boys to girls when it comes to Autism Spectrum disorders is also overwhelmingly slanted toward (or against, depending upon your perspective) boys. Boys have a far higher rate of Autism Spectrum issues than do girls (Yapko, 2003). I'll throw in one more for you. The rate of students with learning disabilities is higher for boys than girls (National Health Interview Survey, 2003). Girls have a distinct advantage when it comes to operating within the parameters set forth by our school systems.

Add to that the fact that we are socializing our boys and girls differently, and we have the emergence of some true differences in the classroom, some of which may be interpreted as acting out behavior for our boys. What do I mean by that?

Take the points I made above and summarize them this way: due to developmental and neurological strengths of girls with regard to communication, and a higher incidence among boys of ADHD, LD, and Autism Spectrum, boys feel more frustration in the classroom than girls. Sounds straight forward enough, but let's look into how boys and girls handle frustration and problem-solving differently.

To begin, let's backtrack a little and switch focus from nature (brain development) back to nurture (how the world around us influences the growth of our kids). We begin by starting to examine how grown-ups interact with little ones (Hargreaves & Colley, 1986). How do we, as grown-ups, talk differently to boys and to girls? Do we even do this? I know we try not to, and may even try to convince others that we are absolutely gender-blind when we are in the presence of a toddler. While this may be so for a really small subset of us, the majority falls into the "guilty as charged" category.

It seems that when adults speak to little girls, they tend (on average) to use more words, they tend to use softer tones of voice, and their words tend to be more relationship or communication oriented. When adults talk to little boys, they tend to use fewer words, their tones tend to be a little harder, and the words tend to be more action oriented. — *How do we talk to boys vs girls*

Think about how adults *play* differently with boys and girls (Hargreaves & Colley, 1986). I think you can probably intuit this part, but I will fill in the blanks for you. The data seems clear on this issue, and I will summarize the findings in my own words: we as adults tend to play with our boys like dogs, and with our girls like cats.

You dog people know how you play with your dogs! You pull their ears, flip them over, and make them bite their own paws. Now, think about how we play with cats. We are more gentle, don't make sudden movements, and we get overly invested in little toy mice that, if alive, would be the scourge of the kitchen. Making a sudden move around a cat sends him shooting to the top of the refrigerator... where it will proceed to give you the stink-eye for two weeks.

There have been a number of studies which replicate this notion. One famous study took a group of toddlers and had adults interact with them. Then they took the children away, and brought them to a different group of adults; only this time, the kids were dressed as members of the opposite sex.

Guess what happened? The adults played rougher with the kids they perceived as boys, and more gently with those they perceived as girls.

Boys interact on a more physical level with others, and particularly with *each* other. Plus, in general, they are not taught the more subtle social skills of identifying emotions within themselves or within others. Therefore, even problem solving becomes more of a physical act for boys. Remember, girls are learning language skills more rapidly as well.

Girls just have more school-acceptable tools in their arsenal when they become frustrated or are in need of problem solving.

So let's tie this all together. You have the coming together of two issues in *any* classroom – even ones without the tougher, harder-to-deal-with students. Even among your more 'normal' kids, the boys will be more frustrated, and will have fewer options to handle those frustrations. The net result is more activity and more acting out on the part of the boys. This natural tendency – and trust me, I recognize that there are exceptions on both sides – will often test the patience of teachers who may (due to frustrations of their own) jump to conclusions about the boys that may or may not be clinically accurate. This conclusion jumping will be particularly true if the teacher is feeling stressed, depressed, overwhelmed, or nearing burnout (see Chapter 6); his or her patience will be in short supply.

I know it seems like I have spent a fair amount of space in this chapter ripping on the boys, but that is certainly not my intent. Merely, I am trying to show how some school issues may be a function of normal differences between boys and girls. Let me try to salvage some masculine dignity here before moving ahead with the chapter; men have bigger brains than women!

(Editor's note: While Dr. Steve is correct in stating the average size and weight of a man's brain is larger than the average size and weight of a woman's brain (Dekaban & Sadowsky, 1978), we here at the publishing house felt it only prudent to provide further clarity to the point. The human brain is made up of two kinds of matter: grey matter *and* white matter. *Grey matter is the part of the brain that, simply put, is involved in thinking and higher order functions. White matter is a fatty substance that acts as insulation. So, while men have bigger brains, women actually have more grey matter (Allen, et al., 2003). Women's brains are built for speed and multi-tasking, and men's brains are built for battle. Men are better able to sustain a blow to the head because they have more packing material up there!)*

Now that we I have restored the balance, let's get back to the point. I have eluded to emotions a couple of times this Chapter. For now, suffice it to say that emotionally, girls have the advantage …and boys are hampered by a phenomenon called "The Boy Code" (Kindlon & Thompson, 2000).

Picture this if you will; a 10-year-old boy is playing little league. He stands in the batter's box waving the bat menacingly in an attempt to fool everyone watching into believing he is not afraid. The pitcher rears back and, as hard as his fifth grade arm can possibly throw, lets the pitch fly with all of the laser-sharp accuracy of an airplane missing its wings, tail section, and a significant portion of the nosecone. The pitch, with a *thud* that could be heard from outer space, sinks into the batter's rib cage like a baker's fist into a mound of bread dough. Can the batter cry?

Heck no! This little guy has learned early Rule #1 of "The Boy Code"; show no pain. Or to put it metaphorically, "There is No Crying in Baseball!" And for that matter, show no hurt feelings, sadness, embarrassment, shame, etc. All negative feelings have to be protected by a shield. What is this shield? Think about the emotions that boys are taught they *are* allowed to show. More than likely, the pain the batter is feeling – and make no mistake about it, he feels *pain* – will be protected by a shield of anger.

Anger is an emotion boys are allowed (dare I say *encouraged?*) to show. When I deliver seminars to men's groups, I always open with the same line, "Men have three basic emotions ... Happy, Angry, and Horny. Everything else is protected by one of these three shields."

And it's true. Boys learn early on to not show pain. The hot little radioactive nugget of pain in that batter's gut will be protected by anger, so he will not cry. Fight back tears, sure, but he'll put on a little show that may include yelling something ugly toward the pitcher, challenging him, or at the very least giving him the stink-eye on his way down to first base. Then while standing on first, he will wear a good, stern look to once again convince the crowd that he is not a sissy. He is not hurt.

No one is worse at defining and reinforcing The Boy Code than other boys. Boys police each other closely to maintain the status quo when it comes to the rules of emotional expression. Parents, though, are not immune to this reinforcement, with Dads typically worse than Moms at honoring The Boy Code (Ruble, 1988).

In any case, The Boy Code dictates that boys learn to deal with pain through anger. And the hotter that radioactive nugget of pain sitting in his belly, the thicker the shield of anger will have to be to protect it. Now, think for a minute about the students in your classrooms who come from a train-wreck of a home. The nugget of pain they carry with them is *burning white hot*, so they have to encase it in a lead box called anger… and they do a fine job of it! Anger, toughness, or just carrying a chip on one's shoulder can result from some sort of spin-out in the home. I'll address this in more detail in the next chapter.

Shifting gears, hormones are naturally occurring chemicals in the body that play a role in growth, maturation, mood, and various other daily functions. And yes, they can have a profound impact on behavior. Even from an adult's perspective, think about how hormones can play a role in how you feel. How you feel plays a role in how you behave, doesn't it? Of course!

In our kids, there are three hormones we see as having the most impact in bad behavior. The first is a drug that (once again) our boys are saddled with ... testosterone.

Girls and women have testosterone in their bodies just as boys and men have estrogen in theirs. But throughout their lifespan, boys and men have higher circulating levels of testosterone than girls and women. And higher levels of testosterone are related to higher levels of aggression and higher activity level (Simpson, 2001). Higher testosterone makes your motor rev just a little hotter. This side effect of testosterone is evident all across the species. It is not just evident in humans.

Applying this to school, we have seen cases where elevated testosterone levels in boys take on the appearance of ADHD, as this elevation tend to make them more hyperactive and more impulsive. The physiological signs to look for are not 100% clear-cut, but typically high testosterone will affect boys rather than girls, and particularly pre-pubescent boys. These are boys who tend to be a little bigger than their same-age classmates. Or you may have a fourth or fifth grader starting to grow facial hair and appears to be revving a little hotter than peers. With these kids, again, getting a medical work-up is vital, as we can deal medically with a hormonal issue... and this will be easier than hanging a psychological diagnosis on the child. *Could this be Trevor? Bigger, delayed, onon, violent*

I will cover the other two hormones in the proceeding paragraphs, but want to issue a general heads-up to school personnel when it comes to psych diagnoses with children: almost every psychological issue in kids – particularly prior to the completion of puberty – *will look like ADHD*. I'll talk about the diagnostic process in the next chapter, but suffice it to say that hyperactivity and impulsivity are symptomatic of nearly every diagnosis, and as it pertains to the current discussion, hormonal fluctuation.

The second hormone that can have a profound impact on behavior is Thyroxine.

Thyroxine is a hormone that governs metabolism, so if kids have *hyperthyroidism*, or abnormally high levels of thyroid hormone, they will (once again) appear to have ADHD (summarized in Stein and Weiss, 2003). Their metabolism will be buzzing like a hummingbird, and they will be very prone to hyperactivity and impulsivity. These are kids who will eat two or three lunches in the cafeteria, but never gain an ounce. We had a teacher with one of these students in her room tell our private practice that she has to take her student out and, "...run him like an Alaskan Husky dog" just to burn off the excess energy so he could sit down and focus in the afternoon.

Again, these are not bad kids, but the accelerator to their motor is stuck to the floor due to hormones.

As an inside, the way Thyroxine tends to affect adults is usually in the opposite direction. For the most part, grown-ups don't complain much about extra energy and the ability to keep weight off. Where we see thyroid affecting adults who come through our practice is if they have *hypothyroidism*, or *low* levels of thyroid hormone. This condition will look, feel, and act like depression. In fact, it is a hormonally induced depression that is not related to childbirth. These grown-ups tend to be a little heavier than those around them, and will complain that it does not matter what they do, they simply cannot lose an ounce. Their metabolism, due to low hormone levels, is slogging along rather than operating at a normal speed.

Lastly, we will examine how the hormones associated with *menarche* can mimic a psych diagnosis. And for those of you without the same "Word-of-the-Day" calendar I have sitting on my desk, 'menarche' refers to the first menstrual period in a girl's life.

This issue became apparent to me after we had had a number of referrals to our office for mothers who wanted their daughters evaluated for bi-polar disorder. The girls were in the same general age range, and all were just embarking on that journey toward womanhood (if you know what I mean). Having never been an 11-year-old girl myself, I did not have a point of reference. But I did come armed with the knowledge that Bi-Polar Disorder does not typically spring out of nowhere when a girl hits puberty.

As it turns out, when a girl hits the runway leading to menarche, there is a good chance that her hormones have not quite hit their rhythm in the cycle. This actually is pretty common, but some girls can have severe fluctuations in hormones, leading to some unpredictable and at times downright *nutty* behavior! The symptoms have some common denominators if there is an imbalance that warrants attention, and these include unexplained crying spells, anger outbursts, feeling "high" some days, or bouts of truncated periods of depression. Until her body hits its stride with her cycle, she may be struggling mightily with being at the mercy of these seismic shifts in hormone levels.

To summarize the hormone section, these profound imbalances are not typical, but if they exist, can look exactly like a psychological issue. I let teachers in on this knowledge because often parents will turn to educators for some direction. Always recommend a thorough medical work-up through the Pediatrician either before we explore psychological issues, or concurrent with that exploration. If the kids are being seen or will be seen by a psychologist, this recommendation will be reinforced by one of us.

From here, we transition to speaking directly about the different psychiatric or psychological diagnoses that you may see crossing your desks. Or, they may be bandied about by colleagues, professionals, administrators… or simply by moms and dads. Even if you don't see the technical terms on any paperwork, you will probably see them play themselves out in their natural habitat – your classroom.

Chapter 4
Diagnoses Crossing Your Desk

Diagnoses of Interest to Teachers I: Learning Disabilities, ADD/ADHD, and Oppositional Defiant Disorder
Aha! I Know that Kid!

Chapter 3 covered some normal variations in behavior and then moved to addressing some physiological issues which may contribute to poor behavior. We transition now to talking a little more technically about some of the different diagnoses which you may bump into during your tenure as an educator. I will go over the symptoms which are required for a particular diagnosis, speak a little about different medications which are used to treat these issues, address the etiology of what typically leads to said diagnoses, and begin discussion of how to handle some of these kids.

Before embarking, let me say this: I will provide information on some of the medical interventions I have seen administered to my private practice clients by their physicians and/or nurse practitioners. I will say, however, that I am not a physician (a psychiatrist and a pediatrician are medical doctors). I am a *Psychologist*, so encourage everyone to speak to a physician or nurse practitioner if you have follow-up questions or concerns about medical issues brought up in the ensuing text.

Here, I will use the pronoun "he" in a generic sense. Adding to that the fact that many of the disorders I will discuss seem to lean more heavily toward boys than girls, this may not be all together inaccurate. I will, however, shift pronouns in sections where the disorder is predominantly geared toward females.

Learning Disabilities

It may seem strange to include learning disabilities in a book about behavior problems and interventions, but remember one of the themes from the gender section of Chapter 3; *frustration* can lead to all sorts of creative bad behavior. Students with learning disabilities – particularly learning disabilities which go undiagnosed – feel tremendous frustration. Believe me, the only thing worse than the feeling like you "don't get it" is feeling like everyone around you does. These kids experience this same frustration on a daily basis, and need to come up with a coping mechanism to deflect that feeling of shame. Eventually, these students learn to punt on second down... school will always be a disaster, so why bother?

At this point, many kids come to an important crossroad; "am I going to be known as the 'bad kid' or the 'retarded kid?'"

And yes, I know that all of you understand the important difference between a learning disability and mental retardation. Mental retardation is global, affecting all aspects of cognition and learning. Learning disabilities (LD) are specific to a single task of learning. Thus, we have several different categories of LD. We have disabilities specific to reading, writing, mathematics, receptive language, expressive language, and a few others which lean to the less common side of the fence.

But what *you* know to be true is not the issue... the issue comes in when we examine what the *student* knows to be true. Even though this sixth grader only has trouble with reading, he essentially *feels* retarded. And believe this; his buddies are calling him a 'retard' out on the playground. To this boy, his trouble with reading will begin to generalize to *all* aspects of school because he has find a way to cope with that awful feeling of, "I'm the only one who can't do this... and it will never get better."

This brings us back to that important crossroad. When faced with a choice of being a bad kid or looking shamefully inept in front of his classmates, the student will choose to be the *Bad Kid*. There is more dignity in being the bad kid. Plus, this label carries the added bonus of being able to get the student kicked out of the classroom if he acts out – thus deflecting the spotlight from falling directly onto his deficit instead of his newfound identity. You never have to read out loud in front of the classroom if you are in the principal's office!

The challenge for teachers is to recognize some of the warning signs for LD. Over time, you all get a sense of what the range of normal is for your grade level. For example, if you teach second grade, you know how some kids are a little slower on the uptake, some a little quicker... but there is a range of normal. If a particular student is struggling (suffering?) outside of that normal range, get Mom and Dad involved and get an evaluation underway. By fourth or fifth grade, if the LD has not been caught, kids will begin to cover their tracks and make it more and more difficult to differentiate the LD from the bad behavior.

Furthermore, once the LD child reaches middle school or high school, the horse has left the barn. It is hard to get these students back, as they have made up their minds about the success potential they don't have. The earlier we catch them, the better the prognosis.

Catching a problem early makes sense in so many arenas. Thinking specifically about learning disabilities, if a child has a learning disability in reading, can he still learn to read? Of course! What he cannot do is learn to read the way everyone else is, or at the same pace. But that's why we have reading specialists; they figure out how the student's brain works and design a program to teach him to read in a way that will stick.

I'll add one more for you to think about. We are getting better at spotting and evaluating students who have processing deficits. "Processing Deficit" has become somewhat of a catch-all category to mean that there is a slower processor chip in a specific, task-oriented part if the brain of these students (Disability Online, 2004). Again, this is a light year away from mental retardation, but still has classroom implications. These students are able to take all of the information in, but cannot process through it at the same clip that students who have a Pentium chip are able to. The deficit students have an old 486 processor rather than the Pentium!

Let me explain... We'll take a receptive language disability. For these students, they can actually *hear* every word you are saying at the front of the room. But, the part of the brain that processes incoming language (located right behind your left ear), is spinning at a slower rate. The "waiting room" of information begins to fill to capacity, and then overflows. Some of the information gets restless, and may walk out or get pushed out before it gets registered.

Thus, the *meaning* of what you are saying starts dropping out because that student understands what you are saying at a pace that leaves him about three or four sentences behind you. Over time, frustration will develop, take over, and lead that student into either drifting off, or engaging in bad behavior.

These are students who constantly feel pressure because they can be prone to panic when called upon to perform. Rather than feel like they have caught up to the flow of instruction, they feel bombarded by a barrage of words that get jumbled and tossed out of their mind.

Your ability to recognize these deficits will help tremendously stem the tide of bad behavior, as you can create a classroom environment that takes into account the differences in processing.

ADD/ADHD

Symptoms common to both ADD and ADHD (APA, 2002):

- Easily distracted, frustrated, and forgetful
- Difficulty with attention (focus), listening, organization, and follow-thru

Symptoms common to ADHD (APA, 2002):

- Fidgets, squirms, or leaves seat often

- Difficulty engaging in quiet activities

- Runs or climbs excessively when inappropriate

- Often "on the go" or acts as if driven by a motor

- Often blurts out answers of vocalizations

- Difficulty awaiting turn

- Interrupts others

As somebody in the educational field, what words spring to mind when you hear ADD or ADHD uttered?

Do you think about hyper kids – constant motion and impulsivity? Kids who drive you absolutely insane; the kind of insane that makes you actually *pick up* an application to Home Depot® to carry around with you in the car *just in case*?

Let's get down to the nitty-gritty. You are being polite because you are thinking to yourself, "Dr. Steve is a Psychologist, and may get offended if he knew *The Truth* about what comes to mind when I hear these terms." Do you during moments of weakness think one of these words or phrases to yourself – over-diagnosed, a crutch, a shield for parents, or students to hide behind, etc.?

Of course you do! ADD/ADHD has historically had a somewhat tenuous co-existence with the school systems since it exploded onto the scene in the early '90's. Some of you readers have been around long enough to recall that point in time. There was a fellow in Massachusetts named Russ Barkley wrote a hugely popular book on ADHD (Barkley, 1997), and low and behold – suddenly, every kid with a behavior problem magically became ADHD overnight. Well, so far, so good. In fact, we haven't yet come to the problematic part of the equation. I'll get there, but first we have to make a few points about the *treatment* of ADD/ADHD.

Try to think about all of the ADD/ADHD medications you can think of. A few of the most popular ones are Ritalin, Concerta,

Cylert, Focalin, Stratera, Adderall, Metadate, and a few other less common ones you may have encountered. Most of these medications fall under the broad umbrella of the popular generic drug called *Methylphenidate*. But, to ease the burden on your eyes as you read on, I'll just refer to "Ritalin" when writing about the ADD/ADHD medications, because that's the one that most all of us can relate to.

The tension between ADD/ADHD and teachers started due to a couple aspects of Ritalin. First, Methylphenidate (and all of its name-brand derivatives) is a stimulant. No, it's not like crank or speed or ecstasy or any of the dire street drugs the doomsayers want you to believe it is. But I'll say this much: it *is* a pretty strong stimulant. Certainly more than the cup of coffee some of you are enjoying as you read this. As a result, we do not want to be cavalier or haphazard in prescribing it.

Now, to the uninitiated, the concept of stimulant medication for ADHD seems to be totally ludicrous. I can hear a few of you thinking to yourselves, "Geez Dr. Steve, these kids are like ferrets on Red Bull... why the *heck* would we want to stimulate them?"

Great question... and the answers lie in the nature of ADD/ADHD as a neurochemical problem. In the brain of the ADD/ADHD person (child or adult), there is an underproduction of a certain neurotransmitter called *dopamine* (Barkley, 1997; Geller, 2003). Dopamine is a chemical that acts as a carrier pigeon in the brain; it takes messages from one brain cell to the other, thus allowing the cells to talk to each other. If we do not have enough of these carrier pigeons, our cells have a hard time communicating. They cannot huddle up and form a game plan, or line up in a cogent train of thought. Nobody knows what each other is doing up there, and we have a difficult time staying on track because all the brain cells are doing their own thing.

Ritalin signals the brain into manufacturing more dopamine, which delivers more messages. More messages being delivered means the brain cells all being aware of what their neighbors are doing. This allows them to line up as cogent trains of thought and sustained concentration. They all talk to each other, and a plan is formed.

One message I want to emphasize in this section is to encourage all of you to not throw the baby out with the bathwater. There are some students who truly have a neurochemical disorder called ADD or ADHD. For them, the medication more than likely *will work*, and will work well. I will never forget the words of a mom whose son had gone undiagnosed (and therefore untreated) until high school. When we finally began proper treatment, she said to me, "Dr. Steve, that pill is from God's hand to his tongue. The medication saved my son's academic career." These are not the kids who give teachers grey hair. The problems emerge from kids who were mis-diagnosed.

Let's say now that we have a student who is not ADHD, but rather is angry. He is defiant, stubborn, and acting out all over the place. If we hang an "ADHD" diagnosis on that kid, we start a regimen of stimulant medication. Now think this through: what happens to a kid who is angry, acting out, and now in the throes of a rather strong stimulant? You got it; *disaster*! Particularly with boys, the stimulants began to lead to increases in aggression.

For the misdiagnosed kids, the treatment actually made a bad situation worse. But there was more…

Even for the truly ADHD kids, Ritalin had another aspect that made it somewhat problematic. Back in the day, Ritalin was only a four-hour medication. As with many stimulants, Ritalin is pretty water soluble, and passes out quickly through the urine. So, a kid would take his medicine with breakfast, then peak out around 9:30 or 10:00 in the morning and begin to backslide into lunch. He would then go to the nurse's office for another dose, peak out around 1:30 or 2:00 in the afternoon, and then slide backwards into the bus ride home. These kids were still having ups and downs during their day as the medication cycled between being more and less effective.

So, you have the ADHD kids going up and down, then you have the non-ADHD angry kids being stimulated, and teachers began to shout, *"Enough Already!"* The treatment became more problematic than the problem itself!

In the past few years, we have worked out a number of the kinks with the medication side of the equation. First, we have more options than ever before. There are different derivatives of the base drugs we can try if another is not effective. Plus, we have *sustained release* (SR) and *long acting* (LA) medications, so you may not be aware of the fact that one of your students is on the medication. He will take his dose with breakfast in the morning, and it will sustain until he is home in the afternoon. Be aware that students may still be given the four-hour medication if his or her insurance dictates a specific course of treatment.

The only side effect of the stimulant medication we cannot get rid of is tied to the nature of stimulants in general; they kill an appetite. This makes sense when you consider that diet pills are all stimulants in some form or fashion. With reduced appetite, some kids will slow down on the growth curve. This will be particularly salient for kids who are younger, smaller in stature, and on higher doses of the medicine. With these kids, we tell parents a couple of things; first, be sure to watch what your child eats. He may not feel hungry as often, so you may need to be more definitive when it comes to snacks and mealtimes. Plus, unless you have a kid who is extremely impulsive and may hurt another child, or may run out into the street, or may do serious damage to property or himself, you can give him a vacation from the medicine on weekends or holidays. "How can we do this?" you may ask. Good question.

We are able to give these vacations because of another nice aspect of many of the stimulant medications. That is, they don't build up in the bloodstream like antidepressants. If you are on Prozac or Lexapro, or Wellbutrin, or any of the Serotonin-Reuptake medications for depression, you will have to take them for two or three weeks before they build up to a therapeutic level in the bloodstream. In other words, you don't take your happy pill on Monday and then start singing *Zippedy Doo Da* on Tuesday... they take awhile to work. Likewise, you cannot just stop cold-turkey from these medications. Rather, you wean off of them. There is a residue (or build up) in the body that must be accounted for.

Ritalin works in a different way. Therefore, when the child is not required to sit still or pay attention, you may be able to keep him off the medication. If you want to allow your child to be a nutty 8-year-old in the backyard on weekends or holidays, more power to you. As always; ***CHECK WITH YOUR PHYSICIAN BEFORE MESSING WITH THE MEDICATIONS, DOSAGES, OR DIRECTIONS AT ALL!*** But this information is offered as an option to discuss with the physician to help the child's appetite have an opportunity to rebound, and to not have as dramatic a slow-down in growth.

There are a number of parents who do not wish to put their children on medication. I have two children myself, and so I totally understand that point of view. We do feel responsible for protecting and maintaining the innocence of youth, and launching them prematurely into the adult world of medication seems to violate that primitive imperative. That is why I share this information with you, the educators. Sometimes, parents don't want to try medication because they are scared. They have read some horrific tidbit on the internet; or caught the tail-end of a doom-and-gloom report on television; or talked to someone at the mall who had *her* kid on medications, and the chaos that ensued… lots of bad info out there. At least if the parents make an *informed* choice, they can at least choose from the options with data in hand.

Now the big question, "If the parents of my student opt out of medical management, what do I do?" To the teachers who have non-medicated ADHD kids in their classroom, I say a couple things. First, take to heart the behavioral interventions discussed later in Chapters 13-16. Always stick to the basic premise – "Make it better to be good than to not be good." Reinforce the positive and tend to the tenants of Positive Behavioral Supports. But in addition, try to instill *self-regulation* into these students.

A good way to do this is to begin emphasizing how *you* are experiencing his or her behavior. To put this into motion, as you give the student a warning, and before the consequence is initiated, ask aloud, "What am I about to say?" Or maybe, "What am I thinking?" Help him begin to anticipate the way you are seeing his behavior. Ultimately, you would like to have his brain give birth to a

self regulation within
for him
"what"

little version of you in the back of his mind that will give him the warning to pull back on the behavior before the real you has to. The more repetition of this exercise, the better able the kids will be able to know in a moment, or with a mere look, what you are thinking, and what you are about to say. Over time, your goal is to have that self-regulatory mechanism be automatic, and not involve your intervention at all.

Another idea is to place a wedge of time between the thought and the action. With many impulsive kids, the light bulb will flash on, and they will immediately go into motion. A brief pause to allow the filter to do its job can be remarkable. For these situations, we also suggest having the students say, "One, two…" to themselves before engaging in any action. It would, if spoken aloud (which many younger kids will do!) sound something like this: "One, two… pick up my book. One, two… turn to page 37. One, two… sit down and read…" etc.

The resulting cadence will even sound somewhat rhythmic to younger kids, but again – the goal here is to wedge a beat between the thought and the action. The more you reinforce this self-management, the more entrenched the pattern of thinking and acting will become. It will not be evident 100% of the time, but the more it expands into the general patter of the student, the better the behavior will become.

Before leaving the ADD/ADHD segment of this chapter, I need to clean up a few points.

Having an ADHD student in your classroom will be relatively easy to spot. He is the one who is not terribly unlike Hammy (the Squirrel) in the movie *Over the Hedge*. The parallel is especially evident in the famous final scene, where Vern gives him a can of high-caffeine energy drink.

The "H" in ADHD actually stands for "Hyperactive." This is not the kid I want to draw your attention to… because he is already doing a bang-up job of that! Rather, I want to at least give you a heads up about the ADD (i.e., *without the "H"*) student. What does this kid look like in your classroom?

Traveling around the country doing the seminars for teachers has afforded me the opportunity to be able to anticipate a number of their reactions. And most often, when asked that very same question about how to spot an ADD student in the classroom, most teachers use the same word to describe them; *Daydreamers*.

Not a bad kid… for sure. Not a student who is doing something with a sharpened pencil to the kid in front of him. Certainly this is not the kid who is out of his chair nineteen times before lunch. Rather, this will be a student who is not on your "Behavior Problem" radar screen. He is a kid who has what I refer to as, "The Drift."

This will be a student whose attention meanders out the window for extended periods of time, or he becomes intensely interested in his thumb for a spell. Or he can't seem to tear himself away from the shoelace he seemingly forgot to tie for the 675th day in a row. Or, this is the student who magically loses a math worksheet somewhere between his desk and yours – and that sucker is *gone forever!* This is the student whose desk or locker looks as if a family of badgers has been living in it for two years.

Here's the point; this is a kid who can quite possibly slip through the cracks because he is not a behavior problem. But make no mistake: he is struggling because (to repeat) those neurons upstairs are having a hard time talking to each other due to a shortage of carrier pigeons.

I refer back to the "misdiagnosis" discussion of putting kids and teens on the wrong medication and the bad situations that can develop as a result. The main problem we have in the mental health field is properly diagnosing *children*. Once kids pass all the way through the vicious doorway of puberty, the cement in their heads begins to dry, and they look and act (from a neurochemical standpoint) more and more like grown-ups. Unfortunately, prior to that point being reached, most of the Psychiatric/Psychological diagnoses we assign actually *resemble ADHD!*

When kids get stressed, depressed, traumatized, or angry, they will spike on any subscale which measures impulsivity and hyperactivity. That is just the nature of the beast, really.

Couple that knowledge with this one: how do most kids go through the diagnostic process for determining a mental health issue?

First, mom has had enough. She has heard from the teachers, from the babysitters, from her mother, and from a slew of other folks who are trying to offer parenting advice: "Geez, you may want to get your child evaluated." So, she does what most parents do... she takes him to the pediatrician. The pediatrician, who does not have the time to get deep into the family history or observe the kid outside of the office, does the next best thing... she gives the Mom a couple of questionnaires to fill out to gain the perspective of those who have a more thorough knowledge of the child and/or the family (i.e., the mom fills one out, and *you*, the teacher, fill out the other).

A pediatrician does this *not* because she is incompetent, uncaring, or in a hurry to move on to the next patient. In general, I like pediatricians more than any other type of physician out there. They tend to be *more* caring, thorough, and helpful than any other branch of the medical field that we deal with on a daily basis. Unfortunately, they really do not have a lot of time to devote to a psychological diagnosis, but want very much to help ... hence the symptoms checklist (questionnaire).

Okay, so you fill one out, mom fills one out, the pediatrician scores them, and – go figure! There is probably a spike in the columns labeled "Hyperactivity" and "Impulsivity." So, what comes next? We try medication.

Another problem is that many parents stick with a bad situation. In other words, even if the medication is not correct, parents, for whatever reason, tend to be reluctant to bring this to the attention of health professionals. They may just keep plowing ahead with the plan.

Because so many of the diagnoses demonstrate as hyperactivity and impulsivity, ADHD tends to be the diagnosis that gets used most often. Digging into family history, observing the kids at home and at school, talking to teachers, and ruling out other possibilities are all necessary when diagnosing kids. In fact, the professionals who are (truly) in the best position to diagnose kids, short of hospitalization for more serious conditions, are either; a) somebody in private practice who can put the time into it or b) your school psychologist. Hopefully, the pediatrician will make the referral… but sadly, many parents are reluctant to follow through.

To finish and move onto the next diagnosis you may run across as an educator; let me give you a little *rah-rah*. The person whose perspective we rely on the most – believe it or not – is *you*. We do the family history and the observations, but the teacher's point of view is invaluable when it comes to helping us move through the diagnostic tree. This is true for two reasons; a) you see the kids in an environment different from where their parent sees them. You see them in a setting where they have to sit still, pay attention, get along with peers, etc. Not that Moms and Dads are biased, but your job affords you a unique perspective and b) you have a good feel for the "normal" range of behaviors for the age group you teach. Some kids are a little nuttier and some are a little steadier, but there is a range of normal. Like Learning Disabilities, if you have a student who is blatantly outside of that range, we need to know that.

And for the most part, the gut reaction of a teacher to an ADHD student is something like this, "Great kid… bright, creative, but *whew*! He wears me *out*!" And ADHD students will make you *tired*. The kind of tired that may require a bubble bath with lit candles at the end of the day just to help you recharge you battery so you are able to deal with him the next day.

Have you ever had one of those kids? Thought so!

Oppositional Defiant Disorder (ODD)

Symptoms (APA, 2002):

- Often loses temper
- Argues with adults

- Deliberately annoys others
- Is touchy or easily annoyed
- Is angry, resentful, spiteful, or vindictive
- Blames others for his or her misbehaviors
- Often actively defies or refuses to comply with rules or requests

As a rule, these are kids who come from some sort of breakdown in the authority system at home, and they are angry because of it (American Academy of Child and Adolescent Psychiatry, 1999). There may be an exception to the rule somewhere in the world, but I have not met him yet.

The breakdown in the home does not have to be abuse, alcoholism, abandonment, or any other bad word that starts with an 'a'… but it *could* be. On the other hand, it may also be a single mom who is working two jobs, and is either too tired or working too many hours to be present physically and emotionally in the home to provide the structure kids need. Or, we could have the same single mom who is very overwhelmed and depressed, and not emotionally present for the children.

Or, it might be two parents who love their child, but hate each other… so there is constant tension or bickering in the home. Kids positively *freak out* if their parents constantly quarrel.

Or, it might be two parents who dote on their children, but go overboard and end up creating narcissistic tendencies in the kids by setting the expectation that life will always give them what they want, when they want it. These are parents who dote to the point of not doing the hard part of parenting. In our private practice office, we have been seeing more and more of this. I think part of it is the new form of "keeping up with the Jones'," where parents battle each other to see who can have the kids who have the most stuff. Maybe they are trying to deal with their own feelings of inadequacy through their kids.

Part of it too is the "age of information" we live in. Ordinarily, I advocate for an informed consumer, an informed voter, an informed parent, etc. Too much information available to parents, though, can also have some adverse effects. Parents get their brains tied in knots trying to figure out what is the 'right' thing to do. As an example, think about how many sources of "Parenting Information" are available today. You have the old stand-byes of; a) your parents who relish the thought of Karmic Payback and b) everyone you come into contact with who has children of their own and therefore feel qualified to disseminate the "Wisdom" they have garnered over the years.

Add to that the fact that we now have numerous parenting magazines, Internet sites, parenting classes, and support groups at local churches. Parents are inundated with advice, so when a conflict arises at home, they can be so overwhelmed, they opt to do nothing. Or, they go to the extreme. They do something for a while, then give up and try something else before giving the first program adequate time to work; and now they're into the second program which frustrates them; and they go on to a third with remnants of the first and second still present; and so they get more frustrated, so they find a fourth and a fifth and on and on and on and on…

Listen, giving in to your kids and letting them have something they want is the easy part of parenting… we all love to see their faces light up when they are overjoyed. Even better is when WE are the reason they feel so good! But attending to limits, discipline, rules, and boundaries is the hard part – *but absolutely necessary in the social development of the children.*

Some sort of breakdown is occurring in the home, and kids start to get very anxious (Lahey & Lober, 1994). Children, be they little or big, need to feel like a grown-up is driving the bus. When that doesn't happen, and the kids feel compelled to jump into the driver's seat, they start to spin out. Kids are not emotionally equipped to handle a very heavy life-situation like that (think about why we preach to teens to *not* get pregnant!). That anxiety is obviously more pronounced and more devastating when abuse or addiction exists in the household, and will ultimately lead to resentment, particularly toward grown-ups, or authority figures, or caretakers. And guess who represents these roles in the classroom? YOU!

So remember, when you have the angry student in your classroom, it isn't about you specifically. Rather, it is rage against the figure you represent to the kid. The world has dealt them a bad hand, and they are taking it out on the people in their lives who step into the role of those who have wronged them. You ever had a student who hates you after knowing you for only eight seconds? Is that even possible? No, because again, it's not about you, but rather what you represent. You step into the stencil, and its game-on!

The anger demonstrated by these kids can be vicious at times. In fact, remember when I said ADHD kids will make you feel tired? The gut reaction of teachers to an ODD student is usually *anger*. Oppositional Defiant kids will go out of their way to make you angry – and sometimes within those first eight seconds of knowing you. This will be especially true of the ODD kids from abusive or addicted parents. While this may seem like a bizarre irony (i.e., why on earth would a child with an abusive parent become skilled at making people angry?), your anger serves two very important functions for them: a) if you are angry, that kid can predict how you are going to act and treat them. In other words, you are now on his or her playing field, and they know the rules of the game. And as an added bonus, once you are angry, they are in control of you – and remember the bus-driving example. When kids come from a home where there is chaos, they fight for control wherever and whenever they can get it. If you are angry, that kid is now yanking your chain, and is in control of you emotionally.

The second purpose is a little deeper, and has to do with intimacy. These students want you angry, because if you are angry with them, you cannot like them. And believe me; they do *not* want you to like them. Because if you like them, they may like you… and that puts you in a powerful position – you can now hurt them badly.

Let me explain. Think back in your life. Have you ever been dumped or cheated on by somebody you really loved? That hurt, didn't it! But now think back again; have you ever been dumped by someone you really didn't care about in the first place? And the only thing you could think to yourself was, "Oh thank *goodness*… that saves me an email!" That probably didn't hurt so badly. When we get close to somebody emotionally, they have power to hurt us. That is the choice we make when we give our love and trust to somebody. In fact, when I see couples for therapy, be they pre-marital couples, married spouses, or life partners, I give them the same speech about developing trust and emotional intimacy in the relationship. And that speech includes, the only way you can build trust in a relationship, the *only way* that emotional intimacy can develop, is when you begin to give your partner a chance to hurt you… and they don't. Trust and emotional intimacy can only evolve if your partner acknowledges, honors, and protects your secrets and vulnerabilities.

Now draw your attention to the angry kids again. They have been hurt badly by the people who are supposed to love, honor, and protect them above all others: their caretakers. When that breakdown occurs, these kids learn that not only is real trust with grown-ups not happening, but it is probably *impossible*.

And hearken back in your own life again… when we are little children, our parents are not just human to us; they are like *gods* to us. They are big, and strong, and they seem to know everything, and they fix things and make them better. If ever those gods die in our eyes, we are left with cynicism and anger. And there you have one destiny of the ODD child.

Okay, ADHD kids are born, but ODD kids are *created*; so that makes treatment a little different. There is not a magic pill for ODD kids. They have been developed into the little bundles of joy you are now experiencing, and now need to be re-taught. But I'm not blind to the difficulty in pulling this off. These kids are like freight trains going the wrong way – especially the ones who are in middle school or high school, and have been living the tough life for awhile now. These are kids who might be fifteen years old chronologically, but seem like grizzled, battle-field nurses from Viet Nam. They have lived three or four lifetimes in their fifteen years, and are not afraid to take that out on you.

With a runaway freight train, we can't just stop that sucker on a dime and get it motoring the other way immediately. We have to coast that thing to a stop over a long stretch of track, and then slowly build momentum in the opposite direction. Patience is crucial here, but so is perseverance. In the brief time you have this student, the *best* you may be able to do is to poke a little pinhole of sunlight in the black shroud he is metaphorically wearing over his head. The road you begin to pave may get picked up by the teacher next year, so he or she can continue to get that freight train slowed, stopped, or going the other direction. These kids were not built in a day, and it isn't going to change overnight, either!

When dealing with these students, and as always, work the reinforcement of good and punishment of bad as detailed in Chapters 13-16 of this book (this will be a recurring theme as we trudge through these diagnoses). But one additional step is going to be necessary to forge long-term change. Some of these kids have the capability to be really cool people, but have such a chip on their shoulder, they get in their own way when that little goodness tries to pop out and say hi. And let's face it, as teachers we aren't just here to teach the basics of reading and writing... we are also in this business to help shape these students into productive human beings who can get along in the world as they get older. Parenting aside, we are in a very unique position in the lives of these kids as teachers. Here's one for you; *you* might very well be the healthiest grown-up in that kid's life! Pretty heavy, eh? I know!

I'll give another one to you: for all of you male teachers out there and reading these words right now, you may not only be the healthiest grown-up in that kid's life, but you may very well be *the only adult male* in that kid's life! Male educators have the added responsibility of putting a good, decent male role model in front of these students. And kids *need* healthy males in their lives, girls as well as boys. The presence of healthy adult males is correlated with self-esteem and confidence. It allows boys to have a role model and it teaches girls how to appropriately interact with males.

With some of the angry students, we may never be able to teach them algebra, but the relationship we begin to form may keep that boy from putting a knife into some poor person at an ATM when he's nineteen... or forming a good relationship with a girl may keep her from becoming a stripper when she is seventeen. We may never know the change we initiate in the life of those kids, because we are only the source, or the beginning, of that change. Then, their new trajectory may lead them down a very different life.

It may sound pie-in-the-sky, and I know many of these tough kids will never be reached. But, the few successes we can affect changes the lives of the people around them, and will carry onward to their own children and the choices the next generations make.

How do we forge these relationships? For starters, my advice is always to abide by the three rules of dealing with Oppositional Defiant youngsters; a) go slow, b) go slow, and c) go slow.

One of the biggest mistakes teachers make when they try to strike up a relationship with a truly angry kid is to come on too strong. As adults, we can see some of the potential a student like this may have, and we want to tell them just how 'wonderful' we know they can be. But remember again the basic modus operandi of an ODD kid: *he doesn't want you to like him.* In a nutshell, he is already geared to have a hard time taking a compliment. Further, if you let the flood gates open, and try to tell him how great he is and how he can become president someday, you are going to lose him forever. Almost invariably, one thing is going to happen: he is going to mock you – either out loud or internally – for being so astonishingly dense that you fail to see how rough he is, or how tough and angry he is, or how bad his life or environment is... you basically lose your "credibility."

Compliments have to go easy. It may be somewhat insulting to think about some of our children or teens in this way, but I will risk offending you and proceed to illustrate my point. If a dog has been beaten his whole life, you don't waltz up and grab it around the neck to shower it with petting and nuzzling. That dog has not learned to trust, and furthermore, has learned to defend itself against such advances – they have ended badly in the past, with him getting hurt. Instead, go slow. Put food down to let the dog come to you on his terms, and in his time. Let him know that the door is open, but don't "force" your good intentions. That dog may never get to be 100% over his past (probably won't, actually), but he *will* learn to trust –

slowly and over time. I'll give you a couple of other pointers to help you in building relationships with ODD students in Chapter 16.

Diagnoses of Interest to Teachers II: Conduct Disorder, Bi-Polar Disorder, and Autism

Aha! I Know that Kid Too!

We have spent an entire chapter covering three of the diagnoses you will encounter in the classroom, and have spent some time discussing etiology, how they demonstrate themselves in the classroom, possible medical interventions, and began putting together a plan of action to deal with them. Let's continue that theme, and use this chapter to cover three more diagnoses: Conduct Disorder, Bi-Polar, and Autism Spectrum Disorders.

Conduct Disorder

Symptoms (APA, 2002):

- Aggression toward people and/or animals

- Destruction of property

- Deceitfulness or theft

- Serious violation of rules

ADHD students will make you tired; ODD will make you angry... Conduct Disordered kids will make you *scared*. These are the kids who make your spine tingle, as they generally make you quite confident that, should they make a threat, they *will* follow through with it. These are not kids who blow a lot of smoke.

I often refer to Conduct Disorder as "Oppositional Defiant Disorder on steroids," but there is more to it than that. Conduct Disorder is a far more dire diagnosis to give a kid, so we really try to not assign that diagnosis if at all possible. In fact, it almost implies that change is going to be next to impossible for these children. It is so heavy a diagnosis, that we as practitioners cannot (by definition of the disorder) assign the diagnosis until the child is a teenager.

The reason for such a gloomy prognosis is that Conduct Disordered folks lack an element of the human condition that makes change more likely; *empathy*. Without empathy, they do not develop a conscience. To follow this to its logical conclusion, without a conscience, they have no remorse. And lack of remorse is mainly what makes these students scary (on a primitive level) to deal with.

No good little angel sitting on their shoulder. Conduct Disordered kids typically are created from the coming together of a few forces; 1) some sort of pretty horrid abuse or neglect in childhood – which creates a sense of rage, 2) total lack of bonding with any attachment figure (i.e., caretaker) during their early years. So, what we have is a very angry child who *really doesn't care* about the people around him. He will take, hurt, and maneuver in any way he sees fit. Further, he will not have a foundational *remorse* that helps keep the rest of us at least somewhat in line.

Again, no empathy means no remorse… and no remorse means that we as therapists have no leverage to affect change, at least in the short term. In fact, these folks would never voluntarily enter into a therapeutic relationship. Almost exclusively, any therapeutic contact we have with them comes at the hands of the justice system, as court-ordered counseling is often a requirement during sentencing.

I'll go one step further. At eighteen, the diagnosis will change to the grown-up version called "Antisocial Personality Disorder" (APA, 2002; Lahey & Lober, 1994). In the vernacular, most lay people refer to people with this diagnosis as "Psychopaths," or "Sociopaths." Remember, they do not have a conscience. And the joke (if you will) among therapists is something like this; "The only therapy for an Antisocial is Jail Therapy." To reiterate, change is a very difficult process to enact if the person does not care, and really does not want to change.

I don't want to keep beating a dead horse here, but let me expound in one more direction to try to emphasize how troubled these persons are. The "red flag" we look to as evaluators when we are assessing children for a potential Conduct Disorder is the first symptom put up on the checklist of this section … cruelty toward animals. And we're not talking burning ants with a magnifying glass or ripping off the appendages of a daddy-long-legs spider on a camping trip. Rather, we are talking kids who will torture – sometimes in astonishingly sadistic ways – dogs, cats, rabbits, or squirrels. These are kids who cannot even connect with *animals*. And *that's* saying something.

Even the angriest ODD child, or to take it in another direction, the most handicapped mentally retarded or autistic kids, will usually be able to connect quite well with an animal. The angry ODD child may have a dog or a horse he really connects with. That is if it is just he and the pet, he is fine; it's *people* who drive him nuts. Or the profoundly retarded or autistic child may not be able to communicate well with people, but may well love the guinea pig in the room, or have a cat they have and hold. Kids typically find animals easier to connect to than people because animals are non-judgmental – *they love you no matter what.*

If you are a dog person, think how excited your dog is to see you when you return home from work. Yeah – the whole dog wags, not just the tail… right? And in reality, it has nothing to do with whether you had a good or a bad morning with the dog; he loves you and is delighted to see you, just the same.

For the most part, kids understand this, but Conduct Disordered kids can't. They don't have the internal structure in place to form these connections or to understand the feelings of love or bonding.

Once in awhile, somebody in a seminar will ask about the difference between Conduct Disorder, and another disorder that is tied to early caregivers; *Reactive Attachment Disorder (RAD)* (APA, 2002). Briefly, RAD is a disorder whereby a child has a poor attachment history. Adopted kids or kids raised in orphanages are often studied as examples of RAD. The main difference between a RAD child and a Conduct Disordered child is the rage that the CD kids feel. RAD kids typically do not have the history of abuse, so they proceed with life in a less destructive fashion, merely having trouble with forming relationships. They either avoid intimacy altogether, or they are very clingy with any life raft that happens to float by. This can lead to frustration and acting out, but you will not get the fear reaction that truly CD kids will give you.

So what is the implication of Conduct Disorder for the teachers in the classroom? There are a couple of things to note here. First and foremost, *protect yourself.* This sounds a bit trite, as it should be a no-brainer, but you'd be surprised. I remember one teacher in Texas telling me the story about a seventh grader who stole her identity, and then, of course, proceeded to wreak havoc for her. He was eventually caught, and when she appeared in court to testify against him, she found out that he had done the *exact same thing* to several other women. And the crown jewel of this experience for her was to see that he had absolutely no remorse for his actions, and would have probably kept on going forever had he not been caught.

So these students cannot have access to your life. This again sounds easy, but bear in mind how much personal info you share with your students. They may know the name of your spouse, your kids, where you live, where your spouse works, etc. And while it may not be possible to censor *all* of this information from your daily interactions with the rest of your class, be aware of your audience, and that these students will gladly use that information to their advantage at some point.

Last thing for you to think about with these kids: the combination of Conduct Disorder with high IQ is perhaps the most dangerous we have for children, diagnostically speaking. These will be remarkably manipulative kids who will use people up and throw them away like Kleenex when they are done. So protect yourselves, keep boundaries very clear – if you give them an inch, they will take a hundred miles. It's what they do... and no, they won't care.

Now before proceeding, let me talk you down off the ledge here. While Conduct Disorder is indeed a very dire diagnosis to hang on a kid, it is also pretty rare (around 1-4% of kids, and more prevalent in urban environments; Shaffer et al., 1996). It's easy to panic and think that your student is CD, but in actuality they are not running around everywhere we look. In fact, there has to also be some other factors involved in the etiology of CD (genetic predisposition, or maybe mitigating attachment relationships), as there are children who come from highly abusive or neglectful situations who do *not* develop CD. It may be that they are naturally more resilient, or perhaps they formed a healthy bond at some time during childhood, which, thus, helped propel them away from CD. Having said that, however, some of you do actually work in schools where you will have a higher concentration of them (i.e., if you work at a tough inner-city school or an alternative school or perhaps, teach in a juvenile justice center); but if you work at any typical mainstream campus, you won't see many of these kids.

To finish this thought, if you *ever have* had a Conduct Disordered student, you will never forget that kid. He (or she) will become an anecdote you tell for ever and ever, "amen." They will hold a special place in your history when you recount your "Tales from the Battlefield" around the water cooler or at a family get-together. Yes, these are students who leave a lasting impression, but for all the wrong reasons.

Next, we can try to do an "after-market installation" of empathy, especially if we are dealing with a younger student. I know I said earlier that you must be a teenager to receive the official diagnosis, but I am also not too dense to know that there are some younger and younger children we see who are on the royal road to Conduct Disorder. Interestingly, as we travel around the country and talk to lots and lots of teachers, we get a number of stories about kids who fall into this category. The one teacher who stands out most in my memory described an 8-year-old student in this way; "He was dead behind his eyes." I'll also never forget the details of his story. In a nutshell, he was eventually thrown into "The System" for stabbing his mother with a pair of scissors.

I make a light metaphor when I say "after-market installation," but the reality is a bit more challenging. Empathy, it turns out, is a bit like language acquisition: if you don't get it early on, the window of opportunity slams shut, and it is extremely difficult to open again. Kids with no language skills who have been discovered after the age of seven (either incidences of extraordinary neglect, or there have even been a couple of documented cases of kids *literally* raised by wolves) made only modest gains in language skills in all the time they were treated following their discovery.

As with most problems, though, the sooner you catch them, the better off you are. Here is what we advise teachers and institutions with whom we consult who have younger students that may be careening into the CD tree. When you send them off to time out or to the principal's office or wherever they happen to go, have them go through the following exercise. This is an offshoot of what many teachers are already doing. They have the student take advantage of the time away from peers to write what they did to earn the time out and what they should have done differently. With these students, I recommend adding a third component to the assignment; have them also write about... *how it made the other person feel*. Whether the wronged person was another student, or you, or the whole class... who ever it happened to be, have the kids go through the motions.

In one particular alternative school, the teachers have developed a more structured approach to helping older kids work through this same process. But, rather than having the teens write down the components, they have created a "Peace Table," where the two actors in "the incident" (i.e., whatever the outburst or transgression happened to be) sit down, and then re-create the dialogue of the incident – *but from the other person's point of view*. It works sort of like a "role reversal" made popular in marital therapy portrayed on most 70's sit-coms. The purpose is to force you into thinking and talking through the incident precisely from the other person's point of view. This is not a bad plan to accomplish with all students (not just the CD students), as it is a good exercise into understanding others. But, particularly with CD students, walk them through the motions of empathy.

That is exactly what it will be at first; the first seventy-five times (or so) the student participates in the "after market installation" strategy, he only goes through the motions. He does the assignment in a very mechanical way, because he will want to get out of whatever punishment is being initiated against him. Over time, however, you goal is eventually wear a niche into the gear in his head that helps him make decisions. In other words, through repetition, "How does the other person feel?" will become *a part* of his decision-making process rather than *incidental – or absolutely irrelevant – to it.*

Even with that strategy in place, these kids are going to be tough nuts to crack. Remember, you only have them for a few hours each day. After the bell rings, they have to go back and survive in whatever circumstance they come from each morning. But this is really the only shot you as teachers have to perhaps effect long term change. From a short term perspective, work the Positive Behavioral Supports as always, and make some inroads to build the relationship. Above all, keep your boundaries firm, and stay safe.

Bi-Polar Disorder

Symptoms in Children:

- Moods cycling faster than in adults

- High degree of irritability

- Mania and depression expressed similarly

I am going to discuss Bi-Polar disorder not so much because there is a specific course of action for teachers to follow when they are dealing with these students, but rather because this is the diagnosis I get the most questions about in the seminars. I understand why; Bi-Polar Disorder is, in my humble opinion, the new ADHD. I say that because we have seen quite a dramatic increase in the number of children being diagnosed with this disorder, despite it being a relatively new diagnostic category for children. Well, not new per se – Bi-polar in one form or another has been around forever, but the numbers of pre-adults being assigned this diagnosis has been spiking for the past few years. Historically, pediatric psychiatrists have traditionally been extremely cautious to assign this diagnosis in favor of a few others. Around the country, teachers generally agree that they are lately seeing more students with this particular diagnosis. There are some pockets of America where childhood bi-polar disorder remains relatively rare in the students, but the trend seems to be moving in the other direction. I'll give my opinions about why that is happening later on.

Let me make sure everyone knows what I am talking about here. Bi-Polar Disorder is more commonly known as "Manic Depression." This tends to be a term people relate to more readily, as the words seem self-explanatory and less like *Doctor Speak.*

I'll talk about adults separately from children, as the disorder is far easier to spot in grown-ups. In adults, as the name would imply, manic-depression is expressed with extreme mood swings, from high to low, and vice-versa. As an aside, there are actually three different types of Bi-Polar disorders we can diagnose a person with; but for now, I'll stick to full-bore bi-polar for the sake of simplicity.

These mood swings are not just having a good day or a bad day. Rather, the adult with full Bi-Polar Disorder will swing from *dizzying* highs to *devastating* lows – with very little time spent standing in the middle on "normal" ground. When an adult is in the throes of a manic episode, they are like a person shot up on an 8-ball of cocaine. They may not sleep for three or four days; they will be out detailing the car with a toothbrush; they will be doing remodeling in the house at 3:00 am; they will go on wild spending sprees, or gamble their life savings away, or go out and have a string of sexual conquests... they will be flying, flying, flying, Flying, *FLYING* until **BAM**! They swing to the other end of the spectrum.

Now, the person will not be able to get out of bed for three or four days. They will move slow, think slow, and feel that hope has been blackened by the dark ink of despair. Depression will grip them like a ball and chain.

Some bi-polar adults move through this cycle as quickly as a day or two. With some, it may take a couple of years to go through this cycle. Some Bi-Polar adults never hit the depression part of the cycle; they just go through manic episodes. There is another type of Bi-Polarity called *Cyclothymia* (APA, 2002), where the person will have the mood swings, just not to the extremes of full-blown bi-polar. These folks will still be driven nuts by their highs and lows, but will be functional in life. They are still at the mercy of their shifting neurochemistry, but they will generally be able to hold down a job, relationships, etc.

And, just so you know, the faster a person cycles, the more resistant to treatment the Bi-Polarity tends to be. Its scary stuff, as this is another disorder that is neurochemically driven; the person really does not have conscious control over the swings – medication with therapy is going to be a remarkably helpful solution.

On the other hand, children with Bi-Polar disorder do not act exactly like grown-ups with Bi-Polarity (NIMH, 2000). Thus, this has the effect of making the diagnosis, with a few exceptions for kids on the extreme ends of the spectrum, a very difficult process. In fact, I'll go one step further and say that the National Institutes of Mental Health are still working hard to make the diagnostic criteria for children more clear. We are in the infancy of this being such a popular diagnosis, and while there have been tremendous advances in our recognition of the disorder (and the medications to treat it), we still need to crawl before we walk.

For now, the symptoms we look for in children and teens have to do with extreme irritability. They just seem like they have an electric current running through them. They may explode into a temper tantrum of Biblical proportions, and then in the blink of an eye, be fine – maybe even remorseful or frightened by the fury they had just demonstrated. These are kids who can be fine one minute and over the top impulsive the next.

As was mentioned at the opening of this section in the symptom checklist, children express the mania and the depression in the exact same manner. It all seems like hyperactivity and impulsivity! These kids tend to have a little more "juice" in their acting out, though.

They have more energy or more inertia, however you want to think about it. They will also cycle faster than adults, making their behavior seem less predictable and more problematic for the classroom teacher. They may literally blow one minute and then be fine the next, leading the teacher to wonder, "What just happened?"

Also relevant when we make the diagnosis is family history. There will typically be some evidence of a family history of Bi-Polar or an anxiety disorder with these kids. That history requires a bit of digging and clarification, though, as often times emotional disturbances are known in family circles as either a dirty secret that nobody talked about, or, maybe, by other less clinical names. "Nervous breakdown" tends to be one of these semi-clinical terms that has different meanings to those who utter it! An emotional disturbance can be masked by alcoholism or other substance abuse. Drugs have a funny way of covering up symptoms, or creating new ones! Other times, the parent may not know if the adults in the family tree were on medication, or if they do know, they may not know specifically what medications they were.

And speaking of medications, here is where we start bumping into the problem again, especially with pre-puberty children. In grown-ups, the old standby for treating Bi-Polar Disorder medically has been Lithium Bicarbonate (or, most folks just refer to it as "Lithium"). We have always used Lithium because *it works*! Lithium snips off the ends of your moods, thus having a dampening effect on the highs and lows. The "worse" your Bi-Polarity, the higher the dose you are on, and the more restricted your range of emotional expression tends to be. It becomes more "truncated."

That's the good news. The bad news is that Lithium tends to be a pretty harsh drug on the body, and actually tears up the liver pretty badly. So you will have to go into see your physician at regular intervals, dependant upon the dosage you are on, to get blood drawn and check your liver enzymes. Physicians have to do a balancing act to ensure good quality of life in the present tense, but also minimize damage in the future tense.

We do have other options which have evolved over the past few years. Nowadays, we have drugs with brand names like Seroquel,

Abilify, Depakote, Zyprexa, Geodon, and Lamictal to treat this disorder. We have also seen some adolescents being prescribed Risperdal, which is also used as an anti-psychotic. And to repeat, these are some pretty heavy duty drugs we've got here. So much so that pediatricians won't generally touch a diagnosis of Bi-Polar in kids. This right has been reserved primarily for pediatric psychiatrists, who have more specialized training in understanding the impact of the medications on developing bodies.

The other thing about the mood stabilizing medications is that regardless of the level of severity, *they will work*. We can give a high enough dose that the medicine *will* knock you down a peg. You can think about their effect as being like throwing a wet towel over the brain. It will dampen emotional expression. So until we really nail down a hard-and-fast method of diagnosis, we are in danger of falling into the same trap that was sprung on ADHD in the 90's. The question thus becomes: "Are we merely masking symptoms with these medications, or are we actually treating the neurochemical imbalance with this kid?"

I'll say again, though, that I am not lacking confidence in the physicians who are on the front lines. Theirs is a very difficult job. With the development of more medications, we have more options, and we are always eager to find the one thing that works. Plus, with every generation of meds, we work out kinks and side-effects that tend to be more evident and problematic early on in medication regiments. Still, we need to crawl before we walk.

I'll close by reiterating that there is not a specific, unique course of action for teachers to take when dealing with these students aside from moving toward self-management in ways already discussed. Work the steps of PBS. If it truly is a neurochemical issue, though, self-management becomes difficult. This difficulty will be evident in adults with this disorder. Now take that and up it two or three notches for children and teenagers, who may have some difficulty with self-monitoring in the first place! Also, when thinking of a chemical issue, think about how difficult it may have been for you in the past to monitor and/or control your behavior if your chemistry was compromised by, for example, drugs, alcohol, or hormones.

Whatever the case, when you tickle the delicate balance upstairs, perception, reality, and even awareness can become skewed.

Encourage parents to get a thorough diagnosis so we know what we are dealing with, and work the program of Positive Behavioral Supports. Reinforce self-control whenever possible for these kids. Parts of the acting out will not be under their control, but the parts that are must be taught to be handled. Kids need chances to practice self-control, or cooling down, every chance they get.

Autism

Symptoms (APA, 2002):

- Marked impairment in use of nonverbal behaviors
- Failure to develop peer relationships
- Lack of seeking to share positives with other people
- Lack of social or emotional reciprocity
- Communication impairments
- Repetitive, stereotyped patterns of behavior

Because most everyone who is currently reading this book was around in the late 1980's, I think it is safe to say we all have a cultural icon when it comes to thinking about Autism. That icon is *Rainman*. Dustin Hoffman as Rainman had a significant impact on the world's understanding of autism. He put a face to a disorder that was otherwise somewhat misunderstood by most, and brought autism onto the front burner of understanding. Dustin Hoffman's portrayal made people remarkably uncomfortable, due to the extremely odd behaviors associated with the disorder; but he helped many folks have an "Aha!" moment as they now had a better grasp of what was up with someone they knew from home, work, or growing up.

Think about some of the wild behaviors that made Dustin Hoffman transform into the character of Rainman. I can hear many of you beginning to smile to yourself as you remember some of the quirky idiosyncrasies that made Rainman a delightful, if not frustrating, enigmatic figure. I'll run down a few as they pop into your mind.

When I ask this question to the groups I teach in my seminars, the most frequent first answer shouted out is something about his uncanny ability to calculate numbers or count cards or flash to the number of toothpicks on the floor. The ability Rainman had, essentially a human calculator, is called *Savantism*. Rainman was indeed an "Autistic Savant." But here's the catch – not all autistic folks are savants. In fact, it is a very low percentage.

Still, the fact that there are Savants serves as testimony to how incredible the machinery of the human brain truly is. In fact, medical science still does not know exactly what causes some Autistic folks to become Savants (Treffert & Christensen, 2005). But as science-fiction as Rainman's ability seemed to those unfamiliar with the disorder, there really are folks like him out there. Once in a while you'll see a blurb on Dateline NBC, or 20/20, or the CBS Evening News about a very special yet profoundly autistic fellow who cannot communicate effectively with the people around him, but he can play Rachmaninoff on the piano.

An amazing testament to how parts of the brain can be shut down entirely, but a spotlight of angelic grace can shine on another. So again, while savantism is what caught most of your attention when it came to Rainman, it is a rarity of the disorder. We'll turn now to the most salient symptoms.

First, and perhaps foremost, Rainman had a very difficult time connecting with other people, right? Relationships became strained almost immediately, and despite some witty banter between him and his brother, he could never connect on an emotional level.

The reason for this lies once again in the neurology and chemistry of the brain. Without going into too detailed an explanation, suffice it to say that the emotional centers of the brain do not work the same in an autistic person as they do in you and me. Emotions are not felt or understood on the same primitive level, and thereby, are rendered as rather puzzling to the autistic person. In effect, emotions become a sort of interpersonal Rubik's Cube for them to spin and try to solve. The stress caused by trying to "figure out" what other people are feeling or needing leads autistic folks to avoid the discomfort, and therefore avoid interaction.

Rainman took this avoidance as far as he could, as he would not even make eye contact with those around him. In fact, if you recall, he even walked with a bit of a slouch due to looking down at the floor all the time.

Eye contact is avoided by folks with Autism Spectrum disorders, by the way, for two primary reasons. I will hit the second in a moment, but in terms of emotion, think about eye contact as being a simple and reasonably quick communication between two people; but also as extremely emotionally intense. And if you don't believe that, seek out your spouse, partner, or other loved one and try to stare into their eyes for sixty seconds. You won't be able to do it! You'll invariably start to giggle, or may even burst out laughing. The discomfort you feel after sixty seconds is felt by Rainman after a half of a second, so he avoids the contact.

Taking the emotional issue to its logical conclusion, connect some dots. Without a basic concept of emotion, subtle social "Rules of Engagement" will also be lost on the Autistic person. Without understanding the unwritten rules of interaction (that the rest of us take for granted, and do not even think about on a conscious level anymore), interpersonal comfort becomes nearly impossible.

As an example of the "Rules of Engagement," think about how you shake someone's hand. When two people shake hands, they incorporate seven or eight rules that were learned about a hundred years ago, and never think about anymore. How far apart do you stand? Who holds out their hand first? How hard do you squeeze? What do you say? What tone of voice do you use? At what volume do you speak? All of these are things that seem easy to us, but will be troubling to an autistic person.

The second main symptom Dustin Hoffman perfected involves a trait that resembles Obsessive/Compulsive Disorder. Autistic folks require a high degree of structure and routine in their lives. Everything has to be how it has to be how it has to be. For example, where is the correct place one goes to purchase underpants for Rainman? K-Mart, I hope is your response. Further, what did Rainman have to do at 4:00 pm every day? Yup... he *had to* watch Wapner. If he did not get to watch *The People's Court*, what was the outcome? Bad times, I would say. Rainman required that structure in his life – much to the chagrin of his busy-bodied brother.

Next, Rainman had a "go-to thing" he would launch into whenever he would begin to feel anxious. He would recite something! Yes, he would launch into Abbot and Costello's *Who's on First*. Rainman would begin to feel stress, so he would separate himself from it by (metaphorically speaking) pulling his head into his shell and soothing himself with a good round of *Who's on First*.

The "go-to thing" serves as a coping mechanism when emotional arousal begins to get too high. If that arousal passes a certain point, a meltdown will ensue. Perhaps the most common reason for this overload is related to sensory input. And here is where we bring back that concept of keeping his eyes cast downward. Keeping eyes down limits the amount of sensory input buzzing around in Rainman's head.

For this brief discussion, we turn again to the brain of the Autistic person. The "filter" mechanism we have on our brain allows us to screen out most of the superfluous sensory information that bombards us every moment of every day. As I sit here writing this, I am wearing headphones (Bon Jovi's *Bounce* album playing somewhat loudly on them), I am sitting in a rather uncomfortable chair, I can hear the droning buzz of the ladies sitting playing cards at the next table, I am a little too warm, I have a full belly after a turkey sandwich and small bag of Doritos, and to top it all off, my fingertips are getting beat to heck by pounding their keystrokes on my laptop. For the most part, I am blocking these stimuli out and focusing on the words that are flowing out of my muddled brain and onto the screen. I imagine that you, too, are dealing with a number of inputs that you are filtering out so you can concentrate on the words you are reading.

Auststic folks have a difficult time weeding out the important from the background noise. Therefore, sensory input comes in at a far more intense pace than it would for us. Sights, sounds, and even touch can be overwhelming for an Autistic person. Remember the few times Tom Cruise tried to touch or hug Rainman? That was difficult for Dustin Hoffman. Or, remember the scene toward the end of the movie when the smoke alarm went off in Tom Cruise's apartment. Rainman *totally freaked out.*

As an aside, ironically, while a slight touch will make an autistic kid wince away, *overstimulation* of touch can actually trigger a calm-down reaction. I once had a teacher tell me about a student whom she could not tap on the shoulder without eliciting a harsh reaction. But that same student would at times come up to her and give her a "whole leg hug," where he would – almost literally – wrap himself around her leg. This caused him to calm significantly.

Now, unless you deal exclusively with autistic kids, you will most likely never see Rainman in your classroom. Think about how he would handle a middle school or high school hallway between classes. Kids yelling to one another... lockers slamming without rhythm... elbows ramming randomly into him... figures darting back and forth through his field of vision... in a word, *disaster!*

Or let's spin the time machine backward a bit; what is the typical kindergarten classroom like? I would venture to say that the typical kindergarten classroom is best described as *almost controlled chaos!* Kids laughing and playing... paper airplanes craftily avoiding the instructions from the flight deck... colorful, fluffy stuff hanging on the windows and from the lights... *A Very Snoopy Christmas* belting from the CD player on the teacher's desk... Rainman would be over in the corner hugging himself and rocking. He would not be able to handle the hysteria.

So, as a bridge to the next Chapter, keep in mind that most of you will not see a student who is as seriously autistic as Rainman. Nowadays however, we are thinking of Autism in a different way.

Rather than seeing it is a discreet diagnostic category (i.e., like being pregnant – you are or you are not), we see it more as lying on a continuum. On one end are folks with the more serious version of the disorder (Rainman would be an example of this), and at the other end are milder versions.

The metaphor I use to explain this phenomenon are the old, 1970's stereo rack-systems that would have a slider bar for a volume control. If the bar is slid to the right, we have Rainman... if we slide it back down toward the left, we have folks who still display all of the symptoms Rainman had, but to a much lesser extent. So, what you *will* see in your classroom with some relative frequency is that stepped-down, slider-bar-to-the-left version called *Asperger's Syndrome*. We will discuss this disorder in Chapter 5.

Chapter 5

A Few Final Psychological Possibilities for Acting-out Behavior

Hmmm... I never thought about that...

Break time is over! I would blow a loud whistle, or hit the "POP" button on the air horn I had purchased specifically to write this book... but I know it's getting late in the day. So, I'll keep it quiet. After all, we don't want the neighbors calling the cops on us or anything.

Picking up where we left off, I'll repeat the bridge so as to acclimate you to the direction we are heading. You will probably never see Rainman in your classroom, but you will likely at some point see a student with a scaled-down version of the Autism Spectrum, called *Asperger's Syndrome.*

Asperger's Syndrome (APA, 2002)

- Qualitative impairment in social functioning
- The presence of restricted, repetitive, or stereotyped behaviors and interests
- No significant delay in language
- No significant delay in cognitive development

Apserger's kids really do have about all the exact same symptoms of Rainman, but not nearly to the extreme. Thus, the

Asperger's students are able to survive school with far more ease that Rainman would have. Keep in mind however, like the rest of the Autism Spectrum, these students will also show some variability of where they hit on that slider bar. Some Asperger's kids will slide more toward Rainman's end (or, have more severe symptoms), and some will slide away from Rainman. But for those who are more toward the lesser end of the spectrum, school can be a place where they excel. In fact, these students may actually be the brightest kids in your class!

The reason they may perform at such high levels has somewhat to do with how their brain works. Think about a computer as a good analogy. In the mind of anyone on the Autism Spectrum, their mind works similar to a computer. It is logical, sequential, linear, data-driven, and tends to mimic a flowchart. I'll get to more on that in a few pages. In an Asperger's student, the same principal applies. They can have laser-beam sharp focus on topics they are interested in. And boiling the pieces and parts down to their bare essence, without the background noise of emotions and social convention to distract them, these kids can be sharp as a tack... particularly in the areas of mathematics and sciences.

And I'll go one step further. The main goal we have our sights set upon when we treat kids at the Asperger's end of the spectrum is to just help them *survive the social aspects of school!* For many of our Asperger's clients, if we can just help them limp through the dangerous waters of the elementary school, middle school, and high school social strata, they will end up fine. Once these students get out of high school and go to work – or get to college, if they choose to pursue higher education – they will be fine. They will become comfortably isolative, and excel in mechanics, engineering, the math lab or the chemistry lab or the computer lab. Whatever the case, they will arrange their life to minimize interactions with other people. In other words, they will attack with their strength, and have a high probability of success.

To further illustrate what I am saying, the world right now is actually run, pretty much, by a fellow who seems to have many of the symptoms of Asperger's Syndrome. Who, you may ask? Well, think about the person who has more power than, perhaps, anyone on earth. He is a person who has his hands in nearly everyone's cookie jar and can make changes to how we live our lives at the stroke of a hand.

That man is Bill Gates. Don't believe me? Think about this one; how many times per day, hour, or minute do you see Donald Trump mug on television? Probably too many! But how often do you even catch a *glimpse* of Bill Gates on TV? Next to never, I would imagine! That's because as undeniably brilliant as Bill Gates is when working with computers, he is remarkably uncomfortable in social settings. It takes him out of "his game." Bill Gates has extraordinary power and strengths despite his limitations. And although being the richest and most powerful man on earth probably has its perks, I would imagine that high school was a disaster for him. I recommend the Bill Gates A&E Biography (2006) for more info on his incredible life!

So finding a way to help Asperger's Syndrome students understand themselves better and weave their way through the landmines of being a school-ager can pay off in the long run. Still, due to the nature of the Autism Spectrum disorders, these kids will still bring a couple challenges to your classroom that should be treated a little differently than you would with your other mainstream kids.

There are really two issues that will be practically unique to the Asperger's student. For starters, recall some of the outrageous social faux pas that Dustin Hoffman would make as Rainman. Relationships were impossible not only because he avoided them, but also because he had a hard time "fitting in." The things he would do and the expressions he would embody were immediate beacons to the world around that he wasn't like the "rest of us."

Now, take that same concept and step it down a notch. Asperger's kids may or may not have a desire to mingle with peers, but if they do, these social interactions are going to be fraught with problems, and ultimately lead to acting out behavior as the Asperger's student becomes more and more frustrated.

To illustrate, I'll talk about one of my favorite Asperger's clients of all time; Andy (his name and a few of his characteristics have been modified slightly to protect the identity of the 'real' Andy).

Andy first came to me a few years ago when he was a fifth grader at a local elementary school. His parents were fairly well-off and tried to remain very knowledgeable in the area of Asperger's because of Andy. For this reason, I would act more as a "collaborator" with his folks, as I had an educated and cooperative ally in his treatment (a novelty for most therapy clients). Still, at times they would reach an impasse with Andy and would need my help to come up with a creative solution because they were a bit too close to the situation.

I'll talk more about one of these examples when I cover the second issue Asperger's kids bring to the classroom. For now, we'll stick with Andy and social problems.

Andy was an Asperger's client, so he had a hard time establishing connections with the kids around him. Still, he was far enough away from Rainman on the continuum that he knew he *wanted* to have a few buddies.

To complete this anecdote, you need to know one more thing about Andy. And I bring him up specifically because, not only is he my favorite client with these issues, he has a couple quirks that are very similar to Rainman, thus, making it easy to use him to demonstrate a point.

All folks on the Autism Spectrum will have a "go to thing" they will use to calm themselves under stress. Rainman recited *Who's on First,* if you recall; some kids will be more physiological, and wave or rub or flap their hands. Some will rock their upper torso slower or faster; some may have a blanket or stuffed animal or article of clothing that they will stroke or clutch for tactile comfort. Andy, like Rainman, had a recitation as his "go-to thing."

While it was no *Who's on First,* Andy had an entire episode of *Spongebob Squarepants* memorized... and it would even include commercials! For my money, there is no better form of entertainment than hearing Andy hammer that baby home! I found this quality of his to be absolutely delightful... but on the other hand, I am not a 10-year-old classmate, so perhaps my perspective is a bit skewed.

But it's not that nobody liked Andy in his class. He was a bit of a know-it-all and not afraid to point out the faults of others, but for the most part, harmless. In fact, the one word that I most often hear from classmates to describe Asperger's students is, "Weird." Andy is no different in his classroom. His peers don't hate him... but he's perceived as quite odd, and, therefore, something to be cautious around. Plus, his oddities make the kids around him feel uncomfortable, so they end up avoiding interaction with him. In the end, nobody tends to play with the "weird kid."

Let's get back to Andy's social struggles, specifically. Here is metaphorically, what would happen repeatedly in Andy's life. He would begin to approach a group of other fifth grade boys on the playground, which would immediately put them on high alert. They may have held their ground for a few beats, but they certainly began to get their hackles up internally. *"Oh geez... here comes Andy... we're supposed to play with him..."* may have been whispered between them.

Andy, who is already in uncharted waters with his initial approach, now really begins to feel anxious. So, he launches into the only thing he's got: *Spongebob Squarepants*, Episode 712 (or whichever one it was) – all the dialogue, none of the emotion.

Now, what do you suppose happened to that group of fifth grade boys? Yes, sadly, they would usually bolt. A little wisp of smoke was all that's left where they had been standing. Andy would be left rejected and frustrated. And that was one of the issues which brought him into therapy: he would have bad tantrums as he fought to contain some of the frustration spilling out.

So here is one intervention you as teachers can initiate. If you pull your student aside on a somewhat regular basis and coach him or her in some social skills training, you can have an impact. I understand, of course, that you do not have the same luxury of time or structure that we have in our therapy office. We run social skills groups where the kids can practice with each other, and go through the repetition they need for the changes to begin to stick.

There are two things to bear in mind with this suggestion: first, as I alluded to above, these kids will need a *lot* of repetition. They do not learn through observing others like you and I do. We can pick up pointers not only through direct experience, but also through watching others succeed or fail. Thus, the amount of exposure it takes for a lesson to be learned for us is sharply reduced. Asperger's kids are not as quick on the uptake in this area.

Second, bear in mind that these students will need to be nudged in directions that you and I take for granted. Simple, subtle social "rules of engagement" need to be taught. Remember the handshake example. Or how about this one: how far away do you stand from a person you are speaking to? For most of us, this is a no-brainer. For an Asperger's kid, personal space may be a rule that is totally lost on him. So, we coach… "When someone you are speaking to backs up a step, you don't keep moving forward. They are trying to establish a little extra space while they are speaking to you."

Social skills training is the first issue Asperger's students bring to the classroom, and the first point of intervention you have to truly make a long-term difference with these kids. The second has to do with that computer analogy again.

A computer basically works as a series of flowcharts. You've all seen flow charts, right? They basically list a series of "if, then" statements and "yes/no" questions, and as long as the decision boxes never hit a wall (or a "no" as the answer), the chart keeps right on flowing. The brain of an Asperger's student works much the same way. It is data driven, and the chart needs to keep flowing.

If ever he hits a wall and the flowchart comes to an end, he is forced to either adjust – to move in a different direction and start up a new series of if/then and yes/no – or drop that series entirely and go to a different flowchart. Here is the rub; if an Asperger's student reaches that wall, he can make a decision that is terribly far from where you need him to be.

I mentioned a bit earlier in this chapter that Andy and his folks would occasionally get to an impasse, during which his folks would get extremely frustrated, and they would need me to help them see their way clear of the wall. One of the issues that created an impasse with his folks (and with his teacher) was when Andy decided he was not going to do a rather significant English assignment.

I, being the astute and resourceful clinician that I am, asked a provocative and insightful question of Andy: "Why the heck aren't you doing your English assignment?" Brilliant! His answer was very telling, however, and taught me a good lesson about the legendary sense of stubbornness that Asperger's kids can have. He said, "Because... when I'm thirty five years old, nobody will care if I have done this assignment."

I was flabbergasted for a second as I tried to come up with a witty retort to his proclamation. But in the end, his logic was watertight: when we are grown-ups, nobody actually *does* care if we have completed the English assignment for Mrs. Drayna's sixth grade class. So, we cannot use pure "logic" to work our way around that flowchart wall.

And with Andy, as with many Asperger's kids, his unwillingness to do the assignment was a purely data-driven decision. It was not about defiance or anger or any of the 'traditional' reasons for our lovely children to not do what they are supposed to do. When I talked to his dad about this later, I called Andy "a mule sitting on the freeway." He would sit there, quite content, with traffic flying around him at eighty miles-per-hour... and that was okay with him. He was sitting there because that was what he decided to do. Sitting there made the most sense. Cut and dry, that was it.

So, we need to help nudge these students toward adjusting their flowchart by using a technique that forms an umbrella over simple logic; we build a broader structure. I'll explain.

Andy is not old enough, or experienced enough to understand the "big picture" nature of any grade school assignment. It feels completely random, or arbitrary. To him, there does not seem to be a long-term upside to doing the assignment, so he isn't going to do it.

For right now, it seems to Andy that the teacher gave it to him just because she gets paid to make his life miserable. To you and me, we see that this assignment is not an isolated event: rather, it is a piece to a puzzle that will eventually lead to a payoff.

So, here's how I conveyed that to Andy. One of the walls in my office is a whiteboard. I walked Andy over and did something pretty simplistic, but, likewise, effective in the long run. I simply drew two islands on the board. On one island, I drew Andy ten sitting here today in my office looking at me like I'm strange for having drawn him as a crude stick-figure. On the other island, I drew him at age thirty-five (still a stick-figure, but a little larger). Between them, I drew a bunch of circles that represented stepping stones.

I asked him what he wanted to be when he grew up, and he answered (in his 10-year-old voice), "A bio-geneticist." As it turns out, he wants to clone himself and eventually rule the earth. I gave him that one and started to move backwards, on the stepping stones, from age thirty-five to the present. I started by noting that, to become a bio-geneticist, he probably would have to go to college. He reluctantly agreed, so I wrote "College" on the stone nearest to his 35-year-old island. Next back, I predicted that in order to go to college, one probably has to get through high school. Again, he agreed. We kept working our way backwards until we found that doggone English assignment resting on one of the stepping stones nearer the present-tense island.

Now for you and me, that exercise seems to be too simplistic to actually work. With Andy, however, it had a *freeing* effect. I could almost hear the wheels turning in his head as he took in the whiteboard. Now, that English assignment fit into a whole different flow chart – one that led directly to his long-term goals. For him, that assignment was no longer "random" or "arbitrary," but a rung on a ladder. In other words, it fit into a "broader structure" for Andy. This freed up the flowchart, and he was able to again move ahead.

Make it make sense, and remember to think like a computer. And to "make sense" means that it has to appeal to the mindset of the student you are working with. Each of them has a unique perspective on the world, and unless you try on their glasses for at least a little while, you will not be able to reach them in a meaningful way.

There is actually a third issue that an Asperger's student may bring to the classroom setting, and it is a little like that stubbornness. With this one, though, neurochemistry makes a return to our discussion.

In the brain of any Autism Spectrum person and Asperger's kids are no exceptions, there is an imbalance. This imbalance particularly involves a neurotransmitter called *Serotonin,* which makes them lean naturally toward anxiety (McPartland, J. & Klin, A., 2006). Some kids have higher levels of anxiety than others, but anxiety will be an issue that each will have to learn to cope with. In fact, in the family history of these kids, you can trace an almost direct path of relatives who have likewise struggled with symptoms of anxiety – even if they were not on the Autism Spectrum per se.

With students who have high levels of anxiety, you may see them occasionally go into "vapor lock," whereby they seem to be "stuck," and cannot move ahead with their task at hand. For example, a teacher we had consulted with once asked about a client of ours that she had in her classroom. This student was taking a mid-term exam in Geometry class, and had 80 minutes to complete the task. Question number one led with an instruction for the students to draw a triangle, and then to perform some operations with it. The student in question took the entire eighty minutes to draw and re-draw his triangle – he couldn't *not* draw it perfectly. He spent his time obsessing (literally) over being perfect in his rendering.

That "loop" he was caught in is a function of chemistry, and must be treated medically. We have to adjust his chemistry to allow him to unlock and move forward. And it is not all or none – brain chemistry has fluctuations, and when these students hit a high or low tide, it can have serious implications. There is not much a classroom teacher can do to break the kids out of that loop once it has begun.

Because of this symptom, some Asperger's kids, particularly those who lean more toward the Rainman end of the slider bar, are at times mistakenly diagnosed with *Obsessive Compulsive Disorder.*

And do you remember how Rainman *had* to have everything in perfect order? Asperger's kids may have a touch of that trait as well.

Before moving from Autism Spectrum, there are a couple of other Autism diagnoses you may bump into. They are exceedingly rare, so I will only mention them in passing. They are *Rett's Syndrome* (girls) and *Childhood Disintegrative Disorder* (boys) (APA, 2002). These are the male and female version of roughly the same issue: these are children who develop normally until they are two, three, or four years old, and then backslide into an irreversible state of autism. If you teach students above the kindergarten or first grade level, this disorder will have run its course, and the kids will appear Autistic (with a couple exceptions that are unique to each of these disorders). Tuck these names into the back of your mind, as you may hear them from time to time. In my travels, it appears that more teachers have bumped into Rett's than Childhood Disintegrative.

That is all I will say about Autism Spectrum Disorders. Anything more would be beyond the scope of a book like this one. For now, I will briefly hit a few other issues which may create some behavioral issues in your classroom

Childhood depression

I want to make a couple of points about Childhood Depression (APA, 2002). I think I have made reference to it a few times over the course of these first five Chapters, so I will not belabor the point. To re-acquaint though, remember that Childhood Depression is one of the array of disorders that can *look like* ADHD, in that when kids get depressed, they tend to accelerate rather than slow down.

When a grown-up gets depressed, they move in the opposite direction, the exception being masculine depression which tends to express itself as anger or hostility. Think what a depressed grown-up looks like. They tend to look... well... *depressed.* They get lethargic, droopy, move slow, think slow, and feel a sense of hopelessness.

Kids, however, tend to spin out when they are depressed. They have all of the natural energy of an 8-year-old, coupled with a big ball of "Yuck" in their belly, and that combination leads to more energy. Hyperactivity and impulsivity are hallmarks of childhood depression.

Even for adults, though, many of the symptoms of depression can mirror ADD (minus the hyperactivity, typically). Most of us have been depressed at one point or another in our adult lives. Maybe not an ambulatory depression, but it was the doldrums nonetheless. If you can recall that event, you probably had a difficult time concentrating, you became more impulsive and more emotional, and you could not pay attention to one thing as your thoughts would wander back to the thing driving your depression… All symptoms of ADD, right? Sprinkle in a little energetic nuttiness that most kids naturally have, and – *wham-o, y*ou've got an ADHD look-alike!

However, that is not to say that a depressed child can*not* resemble a depressed grown-up. It would take a lot to suck the life out of a 7-year-old… but it can be done. We have had (I am not making this up) kids in single-digit ages who come to our office with suicidal thoughts. And some are indeed quite intent on following through with this ideation. If a depressed child looks like a depressed adult, it is a profound depression and needs immediate attention. When we see a droopy depressed child, we take it *extremely* seriously.

The two things I want to stress in this brief section are; first, if you are taking the lead in bringing these issues to the attention of the parents, please emphasize the need for a good, thorough evaluation. We want to properly diagnose so as to properly treat these kids.

And second, don't try to deal with a profound childhood depression on your own. It takes more time and energy than you can handle by yourself. Particularly for kids who come from a disaster at home, they are going to be needy and somewhat chaotic. They may tear your heart out, but surround them with as many professionals as you can to spread out the support that is needed.

Plus, with pre-puberty kids, medication for depression is not an exact science. The traditional anti-depressants don't work in as linear of a fashion with their brain chemistry, so seasoned professionals are required here. You can be the first step, but don't take it upon yourself to be the *only* step.

Angry kids, hyper kids, and nutty kids are going to afford us the luxury of *time* to deal with their issues... serious depression is another animal entirely. It brings with it a sense of urgency that the others do not.

Eating disorders

Traditionally, there have been two Eating Disorders we have studied and treated; Anorexia Nervosa, and Bulimia Nervosa (APA, 2002). Along the way, we added a couple more, with Binge Eating Disorder (APA, 2002) being the most prominent. When it comes to discussing the role that Eating Disorders may play in bad classroom behavior, I will narrow our focus to only the first two.

As another point of clarification, I will break from the structure I set up in Chapter 2 and actually use the pronoun "she" to refer to those who suffer from an Eating Disorder. While I totally understand that there are boys with Eating Disorders (it is actually a growing population), these are still, overwhelmingly, disorders that affect females (Kotler, Cohen, et al., 2001). In fact, the usual demographic for Eating Disorders remains white females aged fourteen to twenty-one. High school and college represent open windows of opportunity for the development of Eating Disorders, but we have seen younger and younger girls who are referred to us for evaluation of Eating Disorders. To date, I don't believe we have seen single digits, but it is no longer unheard of to treat ten or eleven year-old girls for symptoms resembling eating disorders.

Anorexia Nervosa: Not to put too fine a point on it, but Anorexia is a disorder whereby the sufferer does not eat. I am not going to say too much about Anorexia in this book because, frankly, it is reasonably rare. Plus, it is not too hard to spot as a lay person. If you were to have an anorexic girl in your class, you would probably see it in a second. She would look like a girl who (for lack of a better term) *looks like she doesn't eat.*

An anorexic girl will look like someone who does not eat – emaciated, gaunt, withered... all adjectives used to describe girls and women who suffer from anorexia. They do not see themselves in that way, but that's all part of the disorder.

While anorexia is easy for the teacher to spot, I'll part the therapeutic curtain a bit and let you in on a trade secret: it is *remarkably difficult* to treat. Anorexic girls tend to be proud of their "control" (i.e., not eating), and therefore have no motivation to change. Estimates range up to about 25% of Anorexics will die from the disorder (Herzog, Greenwood, et al., 2000), usually from some sort of heart failure due to low, or unregulated, electrolytes. Anorexia may appear horrific from the outside, but many choose to go down with the ship rather than change.

Bulimia Nervosa: Because this is a diagnosis that tends to get a lot of press, it has more possibility to be misunderstood. Therefore, I will open this segment with a definition. Bulimia is the Eating Disorder whereby the girls either binge and purge, or merely purge. While not all bulimics binge, there is a common denominator in the purge.

Binging, of course, is eating... and eating *a lot*. A binge is not just going and having an extra cheeseburger at McDonalds. Rather, it would be like eating an entire cheesecake or a half of a turkey... or a box of cereal and a half gallon of milk... or a loaf of bread at a single sitting. A binge can be legendary in proportion.

Following the binge comes the purge and this is where it really heats up. This is where the girl will "absolve" herself of the binge. A purge, not to put too fine of a point on it, will mean to get rid of the food.

Vomiting is the most common form of the purge, as it is relatively easy to complete, and arguably the most efficient means of removing the food. Some girls who are "good at" making themselves vomit can initiate a gag reflex simply by thinking about it – they no longer need to mechanically manipulate their throat with their finger. The trigger which controls the gag reflex can become very loose and not need physical stimulation.

But vomiting is not the only method we have seen come through our office over the years. Some prefer laxatives (we have had clients who have eaten Ex-Lax by the bar each day), some will abuse or overuse diuretics, and some will utilize a method we have seen picking up some steam in our corner of the world: Compulsive Exercise.

Exercising is not only socially acceptable, but it is actually socially *reinforced*. In order to understand how exercise can play a purge role in Bulimia, you have to understand one other thing about the disorder. Bulimia is sort of like the coming together of *Addiction* and *Obsessive Compulsive Disorder*.

The "addiction" piece of bulimia comes from the reason it exists in the first place: girls use the purge to manage and contain bad feelings – similar to any addiction. Bulimia becomes the dam which holds back the swell of anxiety or other demons lurking in the background. If you are not bulimic, this does not seem to make sense… but that's the deal.

The "Obsessive Compulsive" aspect comes into play when we discuss the binge (or binge and purge): in that they typically involve some sort of ritual, and are nearly cast in stone. When a bulimic girl gets onto the treadmill, she will probably have calculated *to the calorie* exactly what she needs to burn. And she is *not* getting off that treadmill until she hits that magic number. Other purge and/or binge routines will, similarly, have 'rules' surrounding them.

Now here is where the eating disorder can play a role in your classroom. If, for whatever reason, the girl is not allowed to complete the ritual, she will begin to spin out. The dam she uses to contain and manage bad feelings begins to crumble, and the result is spill-over of *yuck*. Maybe she was kicked off the treadmill after a certain number of minutes, maybe someone walked into the bathroom on her, maybe somebody unexpectedly invited themselves to lunch with her, maybe she was around other folks and could not binge like she needed to… something happened to interrupt that "need." Now, she will have all the anxiety of not being allowed to finish off her OCD routine coupled with all of the negative feelings she has been trying to squeeze down via the binge/purge cycle; that combination will spike her anxiety to the point that she may not be able to control it.

Hence, bad behavior may ensue. She may need to get kicked out of your classroom so she can purge (for example, hit the bathroom on the way to the principal's office), or she may just start acting out because she is feeling burdened with mounting pressure.

The problematic feature of bulimia from your standpoint as an educator is that it is the *exact opposite* of anorexia when it comes to spotting these students. What does a bulimic look like in your room? They look like everyone else – normal girls just living their lives… in desperation. From my perspective, bulimia is far nicer than anorexia in that it is easier to treat. Bulimic girls *hate* being bulimic – they feel co-morbid depression and shame almost every single time (Walsh, Roose, Glassman, Gladis & Sadik, 1985). Shame is a wonderful motivator and we as therapists use it as leverage to help pull these kids out of the mess they are feeling inside.

Because of the shame, the bulimic girl is reluctant to let anyone in on her "dirty little secret." In fact, if anyone knows, it is her best friend who has already been sworn to secrecy. Therefore, any acting out behaviors may seem like they are straight out of left field to you, the teacher. Girls who had been just fine and hitting on all eight cylinders prior to these episodes may start acting in ways contrary to what you expect, and all without explanation. In fact, these kids may have been great students prior to the new incidents because they tend to lean a little toward the compulsive side naturally.

Eating disorders, like depression, should not be taken on exclusively by you, the educator. They are complex and will require treatment that you simply cannot provide. You can be an important agent of change, and perhaps a part of her support system, but be careful to not get sucked into the vortex that will be created as she starts getting better.

Let me talk bout one more thing before leaving the kids entirely for a little while, as I turn the focus of this book onto you, the educator. One last undercurrent that can lead to behaviors which will puzzle you is *aggression*.

Aggression

Are girls mean to each other the same way as boys mean to each other? I think we can all agree that the weapon of choice for our boys to act out anger is a good old fashioned knuckle sandwich. Even if you don't see the fight happen right in front of you, you may catch wind that something is going down at recess, or you may see the storm cloud begin to build over little Johnny's head. In a nutshell, it seems pretty clear that boys are not too subtle when it comes to conflict resolution... right?

But then there are our girls. The weapon of choice for girls tends to be *words*. "Bullying" in a more masculine manner is starting to be on the rise among our girls, but social isolation and emotional torture are still mainstays and very much in order when girls go at it. In the eye of the hurricane tends to be a ringleader – a *mean girl*. The problem is that the Mean Girl is probably a sweet angel in the classroom when grownups are around... but sinister and heinous when she is around her peers.

Here is my point to his section: most of the time (yes, there are exceptions), if a boy is being picked on, he learns fast that he has to bloody somebody's nose or else he is going to be picked on for the rest of his academic career. Boys will act out, and once again, be reasonably easy to spot.

Girls, however, tend to turn victimization inward. They will develop anxiety and/or depression, and may start to act in ways you could not anticipate or explain. The girl who was *never* a problem in the past may start to miss homework assignments or have dropping quiz grades or maybe acting out against "safer" peers. The culture of aggression between girls remains hidden, and thus is harder to identify in the room.

So my advice: keep your ear to the ground with your girls. There may be an undercurrent of hostility being played out under the syrupy cover of niceties. There is a great book called *Odd Girl Out* (Simmons, 2002) that details this phenomenon in a user-friendly and readable way. That book should be read by all educators, but particularly the male teachers (who may be shocked to find out how girls do these things to each other!), as they will need to understand how this process works. Most of the female teachers know *exactly* the score of the game because they lived it in their own school experiences.

Part II: The Role YOU Play in Classroom Behavior

Chapter 6

Stress and Burnout

Why 50% of New Teachers Leave within Their First Five Years

We are going to move away from discussing the students for a little while, and focus our attention on *you,* the educators. We are going to form a basic understanding of how you can create the most advantageous atmosphere for growth in your classroom or school.

I am sure you will agree that the manner in which you carry and conduct yourself not only *can* have an impact on student behavior, but it actually *will* have an impact.

Obviously, before we even dip our big toe into this water, we need to agree upon one thing; your leadership and teaching style will not solve all of the troubles your students and you may be having. This section will not serve as the be all and end all of managing classroom misbehavior. Instead, if you follow some of the ideas and buy into the concept of adjusting your leadership style, you will position yourself in the most advantageous way to maximize the potential of your students. No behavioral plan will work unless there is strong leadership, and your kids buy into *your* plan and *your* goals. That takes some strength of character on your part! If the students – particularly some of the tough kids or angry kids – smell blood in the water, you will all lose.

We're going to begin by talking about the real "Teacher Killer," *stress*. I wasn't kidding at the top of this Chapter when I pointed out that, according to the Department of Education, 50% of new teachers will be gone before their five-year hire anniversary. In some of my many travels, I have also heard (although this is not substantiated by anything I have read) that in California, the latency is actually closer to *three* years than five.

The point being, teachers are dropping like flies. They are leaving the teaching profession, and finding other career opportunities that either pay better, or are less fraught with stress. For whatever reason, the stresses of teaching drive a lot of good folks away and *has* to turn around if we are going to initiate long-term change of the system.

Teaching has become one of the professions most prone toward burnout, as more and more gets heaped onto teachers (No Child Left Behind, State mandated testing, demanding parents, disrespectful students, etc.). Many of you are in a position or a district whereby you are *expected* to always know what to do – heck, you went to school to know this stuff! Let's face it; your schooling did not prepare you fully for the gamut of plates you now need to understand how to keep spinning. The "School of Hard Knocks" tends to be less forgiving as a guidepost, but it is the deep end of the pool where most newbies get thrown, right?

So, teachers are bailing out or performing at levels that are far under their potential. *Time* Magazine ran a cover story in early 2008 about how teaching is going to become the new Nursing – that there will be no one to meet the demand in the next ten years because the demand will far exceed the supply. The kids are suffering too, as they need the consistency of knowing you are stable from year to year – that the thing they can count on is seeing the same faces in the schoolhouse when they return from summer break.

And further, some of the roughest students we deal with are the ones who *most* need the sense of consistency from one year to the next! As teachers come and go on a merry-go-around, anxiety and stress trickle down to the students. And think about it – students who lack consistency anywhere else in their lives are most prone toward acting out when they feel flux in the school setting. If you don't want to be there, they certainly aren't going to want to either.

Stress

But let's back up a step… speaking in general terms – not even talking about teaching per se for a moment – what does excessive stress do to you as a *human being*? When I ask this during a live seminar, I get an array of answers including, makes you tired, makes you eat more, makes you eat less, gives you headaches, wears away at your marriage, etc. I always follow up by asking a simple question, "Can too much stress make you sick?"

The answer, of course, is "Yes!" (Cohen, Kessler, & Gordon, 1995). Too much stress, regardless of the source, will eventually break your body down and will make you sick. Think about it this way; there are (literally) cold and flu germs crawling all over you, all over the room you are sitting in, and even *all over this book* right now. That ghastly thought aside, how come we all don't live our lives getting sick every day?

The answer lies in your immune system. We all have little white blood cells running around our body like Pac-Men gobbling up those nasty germs. With increased stress, we start cutting down the number of Pac-Men we have, and thus grow more vulnerable to illness. More stress, fewer Pac-Men… Hence, more stress equals more sickness.

Can too much stress lead to even worse maladies like, heart disease or even *cancer*? Once again, the answer is a resounding "Yes!" (Cohen, et al., 1995).

So take care of yourselves. Your health will thank you for it with years of productivity ahead. But that's not the only reason I bring it up… too much stress, while it will make you miss more days due to illness, and perhaps eventually lead you to don the white apron and flip pancakes at Cracker Barrel®, will also make you a less effective teacher.

Stress *takes up space on your bodily hard drive*. It causes the emotional part of your brain to begin to crowd out the thinking part of your brain. With some of the difficult students we are seeing filter through our hallways nowadays, you really need all of your faculties to be working unencumbered.

The hard drive analogy may be a bit awkward, but probably not altogether inaccurate. For example, have you ever had your car break down on the way to work? That throws your whole life topsy-turvy for the day, doesn't it? Or, have you ever had a fight with your spouse or other loved one in the morning before work? That hangs with you all day, doesn't it! It's hard to concentrate on your tasks at hand when you have those types of issues spinning unabated in the background.

Those are examples of shorter-term, acute stresses. Chronic stress will wear you down over time just the same. Unfortunately, we now live in a world where chronic stresses don't fade over time or go quietly into the somber night. With cell phones, pagers, fax machines, and the ubiquitous internet, we are living on the edge Information and communications are expected to be instantaneous... anything short of that, and frustration sets in. We are living "The Need for Speed," and it's stressing us out!

Plus, all of us are someone's spouse or someone's partner, someone's parent, someone's neighbor, someone's child... we all have dinners to make, lawns to mow, mortgage payments to send, oil to change, laps to swim, calls to return, pets to care for... Goodness! It all adds up and ends up becoming the background noise that makes "living our life" interfere with "loving our life."

And that's not even mentioning some of the stresses specifically involved with being a teacher nowadays. Test scores, screwball parents, meetings, deadlines, No Child Left Behind, and paperwork can all begin to steal away your will to continue on this career path! You may find yourself actually *filling out* the Home Depot® application and tucking it in a nice manila folder *just in case!*

In Chapter 3, I referred to the Sympathetic Nervous System as being the part of us that gets us amped up and ready to rumble. On the flip side, we also have a *Parasympathetic Nervous System* that actually calms us down. When we push the button in our brain that activates the Parasympathetic Nervous Response, our bodies return to a resting state.

Care to guess the quickest and most efficient way to activate the Parasympathetic Response? It's easier than you may think. It's *a deep breath* (Brown & Gerbarg, 2005). Taking in a deep breath, and then letting it out slowly, will trigger a calm-down response, and will mollify internal stress. Have you ever had a really good yawn? How do you feel after a really good yawn? My guess is you feel very relaxed, and maybe just a little high. That deep yawn triggers the calm-down response, and your body dips into the tepid pool of tranquility.

If you're the type of person who is wrapped just a little tighter than those around you or you are in the throes of a really bad week/month/year/… lifetime? Take fifteen seconds out of your day each hour to calm yourself down. Take a breath and give yourself a fighting chance to head into the storm with your wits about you!

You do need to be able to think clearly, cleanly, and effectively to deal with classroom management issues. From a short-term perspective, a high degree ambient stress will sharply reduce your ability to be creative and flexible as the classroom situations change from moment to moment. From a long-term perspective, we need you to hang around and give these kids the consistency from year-to-year that many of them lack in their real lives. With greater turnover comes more unrest among the students.

After all, if you don't care enough to stay, why should they?

Take care of yourself. Having stressful days or occasional speed-bumps in life is not only normal, but they can also be tremendous character builders for you. It is almost nauseatingly cliché, but it does seem to bear out: nothing builds strength of character like adversity. If you are never tested, you don't have an accurate idea of *how* resilient, flexible, creative, or strong you can be.

Too much stress or adversity over extended periods of time with no hope of light at the end of the tunnel will lead to a much more serious condition. We will turn our attention to that issue now.

Burnout

Speaking in broad strokes, "burnout" refers to a condition people can grow into whereby they truly *hate* their job. It becomes a grind just to climb into the car to head off to their workplace, as most burned-out employees describe the worst part of their day as being "the drive to work."

Burnout, for lack of a better analogy, is like an occupational depression. As it becomes worse, that depression can and will begin to bleed into all aspects of the life of the burned-out person (i.e., relationships, happiness, family, etc.).

That's the bad news. And here is the worse news: once a worker arrives at "Burnout," we really can't get them back to "happy." They pass a certain point (and that point is different for different folks), and we can no longer recover a desire to remain in that job.

Here is a good example to drive home this point. I'll preface this by noting that burnout can occur in any situation where you have an emotional investment. For most of us, the greatest emotional investments we make are to the romantic interests in our life. So I ask you to reflect upon this: when you may have been a bit younger, have you ever been in a romantic relationship that you ended up burning out in? You got to the point that you were just *over it?* The point whereby you really did get irritated around the other person *just because of who they were?* Where the way they *breathed* made you want to run away screaming?

If not you, then this scenario has probably happened to a friend. When you reach that point in a relationship, it is time to break-up, right? That's the "circle of life" as early romantic relationships go. They run their course, and you end them.

Occupational Burnout is the same. Once you've lost that "lovin' feeling" for you job, it is really hard to get it back. Almost invariably, we psychologists end up doing career counseling with burned-out clients, and help them to find new careers to begin fresh rather than hang onto a declining situation.

Before proceeding, let me list and describe some of the predominant symptoms of burnout as they pertain to all workers (Greenburg, 1999). Teachers should pay particular attention, though, as their high turnover rate has been documented at the beginning of this chapter (Wood & McCarthy, 2002).

1. *Feeling like not going to work or actually missing days*

Obviously, we have *all* had days where we didn't feel like going in to work. That feeling is a part of the normal ebb and flow of life, and it does not matter if the employee in question works for Chuck E. Cheese® or The Supreme Court; we have all experienced that feeling.

What this symptom refers to, however, is not an acute state of "Holy cow, the weather is so nice out today." Rather, it is a chronic shard in the pit of your stomach whenever you think about being at work. It is calling in sick not so much because you're ill, but because you're sick of the gig. It's finding any excuse to leave or not go in the first place. It's you not wanting to choke down a final cup of sorrow before slogging your way to the job you hate.

And the difference between true burnout and just having a bad run is *hope*. If you can still hang on to some perspective and feel as though it is bound to get better next year or the year after, then you are not burned out yet. If, however, you feel as though this will never get better, then you are burning out.

2. *Difficulty concentrating on tasks*

Here is a prime example of how occupational depression and personal depression begin to resemble one another. With this symptom, your mind has trouble latching onto the task at hand because you *hate it*. You may not have descended to the "hate" level yet, but you are exhausted and are losing your ability to care anymore.

3. *Feeling overwhelmed by the workload, with a related sense of inadequacy*

The inadequacy and feeling overwhelmed typically stems from the sense of hopelessness you have with burnout. If the snow keeps falling, you never feel like you can *ever* shovel your way out. So you begin to develop resignation with the sense of being buried. When that happens, you turn on yourself and feel it is somehow linked to your inabilities or inadequacies that you are in this situation – or, that you are stuck with such a lousy job in the first place.

I always think of this symptom in the same vein as I conceptualize abusive relationships. Obviously, creating the mindset and esteem levels of a person who enters into abusive relationships is remarkably more complicated than this, but follow me for a bit on simplifying this one for the sake of the metaphor. The person being abused, in order to rationalize why they are in this relationship in the first place, comes up with idea that they are to blame. They believe that somehow, if they were a better person if they could just make changes if they could just have chosen a better partner to begin with... *then* they could make it work. But, with all of those "ifs" in place, they are buried and hopeless. Incidentally, this rationalization is also an attempt to regain some control over an out-of-control situation – i.e., if it is *my* fault, than I have some power to change.

This sounds like an odd stretch, but folks continuing on in a bad burnout job *do* feel abused by that job. The absence of hope leads to all kinds of negatively spiraling thoughts.

4. Withdrawing from colleagues or maintaining conflict with co-workers

This one is pretty self-explanatory. Withdrawal is the manifestation of "circling the wagons" as one feels bludgeoned by the job. At some level, these folks would like connection, but feel as though nobody will understand what they are going through. Plus, the irritation and agitation they feel on the jobsite must be kept at bay – thus, the person does not want anyone to even approach or ask about their pain for fear that the dark tidal wave of occupational despair will wash them out if that dam begins to crack even just a little. There is a certain narcissistic element of depression, as depressed folks collapse inward, and feel trapped with the bad emotions and hopelessness.

The conflict with co-workers is probably more of a masculine quality than feminine, as men tend to act out their depression with more overt aggression than do women. Still, conflict guarantees emotional distance (while simultaneously blowing off steam), which is ultimately defined as "withdrawing from co-workers."

5. Having a general feeling of irritation regarding work

Once again, this is a symptom of depression. I described this in the preceding sections.

6. Experiencing insomnia, digestive disorders, headaches

The problems above represent just a few on the longer list of maladies called *psychosomatic*. Literally, meaning physical symptoms caused by emotional turmoil, stress, or pain. Recall the discussion earlier about how too much stress can make you sick. The express bus to *Burnout-Ville* still stops at a few terminals along the way, and the development of psychosomatic problems is going to be one of them.

By the way, the most common stress-related illness is headache. Probably the vast majority of us have developed a "stress headache" at some point or another during our lifetime. Your mind has a great deal of influence over your body

Indulge me with a word about insomnia to end symptom #6. I don't think I need to define insomnia per se, as we could all probably identify that it means to lose sleep. What I *do* want to clarify for you though, is the *three types* of insomnia (Roth & Roehrs, 2004). The reason I am going to hang on this point a bit is because *sleep* is absolutely essential to the function of all other systems in your body. If your sleep starts to collapse, a giant magnifying glass is going to be held to the other symptoms of anxiety, depression, and burnout you may already be feeling. Your brain needs to re-set the hard drive every night in order to keep functioning smoothly.

The first type of insomnia is the one we can all identify with … not being able to fall asleep. You go to bed at 10:30 p.m., and before you know it, you're watching *Leave it to Beaver* in Spanish at 3:00 a.m. You may lie in bed for long stretches of time staring straight up, but the blank ceiling becomes a canvas upon which you paint brilliant portraits of all the stresses you feel throughout your days.

The second type of insomnia is: not being able to *stay* asleep. You may fall into an exhausted heap at 10:30 p.m., but you end up waking at 11:07 p.m. … then again at 12:22 a.m. … then again at 2:55 a.m. … then again at 4:15 a.m. … then at 5:05 a.m. When the alarm goes off in the morning, you feel even worse than you did when you went to bed the night before. Plus, the sleep you grab in the middle of those waking spells really isn't good sleep anyway, so you go on with your day feeling like a truck hit you.

Finally, we have *waking too early*. In this type of insomnia, you fall asleep as scheduled, but wake at 3:00 a.m. or 4:00 a.m., perhaps to hit the restroom, and the switchboard in your head suddenly lights up… and you know it is all over. Your brain begins to spin with everything you have to do today or tomorrow, you focus on deadlines or meetings, and you cannot fall back to sleep. Or, if you do actually fall back to sleep, it is fourteen seconds before the alarm goes off, or perhaps even simultaneous to the alarm ringing and you're off to the races.

Once again, bear in mind that sleep is *foundational* for good mental and physical health. If you are not sleeping, you are going to accelerate the burnout process and find yourself in quite a pickle. Take the steps necessary to maintain good, solid sleep so you can be all you can be!

7. *Incapacitation or inability to function professionally in stressful situations*

Here again, we have a good manifestation of being overwhelmed... just tied to the tracks and waiting for the train. This feeling of incapacitation arises from just generally being on a hair-trigger. You feel constantly "on edge" internally, so when a stressful situation develops externally, it magnifies the unceasing stress already banging around in your head; and you collapse. On the flipside, the more relaxed you are, the more you are able to roll with stress and not fall victim to it.

Plus, stress has an *additive* effect. From minor daily hassles all the way up to more serious life issues, stress can either peck away or downright *blast* away at your reserves, and eventually wear you out! At school, the same principle applies. You each have daily maintenance issues that float around in your life, in the classroom, and in the building; and then there are more major crises that arise which cannot be ignored. Over time, if you begin to feel hammered repeatedly by these stressors, you will burn out and we will lose another potentially great educator.

Burnout – prevention and treatment

When it comes to dealing with burnout, we have two options; nip it in the bud before it happens or deal with fixing it once it starts to set in (adapted from Wood & McCarthy, 2002). Put another way, proactive vs. reactive dealing or prevention vs. putting out fires. As a final word before hitting prevention, I will also mention that, due to genetics and upbringing, some of us are naturally better at dealing with stress than others. The exact same stressor may hit one person very hard, while it merely rolls off the back of another. Think about your own resilience to stress as you read on.

Prevention: There are two main facets of burnout prevention. Neither will shock you, as these are probably the main ingredients of living a happy and healthy lifestyle in general. First, have good relationships with the people around you. Having close, intimate friendships can buffer you against many of the harshest blows life can deal. In the Pop Psych culture, these folks make up your "support system," and basically are the couple or few friends you turn to when you need a hand. These are the friends who will not only take a punch for you, but will throw one as well if you need it.

The second element of prevention is a little more complicated, but is still very reachable. It has to do with the way you *interpret* a situation. An example of what I am saying is written right into the title of this book: are these bad kids, or is it bad behavior? The answer to that question is profoundly important when it comes to dealing with the students. If you feel that these are bad kids, there is an implication of pessimism over long term change. In other words, very little can be done to change a "Bad Kid," so why bother putting in the effort? It is almost like the "badness" is woven right into the fabric of their personality. If, however, this is merely *bad behavior* we are dealing with, change seems to be vastly more possible. These students would be like having a ketchup stain on a shirt. You hit it with some club soda, or spray a little Spray-N-Wash® or Shout®, and we have a perfectly good shirt again. Behaviors can be learned, unlearned, and re-learned. Therefore, your *perception* has power to shape your motivation.

Here's another example, then I will say more about how it pertains to burnout. Let's take the oppositional defiant students. For many of these kids, they develop the reputation of being a pain in the neck early on in their academic career. They effectively get the label "Bad Kid" hung on them in kindergarten or first grade. For those of you who teach third or fifth, or seventh grades (or whatever), you know that you occasionally catch yourself peering upstream to see who is swimming down the pike, right? You look because you want to know who you may have to deal with in *your* classroom next year or the year after.

Here is my point: there are some kids whom you don't like *before you even meet them*. Or at the very least, before they set a single foot into your room. And there has been a lot of research conducted that, in different forms, says that the way you *feel* about a student *will* have an impact on how you *treat* them. You can call it "Self-Fulfilling Prophecy," or maybe "The Halo Effect," or whatever other catchy moniker we can use, but it all boils down to the same concept.

The way you treat them differently does not have to be overt. In fact, I would argue the opposite. None of you goes to work planning to be mean or ugly toward a "Bad Kid." But in very subtle ways, you send strong messages to them that *are* different from the "Good Kids." It may be in a facial expression, or the tone of your voice, or in a barely perceptible change in how long you wait for a correct answer. That difference, regardless of how subtle, will be picked up by the child in question, and again may lead to even worse behavior.

Your interpretation leads to a change in emotion and behavior. Let's hook this into burnout. To do this, I have to get a little philosophical on you again. Do you all remember Descartes? He was the guy who said "I think, therefore I am" (Descartes/Cottingham, 1984). For most of us, we learned that line in an attempt to look like we've actually read something substantive. You drop that line at a party, and people look upon you with awe and sincere admiration. But here is my interpretation of what Descartes was getting at. With a little improvisation to help it fit into the point I am trying to make: That each of us has our own way of interpreting "reality." Hence, two of us can look at the exact same thing, and each will have a different point of view about it.

We can illustrate this using any one of a number of ridiculous examples. Take winning the lottery, for example; one person may think it is the greatest thing ever, but don't we all know the person who will chime in with, "Yes, but look at all of the taxes you'll have to pay," or "You'll probably have people befriending you just because of your money," or "They pay it out over time, so you'll probably be dead before you collect on all your winnings."

The paragraph above sounds like the difference between being an optimist and pessimist (glass half-full or half-empty?). It goes well beyond just that, however. The perceptual difference illustrated above affects all aspects of cognition; thus, your emotional state and your behaviors will follow your cognitive state. Depressed people and anxious people begin to literally *think* differently than non-depressed or anxious people (Beck, 1979), so they feel and act differently too.

If you feel as if bad things *always* happen to you. And yes, you can draw a straight line between this thought pattern and burnout. Not to say that this is the *only* way burnout can develop. Rather, I bring this up as a means to *prevent* burnout. Catch yourself falling into these patterns of thinking and try to reinterpret situations to make them less personal, less severe, and less "unchanging." Things you go through may be truly horrific, but unless you focus on the light at the end of the tunnel, you will feel trapped and depressed (burned out).

This advice sounds a little like cheerleading, or the kind of drive you get with syrupy talk show hosts, but on a more serious level, this is one of the ways we help people in therapy. It's called "Cognitive Therapy" and operates under the guiding theory that if you change how a person thinks, you will change how they feel, and therefore how they behave (Beck, 1979). Once that spiral starts to point upward, it will create momentum in that direction, and good things begin to happen.

Symptom Resolution: Prevention is always the most effective means of dealing, but sometimes we can't keep a fire from happening. When this occurs, we can either sit by passively or watch our valuables go up in smoke, or we can grab a hose and start dousing away. Here are a few suggestions.

1. Personal therapy and medication

If you set foot onto the royal road to burnout, I will first take a moment to put in a plug for personal therapy and medication, as that is what the good folks in my profession do! That sounds a little bit glib, but I will add that depression and anxiety are *very treatable* problems.

I always hear people use the line, "Life is too short…" I prefer the exact opposite approach. For my money, life is *too long* to be miserable! If you are going to live to be 80, do you want to spend the next 30 or 40 or 50 years feeling awful? I would hope not! We don't want to lose you, so ask for and get yourself some help, which I know for many teachers is asking a lot.

I don't mean to be condescending. I deal with a lot of teachers all over the country, and I know that a part of the gig for you is that *you have to be the one who is in control!* In your classroom, you *are* the one driving the bus. There is no co-pilot. You've got to control the room. Thus, for many teachers, their personality leans toward having a hard time asking for help.

2. Downshifting

Do you ever get that question at parties where someone will ask you what you do for a living, and you respond with, "I am a schoolteacher"? They may chuckle now, and give you a line that is some version of, "Ah, banker's hours, eh?"

That reply is always infuriating because the *truth* lies far from the *perception* of how hard teachers work. Think about what time you are obligated to be at school. My guess is, for most of you, you rarely *if ever* leave exactly when you are "allowed" to leave. You either coach or tutor or are a faculty advisor to some groups or you decorate or arrange your room, or you sit and grade papers in the quiet. Further, whenever you do finally turn off the lights and close the door, you probably have a satchel of work that you take home with you. How many nights have you spent grading papers on a TV tray while watching *Desperate Housewives* on TiVo?

Teaching, perhaps more than any other job, is not a job you can "leave at the office." You spend time working out lesson plans, revisiting things that happened earlier that day, or worrying about one of your students while you lay in bed and start to doze off. And let's not forget about all the aspects of normal living that occupy your mind (mortgage, the price of gas, getting your own kids back from soccer practice, having a sick dog, etc.).

When it all becomes overwhelming and your hard drive fills up, it may be time to "purge a few files." Prioritize your events and decide what can go. Downshifting may provide just the space you need to catch your breath and get back into the game.

3. *Seek outside interests – become less focused on being a teacher*

Here is a tragedy I tease out in the live seminars: how many of you have a hobby that you can't *quite* remember when you participated in last? It's too bad, but at some point, many of us become a *teacher* and stop being a human being. If you aren't careful with your own personal boundaries, you can become consumed by this job. So strike a balance. I know you can't leave the job at the office, but maintain the things you loved before you started your job. Keep loved ones close, and keep your life in perspective.

4. *Relocation (geographic OR within a school)*

There are really two issues brought out by this suggestion. One is to get to another school; the other is to get to a different class.

It never ceases to amaze me how many teachers raise their hand when I ask if anyone has ever worked for a lousy principal. I'll talk more about this in the next chapter, but suffice it to say for now that the answer lies somewhere around, "a *lot*." Or, teachers may have a decent administrator, but are situated in a working environment (due to co-workers, location, or other factors) that makes the job unmanageable.

When that happens, a geographic relocation (i.e., get a job at a different school) may be in order. If there are circumstances beyond your control that are making you absolutely insane, get out! This is easy for me to say, I know, but one nice aspect of being a teacher is that 50% of your new colleagues really *are* going to be gone in the first five years, so this turnover naturally will create opportunity.

Believe me, it is better for you to be a good teacher at another school than it is for you to be a depressed, stressed out, or otherwise angry teacher at this one.

The second issue has to do with who or what you teach in your current school. Some of you are, by nature, kindergarten teachers at heart. Some of you prefer the challenge of middle school. We can probably all agree that a middle school teacher and a kindergarten teacher are not the same person, right? But we can hopefully also agree that, when some teachers look for their first job, they may grab onto whatever comes their way. Thus, you may have grabbed that seventh grade job, but after a couple years find yourself longing for the first grade class you see when you visit the elementary school.

You can also burn out if you feel mismatched in your classroom. If you are teaching history (because the principal needed a history teacher), but you really studied to be a chemistry teacher, work your way back in that direction. Strive toward satisfaction rather than just a paycheck. It will feel more like a round peg in a round hole, and help stave off burnout.

5. *Re-evaluate the goals and ideals which led you to become a teacher*

Can you remember the day you graduated with that teaching degree and set out, all doe-eyed and idealistic, to set the world on fire? For some of you, like for me, that was about a hundred years ago and trees had not yet been invented. For others of you, that was sometime last month. Either way, you chose teaching because you had a passion for it. The truth is that this job is more of a "calling" than a get-rich-quick infomercial.

Over time though, the rough kids, the screwball parents, the paperwork, the lousy administers, and the daily grind can suck that zeal right out of you, leaving you to feel like you'll *never* get it back.

But take pause during the chaos to recall those idealistic days. What made you choose this path in the first place? My guess is that either; a) you had one (or both) parents who were teachers and you thought that was pretty cool, or b) there was a teacher somewhere in your history that really *got* to you. They understood where you were coming from; they connected with you in a way you didn't expect; their teaching style or sense of humor was *exactly* in line with yours... basically, they were an agent of impact and change in your life.

To borrow and adapt a phrase from Gandhi, *Be the change you see in your students*. Use the power you have and the position you occupy in their lives to become that favorite teacher you remember. *Seize the zeal!*

Chapter 7

Effective Leadership

How to Drive the Bus

A lot has been made so far about how to take care of yourself and to be emotionally present for the students in your class. Further, it has been discussed how to reduce burnout risk to remain physically present in the educational system. Let's take a step to the side for a moment and examine some qualities of effective leadership. This discussion will, perhaps, shed some light on changes you can make within yourself and your teaching style to maximize the potential for positive behavior and all the learning you can shake a stick at!

I will present these qualities in a brief outlined form, and then in Chapter 8, build a bridge between the understanding part of PBS and the behavioral part.

For the remainder of this Chapter, I will discuss each leadership quality individually (adapted from House, 2004; and Burns, 1978). To begin, here are ten qualities of effective leaders… in no particular order.

1. *Vision and a plan for the classroom*

The first day of the semester, we arrive on campus wide-eyed and bushy-tailed, ready for another run at the coveted "Teacher of the Year" award (given *almost* annually by your principal, providing the budget allows for such an extravagance). In your mind and in your lesson planner, you have laid out what appears to be a water-tight plan of action for the class. The books you will read, the formulas you will cover, the historical battles you will re-enact, the number of pseudo love-letters you will confiscate from the red-faced authors, then read out loud to embarrass both the writer and the intended recipient.

The point is, we all start the year with a solid plan. The vision you have follows logically from that same plan. In fact, I am quite certain the vision many of you have involves the entirety of your class being accepted upon initial application to Harvard Medical School; and then each, in turn, thanking you personally over the P.A. system at the graduation ceremony.

This quality of effective leadership may seem a bit obvious, but there is no substitute for careful pre-planning. This way, you do not have to think on the fly, struggle to explain how today's lesson fits into the overall plan, or lose your place in an unwarranted ugly symphony of classroom cacophony. The "educational" piece of your job has been laid out, thus allowing for some flexibility when it comes to adapting to the learning styles or processing speed of your class. This will invariably lead to more *confidence* as a leader and as a teacher on your part. Preparation leads to confidence, no?

Here is how to connect the dots: The more confident and in control you appear to be, the more trust and faith your class will have in you. The more trust and faith your class has in you, the less anxiety and anger, and the more possibility of good behavior.

2. *Not accepting underachievement*

I throw this one in there because I have, as a casual outside observer, noticed that we are tending to lower the bar more and more when it comes to setting the standards for achievement levels. Not that there wasn't *some* room for improvement.

I see it as a trend in the past ten to fifteen years that we are continuing to lower the bar when it comes to academic standards. For example; how much is required in any course of study; what scores are required to gain admittance into college or graduate school, even the norms for the Weschler IQ tests are fluid, and do adjust over time – roughly every ten years! (Kaplan & Saccuzzo, 2005).

And I do have a bit of experience to back up a portion of this point of view, albeit for post-secondary education. I worked for about five years as a full-time college professor in an accredited Graduate Psychology Program during the late 1990's. During this time (before I left for private practice in hopes of fame, fortune, and Heather Locklear's hand in marriage) I sat on a couple committees with members who successfully engaged in heated debate over *not* raising our lax standards for entering into our graduate school. In other words, there was a lot of institutional momentum/pressure to either *keep* the standards where they were, or to *actually lower them!*

You can imagine my growing unrest and cynicism. Needless to say, if some public colleges and universities fight to keep standards low, does this ideology trickle down to the primary and secondary systems? Perhaps!

Administrators and legislators would argue the opposite. With No Child Left Behind, Head Start, Standardized Testing, other federally-funded national programs, and robust data gathering techniques, it does appear, publicly, that we are fighting to raise the bar. You as the front line warriors know what really happens when we pull back the curtain… so I am sure you all have your own opinion about the utility or success of the national programs.

In any case, when we lower standards, we send an odd message to the students. On one hand, we tell them that they can do anything. But, on the other we are telling them that they can do anything as long as it isn't all that hard to do. It's almost like we are telling them that they probably can't handle a greater load, or that they just aren't able to do it. So rather than encourage diligence, we adjust their goals downward.

Now believe me, I did not exactly set the world on fire when it came to academic performance in school. I think I hit a low water mark in life when my GPA fell into the high 1's and the low 2's my freshman year in college. It was quite a wake up call when my financial aid got yanked, and I was suddenly faced with no longer being welcome at Marquette University. But I wonder what it would have been like if they (i.e., school officials) would have come up with a creative way for me to continue to fail, but keep thinking that I was doing all right. Which master would that have served?

I will give you another example in secondary education. When you all were in high school, was there a teacher who was *tough*? That person would probably have been a teacher most or all of the kids tried to avoid, right? Did you have that teacher in your school? We did. The other option for the course was one of the football coaches, and rumor had it the class spent most days watching movies on one of the school's new Beta Max players.

But here is the deal, if you passed these teacher's classes, you had accomplished something. These teachers didn't pull any punches, didn't reward incompetence, and most certainly didn't adjust the curve down if the class was struggling.

On the other side of the coin, I have been in classes where all the grades were good, and nobody really knew if they learned anything or not, because that didn't seem to matter to the teacher. We didn't get a lot of reality-based feedback on our performance.

If you ask most any student how much work they want to do in a given class, they will respond with some version of, "Whatever I've got to do to get out of here!" And think about this, if whatever they've got to do isn't very much, then that is precisely what they will do – not very much. But if whatever they've got to do is more, then they are forced to adjust their game to pass muster and move on to the next level.

Consider the message you send to your class when you set the bar. Whether subtle or overt (or a little bit of both), you convey confidence in the students when you let them know you require them to be the best they can be. And once again, that confidence and trust in them reflects strong leadership.

3. *Offer kindness and encouragement*

I always ask, semi-rhetorically, if there are any kind and encouraging people attending my seminars. I get a few chuckles, a few snorts, and a couple brave souls who actually (yet sheepishly) raise their hand. In general though, you are reading this book or have attended a live show because your gas tank is running low – maybe even on fumes. Kindness and encouragement may have been wonderful qualities you held dearly at the beginning of your career, but after a few years of being worn down by the poorly behaved, under-motivated, challenging students in your classes, your kindness level has been put to the test.

I hate the gimmicky quality of this move, but I am going again to ask you to remember the favorite teacher you had growing up. As a youngster, you may have been vastly more intrinsically motivated than some of the students you see looking back at your every day, but you favorite teachers also had a quality that inspired you. You looked up to them, and he or she reflected a belief that you really could do *anything*.

You have, I am quite certain, heard the famous quote by William Arthur Ward: "The mediocre teacher tells. The good teacher explains. The superior teacher demonstrates. The great teacher *inspires*." Some of the rougher kids in your presence may come from a home where kindness and encouragement exist in remarkably short supply. For that same reason, they will have a hard time accepting some of your encouragement, but that does not invalidate its power.

Become a positive force in the lives of your students, and they will grow to respect you. Some may never let you know you have reached them, and yes, there are a few who may have descended to a level below that which you can reach in nine short months, but capture the energy of the kids who are open to the inspiration.

And think about this: even those kids who are jaded and wounded past the point of promise will never have an opportunity to grow if their teachers treat them like a lost cause. Leave the door open for them. Whether they elect to pass through or pass entirely is up to them.

4. *Visible and interactive*

I can always tell a school where teachers love to teach when I stroll down the hallways in the morning or during breaks between classes, I see the principal out and about. These are leaders who walk among their people and form relationships with all folks they meet. These principals are greeting the kids, the teachers, and the support staff. They are out mingling and probing, curious about the lives of their students, modeling appropriate relationship behavior, and slapping high fives, hitting rocks, and patting the shoulders of everyone. If anybody has a concern, there is no doubt about the availability of that principal.

As teachers, I hope you take some time to greet your kids as they filter into the room at the beginning of the day, or as they change classrooms. Not only does that presence instill confidence in you as their leader, but it also demonstrates concern and care – it builds rapport.

Plus, if you touch your kids as they filter into the room – pat a shoulder, strike a high fiver, or hit rocks (some of the kids may need a playful smack in the back of the head once in awhile!), you communicate warmth and acceptance in a way that words alone cannot do.

If you don't believe in the power of touch, think back for a moment and recall a time when you received a cold, slimy, dead-fish type of handshake. You got that memory etched in your mind? My guess is that you cringed, and possibly even contorted as you remembered that desire to take an extended, hot soapy shower after the handshake ended. The handshake you are remembering may have happened three years ago, and it took a half-a-second to complete. But, sitting there in your easy chair today, your body has a visceral reaction to the awful memory.

Further, you may not even remember where you were or who actually gave you the foul handshake. But, that residue hangs with you forever.

Good touch works in a similar manner, but in a more positive direction. Your students may not even notice your patting their shoulder as they pass by you in the doorway, but the residue of that positive interaction will hang with them.

Now I also understand that a few of you work in an environment where touching is not allowed, or at times I have heard of male teachers who either have been advised, or have made the personal choice, to avoid *all* touch so as to not encourage a crazy lawsuit from a spiteful teenager or parent. Some of the angry students in our regular schools, too, may react in a bad, or aggressive, way to being touched. In these situations, of course you utilize common sense.

Still, for the rest of us, I am afraid there is a trend developing whereby teachers will eventually be forbidden to touch their kids at all. A few bad apples always seem to spoil it for everyone as our world continues to put tremendous power into the hands of the few who reside in the splinter minority. Most (and by most, I think I am speaking darn close to 100%) teachers are caring and appropriate when they interact with their kids. In fact, the Associated Press found that, between 2001 and 2005, there were 2570 reported cases of sexual misconduct by teachers (CBS News, 2007). That number, without debate, is staggeringly higher than it should be – it should be zero. Still, given that there are somewhere between 3 and 3.6 million teachers in America, this means that about 1 out of every 1300 teachers engages in this grossly inappropriate behavior. The others are doing their jobs like decent people are supposed to. Many kids, particularly younger ones, relate to others in a physical way. Touch has primitive importance upon it.

Here is the other reason to greet kids at the door as they change classrooms, or arrive in the morning: in doing so, you are setting a boundary at the doorway. That boundary can deliver the message that the rest of the world ends here, and that there is a different set of rules in *this* room. To put it another way, "Leave your baggage at the door!"

Especially for the angry students or those who you see are struggling through their day, that boundary is important. Let them know that they leave their worries out in the hallway. Whatever happened in that hallway or on the bus or on the walk to school or at home this morning doesn't enter this room. In this room, there is a new sheriff and you will protect them from the stressful parts of their life for as long as they are here.

Again, maximize the opportunity for the kids to respond well to you. There are some kids who will decline the chance to have a better day, but they cannot go through the door if it is not open to them.

5. *Know each of your students*

I'm not sure how much needs to be said about this quality of an effective leader in that it is pretty self-explanatory. I will refer you back to the passage about the really good principals: taking an interest in the lives of the students will unlock potential.

Bear in mind that some kids, and this may not be the case for just the behavior problem kids, may come from a place they are ashamed to talk or think about. If there is a family secret that is buried pretty deep, or there is an embarrassing element (i.e., alcoholism, sexual abuse, etc.) the kids may be skiddish to talk about their life outside of school. And frankly, there may be skeletons hanging out in those heads that you don't want to know about. It's an eighth grade Pandora's Box.

Do take an interest. Open the door for them to talk about lives or dreams or feelings. They may not ever do it, but it can build trust if they know the chance exists. And be prepared for the things you hear. Even kids from sparkling, middle- and upper-class two-parent families may harbor a secret that is quite disturbing. Remember again that is any school or neighborhood situation, you still have the possibility of being the healthiest grown-up in that child's life.

6. *Have a sense of humor*

Sure, sure... everyone knows how a good sense of humor can add years to your life. Laughter reduces stress and builds your immune system, we get that. But I ask you, educators: have you *ever* tried to interact with somebody who has absolutely *zero* sense of humor? It's nearly impossible to do, and even if it happens, it is really close to impossible to *enjoy.*

Humor is the axel grease that keeps the gears from grinding in social situations. People with no "give" or no "play" in their personality are very difficult to hang with for long periods of time. We need a little sense of relaxation when we relate to others, and humor is a wonderful way to convey that. And when you deal with kids, a sense of humor can be just the lynch-pin that ties you all together.

There is another reason to employ humor in the classroom: humor engages the thinking part of the brain. You can use humor to de-escalate a tensing student or an evolving negative situation (McFarland, 2000). You don't have to make an angry student bust out laughing – that emotional state is probably too far removed from where he is at right now. But if you engage that part of the brain for just a moment – just enough to rock him back out of his escalation and make him say *"huh"* you have bought yourself time to intervene. You have, in essence, placed a brief wedge of time in his game plan, and thrown him temporarily off his axis.

This beat or two is a brief eye of the storm, and the window for intervention will soon slam shut, but without the humor, the window would have never existed in the first place. Your next move is equally important, as you need to hastily intervene to continue the calming momentum. Little Johnny is going to quickly re-establish that anger unless you act to remove the actors from the stage.

7. Help develop leadership in your students

This quality of effective leaders may seem somewhat out of place, but remember that strong leadership begets strong leadership. I remember that from the Beatitudes in my catechism classes at St. James Elementary. I also recall something about "Thou shall not put anything nasty into thy mouth, regardless of how it may impress the girls."

When you manage your classroom, you are also modeling for your students the qualities of leadership. And even if they aren't geared for leadership roles necessarily, they will be better equipped to recognize *appropriate* leadership in authority figures long after they are out of school. Nothing is worse than when kids grow up into adults who don't recognize a raw deal before they enter into it because they never had role models who taught them to spot it.

There is another reason to develop leadership in the students who seem inclined to become leaders, and it has to do with some of the ODD students who grace the tiled floors of your classroom.

One thing about being "The Bad Kid," is that this label gets hung onto them pretty early on in their schooling. Therefore, many of the cool qualities these kids may exhibit somehow get washed through with the explanation, "Ah, he's just a bad kid." In other words, a bad kid must have only bad habits, tendencies, and qualities because (let's face it), he's *the bad kid*.

But one thing I hope you take from this book is that even "The Bad Kids" may have some wonderful qualities that end up buried over time, or they may demonstrate these qualities in manners which really are inappropriate. I'll let you in on a secret, though, that pertain directly to leadership; Oppositional Defiant kids, and particularly those who come from a lousy situation at home that may include abuse or parental addiction, develop a quality that can make them into remarkable leaders.

That quality is the ability to read people – fast, and amazingly accurately. The radar antenna sported by these kids is extremely fine-tuned, as that ability is a necessity to survival at home. They have to be adept at interpreting the general barometer in any given situation.

"Is mom high?" "Is dad going to hit me?" "Do I smell booze?" These become questions and situations that not only hold some value from a philosophical or academic sense, but more importantly because that kid's health and safety rely on his or her ability to come up with the correct answer.

How this relates to leadership is yet another quality of leadership; knowing how your people are feeling, what they are thinking, or where they are at on a given issue. A great leader is able to assess what's on another person's mind, and also what that person may need in that situation. A good leader can read this and adapt his or her response based upon their evaluation.

ODD kids from disastrous homes nearly always have this ability. Sure, they may use it for evil purposes (like revving up the other angry kids in an attempt to overthrow your power at the front of the room), but in another setting this is a great quality.

Take some time to re-frame these leadership qualities. And for that matter, take the time to find *any* positive qualities embedded in bad behaviors. Rather than constantly making the student feel like whatever he's got has got to be bad, start to spin the same behavior in a different direction.

And I mean call it out directly. Even if the end result was bad, let the kids know that he just demonstrated some pretty awesome leadership out there. Punishment may ensue because of the choice he made in applying this talent, but start turning that oil tanker around, and let him know how you can spot a gift when you see it.

Another suggestion for teachers has to do with classrooms that may have five or six of those angry little gems in your class at once. If you try to take them all down independently, you are going to lose. You don't have the time or the energy to develop a strategy for each, and then to implement it in the face of trying to teach the rest of the class at the same time.

So a solution can rest within the social structure of the classroom. A leader will almost invariably emerge from the ranks of the angry kids. There may be a couple, but there will be a head of the snake. If you don't align yourself with the leaders, you leave yourself vulnerable their quickly burning you out.

Align yourself properly by working with the leaders to create a different set of rules for them, and note, I did not say *ally* yourself – big difference… they should still not tread onto the level of power you hold within the room. And, I do *not* mean that they are allowed to get away with anything, either. That would erode the confidence the room has in you as the teacher, the authority figure (the one driving the bus!). I mean rules that set him apart from his peers. Some rules may be more strict, some less, but the important thing is that he holds a separate designation within the room.

Here is an example. Maybe the leader is allowed to get a drink at the water fountain before any of his "peers," as a tip of the hat to his status within the group. But because you also want him to model appropriate behavior for the rest of the boys, he will lose two tokens instead of one in your response cost system (more on those later) if he talks out of turn during class.

If the leader ever gets frustrated by some of the stricter rules and hands you some version of, "You're treating me different!" you reinforce that notion. You say something to the effect of, "You're darn right you have a different rule. Those other boys look up to you, and that carries some responsibility with it. You are the leader of that group."

Reinforce that status through your classroom rules, and the rest of the kids will fall into line behind him. Another thing that may begin to happen is another leader may emerge from the group if the current leader starts to fall. If or when that happens, follow the same plan with the new leader.

Again, your only shot is to work within the structure that presents itself. For you to try to break the back of the social strata would be an almost guaranteed futile action. Plus, it would quickly erode at the relationship you are trying to forge with these kids. You won't reach them if there is a constant undercurrent of power struggle going on.

8. *Show who is in charge*

Again, this point seems like a no-brainer, as I am quite certain you all have a special tone of voice which is reserved for when your students hit DEFCON 1... Or is it DEFCON 5? I can never remember... sort of like those color-coded security warnings at the airport – does ANYBODY know what those mean anymore?

But there are a couple of things for you to keep in mind. First, if you use sarcasm when you mess with your students, and I am sure there are a number of you who do, practice your sarcastic tone and your "I mean business, Buster!" tone so that you are able to make the two distinct and unique from each other. In other words, sarcastic and "I mean it" tones cannot resemble each other, or it will cause confusion among your students, and may make a bad situation worse.

They have actually done a pretty interesting study to demonstrate a point not dissimilar from the one I am trying to make. In the experiment, they took a group of dogs, and then exposed the dogs to two different shapes, or they heard two different tones (Dworkin, 1939). In the shapes experiment, when the dogs saw a circle, they received a re-enforcer. Then, when the dogs saw a square, they received an electric shock.

Over time, the experimenters made the circle and the square look more and more alike, until the dogs could no longer tell one from the other. In the tones experiment, same process applied (the tones became more and more similar). The shock the treat would come, and the dog could not accurately predict which he was in store for.

What happened next, as you can easily surmise, is that the dogs went crazy? They became doggy-neurotic, because they could not control the flow of re-enforcers or punishers. Same for your students – if they cannot discern between those two tones of voice, they will have a hard time feeling settled with you, and will not establish the trust you need to maintain management of your room. Structure and consistency build trust and security.

The second thing to bear in mind is that, despite everything you hear to the contrary, sometimes the answer is "no" for no other reason than because *you're the grown-up!* You do not owe the students an explanation for every single instance when you put up a boundary or a limit. If you get into the habit of constantly back-peddling and explaining yourself, it can over time erode your power base.

I sometimes have to explain this concept to parents. It amuses me when they come into my office and feel the need to show me how great they are at parenting as they explain every nuance of the "no" to their two or three year old child. They always look to me with a sense of relief when I remind them who is really in charge here.

There exists a golden opportunity for learning and understanding if rules come with an explanation. Giving the students the nuts and bolts to rationale and logic can help them tremendously when they attempt to create their own sense of order within their lives later on down the road. Authority should not be arbitrary... it comes with a solid foundation of thought, premise, and purpose.

Teachers can sometimes get themselves into a pickle when every interaction that sets a limit on a student tags an explanation to the inevitable question ... but why? Students will learn quickly that they can get you talking. And remember that students who argue are trying to accomplish one of two things: either they are delaying the inevitable, or they are looking for a loophole. And once they detect blood in the water, they swarm like piranhas on a wounded buffalo.

So, nip that process in the bud and remain concise when laying down the gauntlet. Not every time, but at times when you need to reinforce your power base as the authority figure who is in charge in the classroom.

9. *Trustworthy and honesty*

As soon as I wrote number 9 above, I thought to myself, "How can anyone not know that?" But this does afford me an opportunity to give props to you, the educators, and remind you that we are not just teaching basics to the students. Sure, we hope they leave our classrooms with a better understanding of American history, algebra, reading, or the Queen's English, but we also hope that they leave with a better understanding of how to be a good, decent person.

I remind you that not only are we teachers, but we are mentors, we are parents, we kiss boo-boos, we pat heads, and we show our kids an appropriate way to treat others and to feel about themselves. Granted, not all students are destined to perk up and fly right when they leave our classrooms, but we owe it to them to not only be good, but to be *extraordinary*. Recall that you may be the healthiest adult in the life of that kid, so use the chance we get to model good behavior.

Honesty and trustworthiness may not exist outside of the classroom for these students, but they can at least see that, though you, the concepts can play out somewhere.

10. Diplomacy with students, parents, and school staff

Here again we have an example of how to model good behavior for our students, especially the *bad kids* in our classrooms. But before I get into that, I want to make sure we all know what 'diplomacy' means.

Diplomacy is the ability to enter the fray and resolve conflict in a manner that makes all involved feel heard and at least pretty well satisfied. Not everyone gets their way all the time, but making the combatants feel understood and partially redeemed is indeed a skill. But it is not a skill we are born with: rather, it is something we develop by watching. We observe somebody else being diplomatic, and then pattern our own behavior after that role model.

Now think about this: there are kids out there who come from a home where diplomacy is (seemingly) a cuss word. These are the kids, especially our boys, who come from a place where conflict resolution is taken to a concrete extreme.

I remember having a fifteen-year-old client come in for an intake with his mother. Mom sat down and began by reporting that Robert (not really his name, but you get the picture) and his father had "gotten into it at home." They had a loud disagreement over who-knows-what, but his father's solution was to, "Go out back and finish this."

I thought to myself, then heard myself say out loud, "Wow... really? Dad's solution was to step outside and duke it out with his teenage son?" But alas, the answer was "yes." They were to fight, and then whoever beat the other one up got his way in the home. Quite a model for coping with others, wasn't it? Life Skills 101, it seemed.

I bring that example up to say that this particular teen is not an isolated case. There are kids out there with parents of all skill levels when it comes to parenting, and some of the kids never learn that there even *can* be a diplomatic solution. That the art or finesse of resolving interpersonal conflict may never enter into the universe of some households.

So it is incumbent upon us, the educators, to show them how it's done. And remember too when you are in conflict with a student that it is not just observed by you and he. Rather, there are a lot of faces eyeballing you, learning from how you conduct yourself. Teach by example.

And believe me, all of you have diplomacy. You have to, because all of you have dealt with an angry parent at one time or another, right? Of course you have!

The angry parent is usually Mom, in my experience. And you all know this angry Mom… she is the one who is thinking about what *exactly* she is going to say to you from the time she climbs into her car, drives all the way across town, marches through the parking lot, up the front steps, down the corridor, and until she kicks her door open and lambastes you with, "*are you Mr./Mrs. Olivas?*"

Then you make the unguarded mistake of softly mouthing the word, "yes?"

Then, in a brilliant flash of insight, it suddenly occurs to you that you don't exactly fit out the window, and she is between you and the door… so you've got to deal with her. What do you do?

Actually, the first step I usually coach to teachers (or anyone who is entering a potentially explosive situation) is to have everyone sit down. It is harder to be aggressive if you cannot strike an aggressive posture, and sitting takes some of the steam out of that engine. Also, if there is a height differential – in either direction – then there is a power differential (height = power for most people); so sitting down puts everyone on eye level with each other.

And you, through the school of hard knocks, also realize that this is the type of mom who is not only *thinking* of everything she is going to say to you, but she is also *writing* it on an invisible note card in her head. And by the time she gets to your door, that note card is full – front and back, single-spaced, 4-pt. font.

As I am sure some of you are already thinking, the first step in resolving this lies in your ability to listen. Can you interrupt that angry mom before she gets done reading to you that entire note card? Probably not... that would lead to bad times with almost 100% certainty.

But once she has exhausted that note card, the true art of diplomacy kicks in. What do you do next? Your next maneuver means the difference between handling the issue in a positive manner and sending mom off the deep end of anger.

The next step is to connect with the *feeling* that is driving her anger. What is the real issue here? If all you do is hit mom's anger head-on, she is only going to escalate because you are not getting at the *real issue*. That is the issue lurking behind the anger, driving it and fueling it.

And with angry parents in general, figuring out the real issue is actually pretty easy. Most angry parents are driven by some version of exactly the same thing: namely, that they want what is best for their child and you (probably because that darn kid lied about you!) surely do not. Therefore, it is "Go time!"

So what you have learned how to do is to reach behind the anger and get at the *real issue*. You connect with the feeling the parent brings into your room. You acknowledge what they are saying, you agree that you too want what is best for the child, and you proceed from there. Remember again, if all you hit is the anger, it will only get worse.

Let's use another example. For those of you who have ever argued with your spouse, boyfriend, or girlfriend, do you always know what is making them angry? Probably not, but the better you are able to focus on the issue driving the anger, the better the position you will be in to diffuse the anger and comfort your partner. An argument will go on for eternity if all you see is anger – because you will *never* get at and resolve the real issue that way. There is a radioactive nugget of pain giving life, fuel, and purpose to their shield of anger, right?

Apply this notion to some of the angry students in your room. The anger they show you isn't really the deal. There is always something behind that anger that is pushing it; always some other issue breathing life into the anger and propelling it in your direction. The better you are able to figure out the real issue, the better off you will be to handle it in a diplomatic manner. You can show everyone watching that you understand how they feel, and that you will act in a way that does not escalate or do more damage.

That's my suggestion on leadership qualities as they apply to the classroom. Remember that the better the leader you are, the better the probability that good behavior has the potential to bloom. Take a look at your principal, and learn from him or her. Even the best administrators have some qualities in need of improvement! Before we begin to move to Chapter 8, take a moment and put a check mark beside each of the following qualities you know you do well.

Recall that the point in doing a quick exercise like this is not to focus on those qualities you already have... rather, it is to focus on areas you can continue to work toward improving.

Personable	_____	Builds Consensus	_____
Participates	_____	Diplomatic	_____
Sense of Humor	_____	Team Worker	_____
Willing to Delegate	_____	Accepts Advice	_____
Confident	_____	Responsible	_____
Effective Communicator	_____	Accepting	_____
Patient	_____	Sets and Implements Goals	_____
Passionate	_____	Willing to Learn	_____

Optimistic	_____	Productive	_____
Adaptable	_____	Enjoys Challenges	_____
Visionary	_____	Takes Positive Risks	_____
Assertive	_____	Inquisitive	_____
Organized	_____	Energetic	_____
Inspires Others	_____	Proactive	_____
Self Respective	_____	Resourceful	_____
Flexible	_____	Forgiving	_____
Great Listener	_____	Dedicated	_____
Respects Others	_____	Compassionate	_____
Able to Say 'No'	_____	Decisive	_____
Self-motivated	_____	Friendly	_____
Creative	_____	Professional	_____

Chapter 8

The Ten Commandments for Initiating Behavior Changes

Basic Guidelines for Maintaining Control in the Classroom

In this book as in my seminars, I use these commandments as a connector to build a bridge between the two foundations of Positive Behavior Supports, or PBS. We have spent the first parts of this book discussing the students and you. What is the relationship potential that can grow between you? The remainder of the book is dedicated to the Positive Reinforcement aspects of PBS.

Let's structure the remainder of this chapter reviewing the "ten commandments for initiating behavior change!"

1. All behavior has meaning

I'm sure you have heard to "distinguish between the student and the behavior" before, right? In technical terms, we refer to this concept as "Symptom Estrangement" (Redl, 1972).

When it comes to dealing with a troubled or troublesome student, ask yourself the question brought out in the title, "Is this a Bad Kid... or is it Bad Behavior?" The way you answer that question is extremely vital to your dealing with the kid, as it speaks directly to *prognosis*. I'll explain what I mean.

If you answer the question that this is a "Bad Kid," you pretty much kill a great deal of motivation you may have to initiate change – because you have very little hope for him/her to ever get better. Let's use a shirt as a metaphor. If it is a "Bad Kid," it is almost like the problem is woven right into the fabric of the shirt – not much chance to get that out, right?

Now, let's say you answer that important question by noting that the student is demonstrating "Bad Behavior." Continuing with the shirt metaphor, it's as if the problem is like a ketchup stain on a shirt. You rub a little *Spray 'n' Wash*® or *Shout it Out*® on the stain and the problem is resolved. There exists *hope*, because bad behavior can be unlearned, and more appropriate behaviors learned instead.

Behavior – good or bad – does not randomly happen. It all contains meaning for the person doing the behavior. This meaning may not be at a conscious level for the kid, but it does motivate (or, push) the behavior. To you however, it may *feel* like the behavior does happen at random because as teachers, we are not always in a position to see what may have led to it. All we see is the acting out, and are forced to deal with the consequences. But, the better you position yourself to understand the *why* of a behavior problem; the better off you'll be to re-direct the energy.

2. *Change bad behavior "before" it happens*

At risk of going to the well with this advice once too often, I'll repeat it for the sake of posterity one more time; If you nip off the bad behavior on the runway, it never has a chance to take off into the majestic open skies of your eventual insanity!

It is easier to diffuse the bomb than it is to clean up the room after the explosion. Whatever the consequence happens to be (hurt feelings, a bloody nose, or negative attention seeking), collateral damage will not materialize if you control the context and never let acting out occur in the first place.

This is hard to do while you are trying to wrangle the other twenty-three students in the room. But, continue to train yourself to ask what happened just before the behavior. Is there some way you can structure the classroom or the experience of this particular student to keep the bomb from going off? Work it as best as you can – the entire class will benefit from not having to deal with the behavior problem as well.

3. *Remain physically engaged; eye contact, physical proximity, and use the student's name*

You get people's attention when you are physically engaged! More importantly, though, you *keep* attention when you *remain* engaged. Use your physical proximity as a tool in maintaining order in your room. If a student begins acting-out, move toward him or her to put that student on notice. Even placing a hand on a shoulder, or tapping lightly with a forefinger on his desktop can be an unobtrusive means of sending the same message without calling the student out.

Plus, remember that as you begin your behavioral planning, you must not forget the relationship building process. Using eye contact, using the names of your kids, and using touch or proximity are all signs of *respect*.

I know a lot of you have classroom rules with your students. Come to think of it, I hope that *all* of you have classroom rules for your students. My guess is that one of those rules pertains either directly or indirectly to respecting others, respecting you, respecting property, etc. Kids will have an easier time knowing how to behaviorally manifest respect if you model respectful behavior and the three means of engagement listed in the title (eye contact, physical proximity, and use student's name) are all good examples.

I don't even mind when teachers use nicknames of students when addressing them, but overall tend to like using names best. When addressing older students (middle school perhaps... high school for certain) a more proper "Mr." or Ms." when talking to the students may set a good precedent. It duly notes status upon them while also reflecting the manner in which you expect to be addressed.

You can even balance respect with familiarity is you use the title (Mr. or Ms.) with the student's first name rather than his or her last. The result will be less formal, and may have a bit more bounce to it. In the end, an exchange will sound something like, "Mr. Jason, please bring me that rubber band," or "Ms. Amber, might I see the note you were about to pass to Ms. Tiffany?"

4. Give students an opportunity for positive interaction

This one may be another that falls into the "Yeah... no kidding... really?" category. But, we tend to forget when we get frustrated that we actually become surrogate parents to some of the difficult kids in our classes. As I am sure you have surmised by this point, some children do not come from a household that has a lot of room for nurturing or guidance. So, you step into an important – dare I say *critical* – role for these students, and have an opportunity to begin changing the rules.

Think about friends or even authority figures in your life. In fact, step that down a notch and think about some clerk you just met at Sears. Aren't you far more motivated to engage and deal with a person who seems to care about you? I'll never forget some of the truly wonderful people I have met over the years of traveling. By the same token, I can recount a number of horror stories about schlumps I have met who have actually made living my life more difficult *just by their being a part of it.*

Let me expand upon the preceding example. When I walk into my local Sears store, I can usually size up in about six seconds which employees are the ones who have been hired just to fill space. They tend to be obvious, even though they probably think they are stellar workers. On the other side of the coin, I feel really good when I meet the employees that a boss wishes he or she had ten more of. Good employees are hard to come by and harder to keep, but hopefully good teachers are more common.

Most everyone is motivated to please those who make us feel good. The guiding philosophy is that you are more motivated to make a person happy if they make you happy. Students react the same way. A solid relationship provides firm footing for that positive spiral to begin spinning.

5. *Watch your words! Students may have heard and internalized negative messages from home and educators before you*

On the surface, this one seems like a reiteration of a rule most of us carry with us anyway. We never set out to treat a student badly, or dress him down in front of the class. As a normal part of our moral compass (I hope) you would not knowingly cross this line with a student. Still, there are a couple subtleties to bear in mind which may come across as negative or unkind, thereby leading to a greatly diminished motivation on the part of the kids.

First, I hearken back to our discussion of sarcasm a few pages earlier. For those of you who use sarcasm to interact with your kids … remember the two crucial elements of a sarcastic remark. To be successful, sarcasm relies on *tone* and *timing*. In fact, sarcasm by definition is rather cutting in nature (e.g., "Hey kid… *nice shoes!*" or "Is this handwriting, or did a chicken with blue ink on her feet walk across the paper?"). If you have a good rapport with your students, and are in control of tone and timing, you can get away with a sarcastic comment as leaning toward playfulness or jocularity.

But, if you are having a stressful day or are in one of those grouchy places we all go to once in awhile, you are not as in control your tone or your timing as you think you are. In fact, what may sound funny and endearing while it is rattling around in your head may, actually, come out of your mouth with a sharp edge. You may hurt a student without even meaning to.

Even if you are having a good day, your student may be having a bad one, thereby rendering them vulnerable to misinterpreting your attempt at levity. He or she may not be able to weed through the subtle quality of your sarcasm, and may be more prone to taking it literally. Younger students who are still very concrete in their thinking may be totally unaware of the double-edged nature of sarcasm, and thereby not *get it* at all.

So if you are feeling "off" on any given day, I advise you to pull back some on the sarcasm. Save it for when you know you will be able to use it as a relationship builder! Your tone, and I'm sure I am preaching to the choir with this one, says a lot of things to your kids that your words may not intend. This brings me to my second point.

Recall that the "Bad Kids" are given that label early on in school, and teachers can inadvertently be quick to reinforce that label. Not only in tone, but also as subtle as facial expression. When you are tired, frustrated, and sick of dealing with a student or two, your tone and expression may be off-putting, even when the kids are not acting badly.

Yes, this is easy for me to say because I am not down in the trenches with you. Remember to pay attention to the way you communicate with the students, even on a non-verbal level. The "Bad Kids" will pick up on your distaste, and will begin to exploit it – they are darn good at being "The Bad Kid."

6. *Balance work with play*

I'm sure most of you do special stuff for and with your students. Play is the fun part of school and gives the kids a chance to unwind with you and their buddies. Special things are important in the context of this book because they hit both ends of PBS – they build the relationship *and* they are positively reinforcing.

Play can run the gamut. Some dive right into the waters of grandiosity (i.e., pizza parties, fun days, or, as I saw in my area a few years ago, watching the principal shave his head because the students hit their goal in a school-wide reading challenge). Some straddle the middle of the road (i.e., fifteen minutes of free time at the end of the day, homework passes, or dropping a low quiz grade). Some are enduring… remaining simple, yet meaningful (e.g., a smiley face on a returned paper, calling out good behavior or performance, or a knowing wink to a student who may be having a bad day). The point is that these are important to incorporate for your students. Some kids may come from a home where they rarely, if ever, feel that glow of acceptance or being special.

7. *All behavioral plans need consistency to gain traction and to be successful*

I know you hear at every staff meeting and training session you attend that you have to be consistent, right? Sure you do. It's sort of a trap we like to set so we can look smart. Here is how the trap works.

We tell you that 100% consistency is the only way that a good behavioral plan can flourish. So, you go out and try it, and, of course, fail miserably at being consistent 100% of the time. So then when you call us to find out what may have gone wrong, we can always tell you that it is because you were not consistent 100% of the time. We end up having a built-in good reason to tell you why it didn't work, without really having to do any work ourselves.

But here's the reality of the situation. *Nobody is consistent 100% of the time!* What a lot of teachers end up doing, though, is falling into a different sort of trap. That's the one where they *think* they are consistent, but are actually giving one warning after another without any follow through. The other side is to have kids perform well over and over without the agreed upon re-enforcers being introduced. Kids learn that game quickly, and will exploit it. I'll talk more about this later when I talk about giving warnings to students (see Chapter 10).

I'll close this one out with a word about keeping promises. I am sure all of us have made a promise that we eventually just kind of forgot about after a couple weeks. Here's the deal … do your kids ever forget? No! They live to trip you up on a deal you struck with them in an unguarded moment, then hoped would slide between the cracks!

Promises can create some classroom levity when the kids catch you in a moment of "Oops!," but on a deeper level, following through with promises serves a more profound function for some students.

Again, I am going to speak of the tougher kids in your room. Kids who approach life, relationships, school, etc. with a cynicism that is born of harsh reality. For these students, the relationship you forge with them *must* be based upon trust – trust that if you say it, you will do it. Walk the walk, not just talk the talk, you know what I mean? These kids have learned that grown-ups are not to be trusted... that if a promise is made, it almost invariably will fall apart in the end – usually when that kid needed it the most.

With many of our students, opportunities for building trust are like buses: if you miss one, another will come along soon enough. But for the kids who have been pulled through the keyhole of life, the next bus is a long way off. If you do mess up and drop the ball, it may be worthwhile to back the truck up, apologize, and process with the class what just happened. Then you can work together to forge a plan to make it right. Teachers are human too, right?

Be the change you wish to see in your tougher students. Make and keep promises so that level of trust can develop. And if you break your word and there is not some follow-up to make it right in the kid's mind, you may lose that kid forever because now you are "just like everyone else."

I've said it before, that you model not just good behavior, but exemplary behavior for all these students. They need you!

8. *Recognize possible learning problems – help the frustrated student*

Not being an educator by trade, this is the one area I am least versed in to tell you what to do or how to do it. You can check out David A. Kolb and his Learning Styles Inventory for a more thorough discussion (Kolb & Fry, 1975). What I do know, however, is that kids come to the table with different strengths and weaknesses when it comes to the *how* of learning. Too, the boys especially will act out the frustration they feel if their learning style is not matched by your teaching style.

Learning takes place in several parts of the brain, and accessing those parts requires various mediums. Using speech (i.e., lecture), hands-on experiential exercises, music, art or visual media, repetition, or even some of the ridiculous mnemonic devices we learned as kids (e.g., "H-O-M-E-S" for the names of the five Great Lakes) can dramatically improve a student's retention.

Remember your most favorite teacher of all time. It was probably almost like the knowledge just fell out of their head and into yours. Somehow, they were in completely sync with how you absorbed information. It was osmosis at work in the classroom.

Now, think of the worst teachers you have ever had. Whatever they may have known might just as well have been locked in a vault somewhere in a bunker in the middle of nowhere. There was no way those morsels were ever going to be devoured by hungry students. And by the way, over time that hunger for knowledge was eventually sated by the complex carbohydrates of anger and disgust.

It isn't just communication or the ability to be an effective communicator. It is also related to recognizing when your students "get it" and when they gaze at you with those puzzled expressions. You know those expressions; it's kind of like how my kids tend to look at me when I ask them who fed a Strawberry Pop Tart® to the goldfish!

The ability to adjust your game plan to maximize the potential to reach your students will reduce the frustration and allow them an opportunity to have a positive experience in school. The less awful their experience becomes, the less the likelihood of bad behavior on their part. And, as an added bonus, if you become that most favorite teacher, you may actually be spared some bad behavior!

P.S. Did you all remember the names of the five Great Lakes once I resurrected that mnemonic device? Thought so! And for those of you who didn't cheat and look it up, they are (in order); Huron, Ontario, Michigan, Erie, and Superior ... HOMES.

9. Realistic with expectations – remain positive and encouraging

I refer you back to the section on not accepting underachievement. Keep the bar raised for your students, but be aware that if it is *too high for too long,* students will learn that they can never hit the mark and will give up before they even try. When students feel trapped on that wheel, they will punish you for putting them on it.

I also use this section to remind you that with some truly awful behavior-problem students, success may have to be measured on a different scale. To illustrate this, I always remember the movie "The Miracle Worker" (1962).

The movie was about Helen Keller and her tutor/mentor Annie Sullivan, who took what was basically a feral child and turned her into a well-behaved little girl who eventually learned to communicate through the written word and eventually through the spoken word. This was all despite Helen overcoming the double-whammy hurdle of not being able to see or hear.

I bring that up as a case study because had Annie entered the relationship expecting Helen to immediately stand up and utter, "So nice to welcome you, Mumsy. When is tea?" she would have felt like a failure. Indeed, she would have actually failed.

Instead, Annie set reachable goals that Helen could achieve and began to feel success rather than failure. Small increments, like just *holding* a fork in her hand. Helen didn't even have to eat with it right away, for that would have been too distant of a goal. Rather, successive approximations were reinforced and small victories rewarded. Success can be addictive, but only if you have experienced it.

10. Get excited about teaching and become passionate ... realize the unique position you have to "change the rules" for these kids

Have you ever been around someone who just simply *digs* what they do? You all know somebody like that, don't you? I'm talking about somebody who carries themselves with a quiet confidence, somebody who just enjoys doing whatever it is they do. That energy – sometimes called a "good vibe" – becomes contagious. It lights up and energizes folks around them.

On the other side of the equation, have you ever been around someone who is just like a human version of Eeyore? They're the kind of person who sucks joy and laughter out of a situation... they are the type who begin to notice that, when they enter a conversation, suddenly everyone else gets real quiet and starts looking awkwardly down at their shoes. I always think of them as a little ray of darkness in a sun-filled room.

Kids will reflect your level and type of energy. The more surly and Eeyore-ish you become, the more the students will act that out and send it hurling back in your direction. If you don't want to be there, they certainly will not want to be there. Granted, not every positive, upbeat, optimistic teacher will be met with thunderous applause and fanfare from some of the angry, oppositional students. But, the more positive you are, the more the door swings open for good behavior.

Part III: Positive Reinforcement as a Proactive Strategy

Chapter 9
Determining the Re-enforcers
What Lies Beneath the Surface

Before launching into the behavioral portion of our program, let's take a moment and throw a few concepts out there for you to chew on and apply as we proceed. Bear in mind that the re-enforcers we try to determine in our planning can be as simple as Sweet Tarts® or more complicated like Power and Control. I'll address this issue in a moment, but will begin with the A-B-C Model, exemplifying the two basic points of intervention we have at our disposal whenever initiating a behavioral program.

The A-B-C Model

I like the A-B-C Model not only because it very simply illustrates a point, but also because I have very little difficulty remembering how to spell it. And again, this model demonstrates the two windows of intervention that open for us when we think about initiating a behavior plan.

As you have undoubtedly surmised, A-B-C is an acronym, and the letters all stand for something else.

"A:" Antecedent. Antecedent means *context.*

The first window of intervention we have opens before the behavior even happens. I have addressed this in the past Chapters, but in a nutshell, this point forces you to think about the situational or environmental variables which set the table for the bountiful feast of bad behavior in which we are about to indulge.

If you diffuse the bomb, you don't have to clean up the room after it goes off. From here forth, this will be referred to as *Intervening at the "A."* I'll give you an example.

A few years ago, a seventh grader was referred to me. He (we'll call him Jacob) came into my office, accompanied by his rather angry-looking mother, because he had started to act out against classmates – disruptive, aggressive, and defiant. Some of this behavior had spilled onto teachers as well, but it seemed to be limited to other students. In fact, the crown jewel of Jacob's bad behavior, the *piece de resistance* which had earned him a three-day vacation at the hands of the principal was something to behold. His mom took the reigns and told me about this one.

His best friend in the world, James, had injured himself at home about a week prior to the incident and had his ankle wrapped. Nothing too serious, but he had to get around with a notable hobble. Jacob went over to his best friend and proceeded to kick him, hard – *on the affected ankle!*

When I heard this, I immediately raised an eyebrow, and tried to catch Jacob's eye. He kept his gaze turned downward, more a move of embarrassment than defiance. His mom's glare was pretty pointed, as she had *no* problem maintaining eye contact with me. Although the glare vacillated between me and the reddening side of Jacob's face.

The other piece of information that is relevant to this example is that Jacob had – literally – *never* been a behavior problem in the past, quite the contrary until now. I do want to throw in that the ankle-kicking had caught my attention because of the extreme nature of the offense. Jacob was clearly trying to say *something*, but the grown-ups involved (teachers, administrators, and parents) were all busy being angry, and didn't bother to try to piece together what was happening in Jake's mind. Not that I can blame them; it is their job to try to steer Jacob right, and frustration mounts when confusion and defensiveness come together.

What was happening, it turned out, had slid under the radar because Jacob, at age twelve, was in Middle School. Therefore, he did not have any one teacher for more than fifty-two minutes at a stretch during his day. Add that to the fact that he had an irregular schedule, it turned out that he did not have gym class on a predictably-regular rotation.

Okay, you've got it now. It didn't take Columbo to solve the mystery, but because the evidence tended to be scattered throughout his week, nobody had been able to piece together the pattern that eventually emerged. Oh, and Jacob being a 12-year-old male wasn't talking. He would rather have taken a sharp stick to the eye than talk to anyone about the trouble he had been having in gym class. He wasn't real close to his mom and his father was a pretty masculine male, thus, making it difficult for Jacob to approach on this topic,

I eventually earned his trust enough for him to discuss with me what had been going on. This came at a cost, as I had to agree to not tell his parents (he eventually did, with me there to smooth things over). We worked with the school to get him out of the offending gym class, and things in Jacob's world started to get better almost immediately.

Teenagers (especially the boys) may have a hard time talking to adults about matters of the heart, but they have no trouble figuring out ways to get held out of gym class.

I recognize that this has been a very clean, clear-cut example of how to spot contextual variables that lead into bad behavior. I also realize that many of the examples you will be dealing with may be more multi-faceted. Jacob came from a good family and had a singular issue driving him crazy. Still, it shows how we can prevent bad behavior from happening if we are able to control key environmental components.

So yes, in case you are wondering, we did make an adjustment to Jacob's schedule, and the problems began to resolve themselves almost immediately. He had some amends to make with his buddy, James, and we began to cover some different ways to handle conflict situations; but in the end, things worked out for Jacob.

Moving right along…

"B:" Behavior. With the "B" we don't have a lot of control. This is not necessarily a point of intervention, as the bad behavior is already appearing before your very eyes. You may at this position attempt to intervene, but once that horse has left the barn, our only true option is to wait for the…

"C:" Consequences. The "C" is the second point of intervention you can elect to hit with a behavioral plan. This is the point at which you control the re-enforcers and punishers following a behavior (good or bad). Another way this concept has been presented in the past has been to call it a "reactive style of discipline." While this position may not be as powerful as intervening at the "A," this may be your only option while you train yourself to look for the context. And don't fret about being reactive at times – this may be all you've got to work with, especially early on in a management program.

Plus, good behavior should always be reinforced, thus by definition requiring an intervention at the "C." Bad behavior should be clipped off at the knee before it even gets off the bench, but good behavior should be reinforced after it has been practiced by the student.

There are about eleven-bazillion examples of consequences or re-enforcers after the fact. We have time-out (or sending to "quiet time"), detention (in school or out), write-offs/punishments (write, "I will not make potion out of glue and magic markers" one hundred times, was my personal all-time favorite) on the negative. We have treats, extra time, and the ubiquitous homework passes as positive re-enforcers. Speaking of re-enforcers, I need to cover just one more issue to help structure the remainder of our time together.

Whenever we talk about behaviorism, even in generalities, I am reminded that, as educators, most of us have taken the basic courses on behavior theory through our coursework in college. Even a master's degree or plus-30 programs tend to force "Learning Theory" upon the students, and these classes typically include a unit on some semblance of behaviorism. The problem is that for many of you, your learning on this subject was limited to Pavlov (see Chapter 2) or a more simplistic model of Skinner. Skinner (at his most basic) was the scientist who worked a *lot* with pigeons – remember the "Skinner Box" – and spent the bulk of his career examining their pecking habits as they were shaped by rudimentary re-enforcers, like food pellets.

When we work with students, though, the needs they are meeting and the re-enforcers they seek or require can be far more complicated than a simple food pellet. If only ninth graders (or husbands) were as simplistic as pigeons!

For example, we could easily teach a dog to roll over on command, right? Likewise, we could probably just as easily teach a 1- or 2-year-old the same trick for roughly the same level of re-enforcers. But think about this, would it be *equally as easy* to get a high school senior to roll over? Or take it back a notch – would it be just as easy to teach a fifth grader, or a first grader the same trick? How about your spouse?

The issue I am getting at is that once cognition becomes a variable in the conditioning process, or perhaps once socialization kicks off those good old Freudian unconscious drive systems, the re-enforcers with the most punch become more complicated – both to analyze and to dole out. A food pellet, doggie bone, or a Sweet Tart is pretty easy; however needs like attention-seeking, power and control, revenge, or displays of inadequacy are not quite so easy!

For this reason, I have spent a good deal of our time and space in this book describing some of the issues that these kids bring into the classroom. Understanding them will best equip you to re-formulate the relationship in a way that allows for that student's needs to be met, and for sanity to be restored to your room. Likewise, I will spend the remainder of this chapter going through some of those more complicated needs that are to be met by many of the acting out students we look at every day... just before we head out to the parking lot to make sure we have an updated resume in the same file folder with that completed Home Depot® application.

Goals of Acting out Behavior
(adapted from Johnson, 2006)

1. *Attention*

We'll start with the easy one; attention. Everyone loves attention! The "good kids," the "bad kids," we grown-ups kids... all of us want – dare I say *need* – attention. In fact, if I were to poll the teachers across the country and asked the Family Feud type question, "Name a reason for acting out behavior," the number one answer on the board would be "Negative Attention-Seeking!"

Incidentally, I think "To Make the Teacher Nuts" would be a close second.

When it comes to attention, remember not only the students from bad home lives but consider also the kids with two loving parents – they still jockey for position with two or three brothers and sisters to gain the focus of their folks.

In fact, I remember reading when I was in college that, on average, working parents spend less than thirty minutes of quality time per night with their kids on work nights. I recall being somewhat mystified by that statistic. But then I grew up and had kids of my own, and I now realize that we are truly in danger of that coming true.

Kids do the math… what is the quickest, most efficient way to get the attention of an adult when you really, really want it? Acting out/bad behavior, of course!

For example, if you want to get mom's attention – right *now* – and she is busy making dinner, chatting with her sister on the phone, trying to watch the evening news, and take care of your baby brother, what do you do? You do something awful… to the cat… with a fork… now *that* will get mom to table all of her other interests for a moment and get down to business.

Kids learn that little trick early on, and then bring their knowledge of it into the classroom. And furthermore, now they don't have two or three brothers and sisters; they have twenty-three. And now they don't have a mom and a dad; they have you. So it's go time for the students, and they will find a way to get your attention when they really want it… but the Bad Kids will have more latitude with regard to the behaviors they have at their disposal.

So kids can turn to behaviors like interrupting, forgetting, or clowning to get your attention. And let's not forget that it's not necessarily *your* attention that can feed that need. Even the other students in the room can fulfill that need. Behaviors for the benefit of the other students can even take on a more subtle nature – it's not always Arnold Horshack pulling the infamous, "Ooh, Ooh, Ooh!" in the back of the room that can grab the floor. Behaviors like dropping stuff constantly, catching the eye of a classmate, passing notes or drawings, or a well-timed chuckle or snort can also draw in the room, and re-route them off of whatever you are trying to accomplish.

And remember, even though a good scold is a negative repercussion, when you are "locked in" with that student, you have just established a very intense one-on-one interaction, whereby the rest of the room may no longer exist. What you see as a punisher may actually be a re-enforcers when you intervene at the "C."

One possibly effective intervention for acting out behavior is to initiate a "Planned Ignoring" (sometimes called "Tactical Ignoring") program, during which you essentially cut off the reinforcement (i.e., attention). This is an intervention that is almost always taught at teacher behavior-management in-services and seminars, but rarely come with the necessary caution labels. For now, suffice it to say that the targeted behavior must meet certain criteria in order for the planned ignore to even be relevant.

First, it must be behavior that is only *solely* designed to grab attention; it cannot be meeting other needs which may still be fulfilled even if the attention is removed. Second, the behavior must not be one that *has to* be dealt with in a more immediate sense. Behaviors that may be harmful, dangerous, or are maximally disruptive are those which cannot be put off for the amount of time required for a Planned Ignore to take root.

While a Planned Ignore will work over time, there are a couple of issues inherent to the models that make it very difficult to successfully pull off in the classroom. I'll just tease you with these for now, and hope you keep reading through Chapter 13 when I discuss the pitfalls in more detail.

The other thing I wanted to bring up in this section has to do with class clowns. Clowning around is a fantastic means of usurping focus in the room and can work to derail both you and the rest of the class. The neat thing about clowning is that it almost doesn't matter who the attention comes from – anyone can fill that void. So, it could be you, it could be his buddies (and class clowns are almost exclusively the domain of the boys), it could be the jocks or the girls or the others students in the hallway – it really doesn't matter.

We have all probably had a little class clown in our room at one time or another, right? But you've got to admit, some of them can be pretty talented! Have you ever had a class clown say something so funny – but so doggone inappropriate that you literally had to turn your back so he didn't see you laughing? The thing that class clowns have going for them that can really be strength (if only they would use it for good instead of evil!) is that they can probably think pretty fast. A sense of humor requires a Pentium chip upstairs. If a student has an old 486 up there, he wouldn't be able to make the connections or turn the phrase lightning fast to be truly funny.

So, one thing we recommend for class clowns – and really for almost all poorly behaving kids – is to teach them to control and contain their bad impulse, and then channel it in a more appropriate direction. If all we try to do is squash in our fists, the energy these acting out students bring into our classrooms, eventually it will start to leak out from between our fingers. Re-directing can allow them the freedom to still express themselves and that energy, while also giving them a skill that can carry them outside of the school setting.

So for class clowns, here is something to consider. It is usually reserved for older students (i.e., middle or high school) whose sense of humor lends itself to this intervention, and secondly, this intervention will only be effective if the student is mature enough emotionally to handle this. But you can try to "Prescribe the Symptom" (Haley, 1993).

Here is what I mean. Let's say you have a class clown who gets too disruptive with his "gift." You sit him down one day, and say to him, "Listen, next Thursday when we are all filing in from recess (or changing classes, or whatever), I'll give you three minutes of open microphone time. Save up, get some of your best material together, and let's see what you've got. I don't want to hear it during the class period. Really – get it together for your floor time."

Your goal in doing this maneuver, by the way, is not to hope that he fails. Quite the contrary – you want him to succeed. You want him to impress and entertain the jocks, the girls, his buddies, or you so that now you have a vital tool – *leverage*. Now you can tell him that if he's good next week, you'll will give him two minutes on Tuesday as well. If he is bad, he is down to one minute next Thursday.

And all of us have three minutes somewhere in our schedule to plug the kid in. Whenever we change rooms or situations, it usually takes the kids a couple of minutes to settle in. Take advantage of this! And if the student hands you the line, "Three minutes, that isn't very much" remind him that it *really is!* Have you ever tried to get up with a prepared speech in front of a group of your peers? Or worse yet, have you tried to be funny only to find that your joke died a horrific death in front of the group? Where a minute can seem like a virtual weekend?

Prescribing the Symptom allows the need to be met in a manner that is more appropriate, provides the student a good outlet for the energy they've got, and affords the student a chance to practice mastery of control and contain.

2. *Power*

Ah, here is the driving force of many of our angry kids; those delightful little ODD students we have grown to love so much! Those aggressive, defiant, stubborn, oppositional kids! Actually, my metaphor for these kids is that they are like good hunting dogs.

Now bear in mind that I am from a small town in Wisconsin, where the school absentee rate among students on the first day of Deer Season can approach 40 or 50%. But deer aside, when you hunt fowl you have to take a good hunting dog with you.

I'll spare you the hunting lesson and go straight to the point. When you are out shopping for a good hunting dog, you need a test to figure out if a puppy is going to work out or not. So here is what you do: you grab the puppy under the belly and flip him over onto his back. If he jumps right up and looks you in the eye and says, "*Hey*! Knock it off!" you have the makings of a good hunting dog.

What you don't want is a dog that stays over on his back, acquiescing to you. You don't want a wimpy dog; you want one with a little bit of *chutzpah*... one that will be appropriately assertive when he needs to be.

These kids are like those good hunting dogs: they will not back down or back off. If you rise up, they will meet you stride for stride. As you escalate, they will match you in kind. So to deal with these students, we have to look at yet another dog metaphor.

For those of you with dogs; have you ever played with a tug toy with your pooch? Either a tug toy specifically designed to be such, or maybe a piece of rope, or a sock, or whatever? Most of us have. As you try to pull on that thing, what does your dog do? My guess is, s/he clenches their jaws, haunches back and digs all twenty toenails in to the harvest gold shag carpeting, right? The harder you pull, the harder the dog adjusts and pulls back. A weird sort of equilibrium is met.

So, how do you get the tug toy away from the dog? Simple... you stop pulling and (*most importantly*) give a little slack. You wait for the dog to relax a bit. Then, as humans are seemingly programmed to do, we yank that sucker away, fake the throw, and feel superior to our canine companions.

But the point is this: if you don't unseat your dog's feet, s/he will never give up the tug toy. You have to get those nails out of the shag carpet. These ODD students operate in almost the same way. If you try to push, they dig in. If you try to pull, they dig in. The only way to get them moved is to unseat their feet – or, by allowing them a little slack.

Here's how we bring that metaphor into your classroom. It has to do with giving *options*. Options are important because they offer at least an illusion of power and control. Even options that are really still on *your* terms can give the student just enough room to "save face" in front of his buddies, or at the very least feel like he is now in control of the pace and/or the direction of the next move.

For example, say you have a student who has been acting out and now has to go to the principal's office. As you push, he rises up a little. Now in actuality, if you continue to push, you will win the battle – after all, you are the grown-up. In the same manner, you could always rip the tug toy out of your dog's mouth because you are bigger. But what are you doing if you "force" the kid into something, and make him feel strong-armed into it? You win the battle, but eventually lose the war because you are creating anger and damaging your relationship with him.

A better solution lies in a bit of finesse. Rather than force the student, offer him a choice; "You can go down to Mr. Johnson's office right now, or you can take a few seconds to breathe and we'll go in a moment."

While this statement still keeps your needs on the front burner, it simultaneously allows Little Johnny some room to look like he a part of the bidding process. Thus, it can free his up feet enough to get him moving in the right direction, while still maintaining a protective relationship between you two.

Oh – and keep the number of options down to two – *maybe* three on special occasions. Too many options can be overwhelming to kids. Worse yet, too many choices can also work to shift the power base to his camp, thereby rendering you powerless You give a choice, but you are still in charge.

3. Revenge

Bring on the Bullies!

Sound like a nightmare you have had at one time or another? It certainly is one that the frail students in your school have had recurring. Most of us have had some dealings with a bully – either as kids or as grown-ups in our schools. Whenever the exposure happened, it was probably not a pleasant one. Bullies kind of have that "gift."

Now, dealing with bullying behavior is ripe for an entire book on the matter, but I will throw out a couple of suggestions to give you something to think about if you are scratching your head, wondering what you may be able to do.

Bullies, almost without variation, are the products of the coming together of two distinct forces: first they come from some sort of abuse at home. Physical, verbal, emotional – whichever it happens to be, the abuse serves two purposes: it creates anger in the heart of the bully, and it robs him of his self worth.

The other force meeting the anger is typically some physical size. Bullies have the genetic influences that allow them to bring the Law of the Jungle to the playground. Or, "Might Makes Right, and I am far mightier than thee, thus I am going to impose my will upon you."

Another aside, I will be using the pronoun "he" again in this section. We have been seeing a rise in the number of girls who are bullying like the boys typically do. By and large, bullying in a physical way still seems predominantly male. Girls, for the most part, are still bullying with words and social exclusion more often than fisticuffs.

Let's look at the bully's point of view. What the bullying behavior is doing, from a psychological perspective, are a couple of things. First, it is re-creating the trauma the bully has felt in his life – only now, he is putting himself in the power position and putting the victim in the position he has felt at home. And let's face it; does the bully usually pick on the linebacker of the football team? Heck no! The bully isn't stupid! He wants to live to bully another day! So he singles out weaker members of the herd who are more easily dominated, thereby making them exactly like he is compared to his own abuser.

The other thing bullying behavior is doing is giving the bully a sense of being respected by the children he dominates. He fuses and *con*fuses fear with respect. And, after all, because his self-worth was stolen from him years ago by the grown-ups in his life, he (at some level) does not feel as though he has anything to offer *other than* his size and strength. In other words, in the mind of the bully, other kids have no *other* reason to respect him, because he really has nothing else of value to offer (Batsche & Knoff, 1994). If you were to ask him to earn respect any other way, he would feel as though he had nothing to give.

I know you tend to get fed up with the explanation of, "A bully is just a misunderstood kid with low self-esteem..." You still have to deal with the fact that he is either creaming or intimidating half of your third grade class! So, to treat the bullies, we have to approach and deal with them on two separate fronts, each addressing a different aspect of the bullying.

First, and as is the case with all behavior problem kids, work the reward and consequences of his behavior plan. Make it better to be good than to not be good. This will work toward curbing the behaviors on a shorter-term basis. For longer term change, we work on the second front.

Secondly, we can effect tremendous longer-term change in the life of the bully if we can instill some self-worth or value in the kid's sense of identity. This does sound a bit "pop-psych" when I phrase it this way, but it does have some legitimacy to it. If we can make school seem like less of a disaster to the bully, and if we can begin to change the underlying energy that is pushing his bad behavior, we can change the rules of how he approaches the world – and remember that this world includes *you!* To accomplish this task, we have a couple options.

To work toward school creating a sense of accomplishment rather than an atmosphere of failure, we can hit him with option "A." To do this, we go back to Gardner and his different intelligences.

Do you all remember Gardner? He was the fellow who took a look at the standardization is intelligence testing, and asked the philosophical question, "What the heck *is* intelligence, anyway?"

Back in my day, there was only one kind of intelligence. It was called "g" and it was measured quite succinctly on a Weschler Intelligence Test (a WPPSI, WISC, or WAIS). The scores were normalized with a mean of 100 and a standard deviation of fifteen, and if you didn't fall within two standard deviations of the mean, there was something either very wrong or very right with you.

So, along ambles Howard Gardner, and he turned the whole ideology on its ear. He started to think and write about how people could be smart in a variety of ways – some of which may not even show up on a Weschler test (Gardner, 1983)!

Blasphemy! Clearly Gardner is not a founding member of the Flat-Earth Society. But think about it for a moment. Think about some of the smartest people you have known in life. For me, I think I mentioned before that I grew up in a small town in Wisconsin. Being a small town in Wisconsin, we had our fair share of farmers. The farmers around me, many of whom were either neighbors or the dads of friends of mine, would never have performed very well on a Weschler test. Quite a few did not even finish high school, in fact. But I'll tell you this: if my car broke down, who do you think I was calling to help me out? Or when the water heater blew in our basements, who do think we were grateful to live near?

Yeah – the farmers! They were extraordinary when it came to fixing stuff and knowing how to problem solve. They could figure things out in a way that I still admire to this day! So… were they intelligent?

Of course! And that was Gardner's point. So, he came up with a number (and the number grows every few years – we're up to nine or ten, depending on whether you include or exclude "Existential Intelligence" of intelligences in which a person can be proficient. Some folks are very smart when it comes to music… or art… or sports… or reading other people. Let's bring this back to bullying.

Are the bullies in your school typically among the smartest students? No, probably not. These kids will never sit on the Supreme Court. But, they may be really good at tearing down a lawnmower engine, building things, being artistic or athletic, or good at other things that they won't admit to because they're "too cool" to engage in them.

As his teacher, you can work toward building self worth by creating success in a setting he has grown to hate – school. Find those activities where he can succeed and allow him to meet a challenge. Perhaps you can create a group project where each participant can contribute based on their unique strength rather than forcing them to feel the pang of individual deficits.

For example, let's say you teach English or Literature. If you create a group project that has them put together a book, you could create a situation whereby the students contribute from a position of strength. So, those who are creative may come up with the concept; the ones who draw well can do the illustrations; those who can write well can do the text; those who are more mechanically inclined may physically put the thing together from a gum wrapper, a Fruit Loops box, six inches of reflective duct tape, and a 26-inch shoelace. You get the picture. However you conceive of the project, allowing the students to choose their own piece of the pie can set them up for success.

The other option "B" is only going to be an option if you have it as a possibility in your school/situation. It involves building self worth by allowing the bully a chance to have others look to him as having something of value to offer besides his strength.

To pull this off, you really have to get the bully out of your classroom. If changes begin to happen, and the bully starts to move – even slightly – off of his position as the bully, the rest of your class will work hard to yank him right back into that roll. They do this because the only way they are comfortable is to understand him as being the bully.

This sounds like I have ripped a page form the *Bizarro World Daily News,* but hear me out. I'll give an example you may be able to relate to on a more personal level. Have you ever gone "home" for Thanksgiving? Your parents, aunts and uncles, grandparents, etc. all gather together at this festive occasion. And when you go into this atmosphere, do you feel like you're 12-years-old all over again? If so, it's because the family system (and all of its members) have a hard time seeing you as a grown-up. They grew really used to seeing you as a kid and now don't see you quite often enough to grant you the dignity of being a grown-up. They will pull you back into that role because the family is stronger than your ability to resist!

Or here's another one: for those of you who may have been rebellious teens: do you feel a little of that rebellion begin to stir whenever you go back into your mom and dad's house? Same principal applies.

In your classroom, even if you start to treat the bully differently, the rest of the kids will be adjusting at a far slower pace. They will still be avoiding eye contact with him, they will shrink away from him in the hallway if he gets too close, and nobody will hang with him on the playground. In essence, their fear and loathing will suck him right smack back into being the bully, and order will be restored in the universe.

To effect long-term change, we need to get him out of an environment whereby everyone knows him as "The Bully." One thing we have been successful with requires a few variables to be in place. First, this has to be available to you in your particular school setting. Second, the bully has to be emotionally able to handle it, and this typically works better with bullies who are a little older.

The plan is to take him down to the kindergarteners or first graders, and have him read to them, help them with some task or assignment, or coach them at gym class, whatever. The point being that you set up a situation where other people can look to him as having something of value to offer other than his ability to beat them up.

Further, we use real little kids because, for the most part, bullies have an unwritten limit as to how small the victims can be. Once a bully reaches a certain age, he won't pick on the really small kids anymore. Thus, the kindergarteners or first graders may not even know that he is a bully – he is just another big kid coming down to mentor or teach them.

Community service projects can also be a good opportunity for the bully to shine in a way he does not in the classroom. One possibility here is for the bully, or perhaps even an entire class in an alternative setting, to arrange to help on a Habitat for Humanity house. If this arrangement can be made, it can also be a reward that the students earn their way up to. But again, use whatever you have available to you.

4. Display of inadequacy

I throw these kids into the mix because they are also demonstrating a lack of self-worth in a different way than bullies. These are kids who do not feel adequate or worthy, but do not have the level of internal anger or the physical size the bullies have.

In the interest of clarity, I'll be a little more specific as to who these students are. These tend to be the kids who, as matter of course, punt on second down. They are the ones who refuse to try because there is more safety in defiance or self-handicapping than there is in trying your best and then failing. That vulnerability (or their belief that they cannot possibly succeed in the first place) is too frightening a force, so they avoid by chopping their own legs out from under themselves.

Another way that this feeling of inadequacy can play itself out behaviorally is in their speech patters. For example, you may know a kid – or maybe even a grown-up – who falls into the category of folks who I call "The Disclaimer People."

These are folks who will preface every personalized statement (i.e., statements they make about themselves) with a disclaimer. Like, "I know this is going to be wrong, but…" or "I know you're going to hate me, but…" or "This is really going to sound stupid, but…"

Even without a clear-cut disclaimer, students can have a speech pattern that belies an underlying depression or lack of worth. These can be kids who are angrily *brutal* when tearing into themselves. They will say things like, "I'm so *stupid*," or, "I can't get anything right" or the all-encompassing, "*I hate myself!*"

As a general rule of thumb, the way we talk belies the way we think. Depressed and anxious people actually think *and talk* differently than non-depressed, non-anxious people. When you hear speech patterns like this, what the person is effectively doing is opening a little window into his or her mind and allowing you to hear the elevator music that they hear constantly playing in the background.

When a student gives you one of his patented disclaimers, what he is hearing in his head is, "You are *always* wrong" or "*Everyone* will/should hate you" or "You *always* sound stupid." The words that actually make it out of the mouth tend to be a watered down version of what they are saying to themselves, believe it or not.

For these students, you can make a powerful intervention without a lot of work. Just start to nudge them cognitively and change the way they talk.

Obviously, I don't mean that you should pull them in front of a mirror and have them do their best Stewart Smalley imitation, whereby they are forced to recite, "I'm good enough... and I'm smart enough... and doggone it, *people like me!*" That technique would have little effect because it is trying to force a mindset onto the kid that, to him or her, feels a million miles away.

Instead, try a gentler touch. With the disclaimer kids, for example, merely snip off the disclaimer. At first, it will require a firmer hand, and a bit more directness in your instruction. Obviously, your goal over time is to have the student catch himself before the disclaimer slips out.

To those who are more straight forward or harsher in tearing at themselves, you may have to be completely overt and absolutely direct – to the point of having them stop, back up, and re-state whatever they were saying from the beginning *without* the self-deprecating remark. If that is too far off, start them by having them repeat the slam in a milder manner. Over time, you can push them to eliminate it all together.

If you change the way they talk, you will change the way they think. This will, over time, change the way they feel and the way they behave. In my business, this is called a *cognitive intervention*. For you, it can be the difference between a student moving forward with a sense of confirmation of all his or her worst fears or moving ahead with a renewed sense of value.

Before fast-forwarding into Chapter 10, I remind you that, for all of the students we examined in this chapter, they still have to go home at night. Whatever environment set them up to aggressively seek attention, to grab power like a dog with a tug toy, to bully, or to self-handicap still exists out there in the "real world." Whoever created that mindset in that kid may still be in the home and may be a far-from-helpful element in the daily grind of your student. So the strides you make with you student during the time you have them throughout the day may be systematically torn down and torn apart while he or she tries to manage at home each night.

Have some patience and remember the oil tanker or the freight train analogy. Some days it may feel like two steps forward, 1 step backward – and you may be right! The parental/caregiver forces are always going to be more powerful than any force you can generate as a teacher in the life of the student – particularly for the younger children. But don't underestimate *your* level of importance in his or her life. Your goal should not be to have a Hollywood ending to the school year. An ending where you and the kid march, hand-in-hand, into the setting sun with some random Whitney Houston tune crooning in the background… everyone is happy… all is well… dog people and cat people living together in perfect harmony, etc. Rather, you are inching and nudging his trajectory toward a brighter destination.

Chapter 10

Behavior Plan Common Denominators

Finding the Common Ground

Let's get down to business and talk about some of the common denominators of any good behavioral plan (adapted from Johnson, 2006). I also place these under the general heading of, "Regardless which plan you begin, this stuff has to be in place."

Bearing in mind that we are going to discuss several ideas for classroom management in upcoming chapters, know that it doesn't matter which you choose... each of you has a different personality and will feel more comfortable with one or another. By the same token, each of the plans is adaptable to your specific situation. All of the plans, though, need to have an umbrella of "behavioral common sense" to protect them from failing miserably! Let's go over what that umbrella consists of.

Specific instructions

1. Make everyone know the rules

Perhaps the most important rule of all is to have the rules clearly understood by all who play the game. I'm sure you all have rules in your classroom. Incidentally, whenever I ask what the rules are in teachers' classrooms, I get examples like; hands to yourself, raise your hand before you speak, come to class prepared, respect others' property and persons, etc.

I actually chose to write "respect..." last on purpose. This is because that concept seems to be the over-arching rule that governs all others. In fact, if you could boil all of your classroom rules down to their bare essence, you would have something like "respect" residue left at the bottom of the pot. It is the guidepost for all good behavior, and in fact is the foundation to the *Golden Rule.*

I would like to take a moment to remind all of you to break "respect" down to behavioral, concrete terms for your students. An ambiguous term like "respect" can be either confusing for the younger kids, or can begin to morph into all different directions for bigger kids (i.e., how many faces does "respect" wear in any given high school?). So, for the sake of clarity, be sure to set aside a couple of minutes at the beginning of the school year to outline very specifically what *you* mean when you say "respect."

Think about it this way: how do you show another person respect? Usually, there are hard signs like these: make eye contact, respect their property by not wrecking or stealing it, don't interrupt when they are talking, use the other person's name when talking to them or referring to them, use positive language or words when discussing another person, etc.

I'm sure most of you are doing this already, but moments of reinforcement to know you are doing a good job can feel good.

Make sure everyone knows *The Rules.* And furthermore, it is an important process to go through and have the students feel like they all have a hand in creating *The Rules* (I'll explain why in a minute). On the first day of class, go through the shell game of making the kids feel like they are moving through the process of developing rules for the classroom with you as the guide.

And I use the phrase "shell game" because it is a bit of a parlor trick to actually create the rules with the students. Some smoke and mirrors has to be applied because, as I am sure you already know, you tend to have a *pretty good idea* of what the rules are going to look like before you even ask the class for input. This way, if one student throws out the suggestion that everyone should keep their hands and feet to themselves, and another kid in the back row insists that they need a water fountain that shoots chocolate milk back there... you can conveniently highlight the hands and feet rule and nudge the rules in that direction.

But having the students feel responsibility for the rules for the room combines with #2 below to create a base of power for you.

2. Have the rules graphically displayed in your room

This rule is pretty straight forward; have The Rules clearly posted on The Wall. Now I will bring together the concepts in numbers 1 and 2 above and tell you what I mean when I talk about establishing your power base.

If the kids know the rules, feel a sense of responsibility for the rules and can see the rules clearly on the wall, it frees you up if there is ever conflict. You do not have to get sucked into the fray because now, the scenario is set up where it is no longer the student versus you. Rather, it is the student versus the rules on the wall. You are now free to be above the chaos; and instead of thinking up the rules on the fly, you are firmly in a position to circle around the fray and merely be the *enforcer* of the rules. From a power point of view, this is a superior position to be in.

I know that sounded a bit confusing, but here is an example to (hopefully) clarify my position on this one.

Let's say you have a student who is acting out and you are forced to initiate a consequence. Rather than getting sucked into an argument with the kid who typically starts with him saying something to the effect of, "You're just picking on me," you can back out of the chaos, point to The Rules, and say, "No... its number 6 up there on the wall."

You can even throw in for good measure, "And furthermore, you came up with number 6! So don't tell me I am picking on you!"

It is now the student against the wall (metaphorically) – and the wall becomes an external force that no longer involves or requires your subjectivity. The class has agreed upon the rules and can see them whenever they choose. You are freed up and above the din!

I also tell parents this if they employ time-out at home. In this example, I tell moms and dads that, if they send their kids to time-out, the parent does not keep the time. Rather, they will now set an egg timer or the microwave to keep track of the time spent. This way, you avoid the power play of kids who will pull this one on you: "Can I come out now? Can I come out now? Can I come out now…?"

If the kids pull that one out of his bag of tricks, you do not have to descend into battle. Rather, you remain outside of the fray and are able to point out that you have not heard the timer go off, so clearly the time is not over. It is now not your child against *you*, it is him against *the clock*. And from a power perspective, this is, again, a superior position to be in.

So utilize points 1 and 2 to elevate yourself out of the war zone of whichever battle happens to be raging in your room. You are not engaging the students in battle; you are only monitoring their engagement with the rules on the wall.

3. *Have positive expectations*

I bring this one up for a couple of reasons, and each has to do with maintaining sanity in the room!

Perhaps most importantly, think about how you begin the morning (if you have the same classroom for the full day) or the class period (if your students change classrooms throughout the day). Do you all start the kids off on a positive note? Some sort of affirmation – or even at its most basic, saying something like

"Good morning!" can help begin the arduous process of moving some of the troubled kids out of their axis.

And I am not Pollyannaish to the point of believing that this can shake a bad mood out of a student who has had a really tough morning or bus ride or transition in the hallway. No, some kids are really going to struggle within a pretty rough bubble of space. But your best shot at creating an atmosphere conducive to positive behavior begins at the pace/tone you set at the onset of your time together. Make it a ritual to leave their baggage at the door. Remember again, if you don't want to be there, they certainly won't want to be, so do your best to create a positive space.

I *know* you each get a good feel for how the class is going to be when your kids are strolling in. If you sense one of those dark clouds over a head or two, do your best to move them in a different direction.

And on a related note, do any of you start the day or the class period with a recitation, either starting with the Pledge of Allegiance or a Prayer or a school slogan or a more formal affirmation, etc? Remember Chapter 7 on effective leadership; you want to create a boundary at the doorway for the tougher kids. When you start the class with a recitation – and it really does not matter *what you are actually saying* – you are creating a collective consciousness and getting all the students marching both in stride and at the same time. In other words, you are setting the remainder of your time together apart by creating a boundary.

It may not even be a recitation. Some teachers begin with a common task in which the kids engage when they arrive. Maybe a question for thought on the board or a fun problem or a relevant task will also get everyone to put the car into gear and move away from their troubling parking spot.

Here is the second reason for starting the day on a positive note: it creates a better situation for your own self-fulfilling prophecy.

By this, I mean that your internal expectations have an impact on how you approach a student or a situation. If you truly believe that today is going to be awful or that one or a few of the students are going to have you banging your head against the wall, your behavior will follow that line of thinking. And it does not have to be overt!

A positive table-setting allows you the best opportunity to approach the day fresh and behave in a manner that will maximize the potential for good behavior.

4. *Utilize a warning system when behavior escalates*

I trust that each of you has a warning system whereby you afford the students an opportunity to lasso the horse and drag it back into the barn without consequence. And I don't mean issuing a smaller consequence before hitting them with a bigger one – rather, I mean truly giving them a chance to practice control and containment before they get the penalty.

The more common ones I hear involve either a direct verbal warning ("Justin, this is your first warning.") or some sort of progressive steps (like name on the board; moving clothespins from green to yellow; having the teacher hold up one finger, then two, then three, etc.).

I also particularly enjoy those teachers who simply stop talking! They grow silent in an effort to stir the pot and get the students to notice. Bear in mind, the humor for me lies in the fact that this system relies on the do-gooders in the front row to hurriedly turn about and issue the more auditory "Shhh! Shhhhhh!" to their slower-on-the-uptake classmates in the back of the room!

As an aside, I always ask my groups if there are any light-flippers in the crowd. You know those teachers – the ones who flip the lights on and off if the classroom as a whole starts to escalate. There are usually a few who raise their hands and admit to this old standby.

Warnings are an extremely important part of any behavioral plan because the practice we can give the kids to work on self control and behavioral containment is a vital developmental concept.

And think about some of the environments your students are coming from as they make their way to school each day. They have all sorts of parenting styles at home, and for some kids, knowledge that they even have the *capability* to reign in their behavior (i.e., control and containment) is indeed a novel thought! For these students, control is always externalized. Here's what I mean by that:

Think about kids who come from a home where they have a very punitive, intrusive, and/or over-controlling parent. For these kids, whenever they begin to act out their parent is immediately on top of them, crushing them and their behavior. The end result is that these kids never learn that *they* can be in control – they never have to or get an opportunity to. Over time, they will learn to rely solely on external forces to gain control for them.

In your classroom, these kids tend to be easy to recognize because they are the ones who will keep prodding and poking and searching out your buttons until finally you snap and force control upon them. It may feel like they refuse to bring themselves down. In actuality, it may be just the opposite; they don't know how to or even that they are able to.

So for these students, and really others too, giving them a chance to practice this skill (control and contain) without immediate punishment can not only develop a skill, but will also help build the relationship with you because trust will begin to develop in an area the student may not expect.

And by the way, what is the right number of warnings to give before hitting them with the consequence? One? Two? Three?

The answer is that there is no magic number answer. The situation will depend upon the ages of your students, their emotional maturity, the size of your room, etc. Factors will influence the number of warnings you issue, but always bear in mind that it is better to err on the side of low rather than high.

What happens if you start to issue seven or eight warnings before you slap them with the consequence? If you give too many warnings, the kids will blow through your yellow lights because there is never a cop on the other side giving tickets.

But here is something I see quite often; teachers who know not to give a lot of formal warnings will *inadvertently* issue quite a few informal ones. I call this developing scenario "The Teacher Trap." In The Teacher Trap, many a good, hard working professional may catch themselves staggering warnings throughout a time period. These are warnings that are not labeled as such, but still have the power of teaching the kids your rhythm or your cadence.

If you catch yourself going through a motion similar to this one: "James, sit-down... I said sit-down... I – hey – I mean it – *sit down* and pay attention... JAMES... Knock it off... Okay, this is your first warning..."

Get the picture? You only issued one direct, formal warning, but you actually fired several warning shots across his bow before you even got to the formal warning stage. This has now taught James that he can push you to four or five before he even gets smacked with warning number one – and he will take advantage of this knowledge! Kids do the math quite well and will respond to the structure you impose.

Give them the chance to practice control and contain.

I also employ the same technique of reinforcing the control, not the acting out, when I help parents of kids who have temper tantrums. And nothing will unbalance a household like one or more kids who employ tantrums as a weapon or a means of manipulation! And I am sure you have all seen a really, *really* good temper tantrum, right? I mean a tantrum that makes everyone walking out of Sears to say to each other, "Now *that* was impressive!"

Before moving on, I will also take up some for the poor parents who are controlled by their three year old. Tantrums have a pretty easy path toward development because almost all kids go through a tantrum phase while they are developing. They do not have the means to wall off frustration, so it flies in all directions like stroganoff in a topless blender set to *puree*. When this happens the first or second time, it may catch the parent off guard and they will swoop in to fix the problem. And now, as they say, the hook is set. The tantrum has been reinforced to the point that it is sealed in as the "go to thing" for when that student wants what he wants.

Do you think kids are in control of tantrums? Sometimes no – these are kids who pass a certain threshold, and they are *gone*. For these kids, it really does require a grown-up to step in and help get them backed down out of the tantrum.

For many kids, however, a tantrum is used as a tool, similar to any device designed to gain control over a situation. And the litmus test I give a lot of moms and dads is to give them the following directive; pay attention to your kids next time he tantrums, and notice if he *scans the room* every once in awhile.

I ask this, and parents have an "Aha!" moment. I ask if he is throwing tantrums at home, does he have the tantrum on the linoleum or on the carpet? Or for teachers; I ask if he is flipping out on the playground, is it on the pavement or on the grass?

Again, I hear a lot of "Ahhaa's" coming from folks. But for tantrums, we treat in the same conceptual manner I have been describing when I talk about warnings. Once again, we reinforce the control and contain, but *not* the tantrum.

To do this, we take advantage of one of the wonderful qualities of every temper tantrum – and the worse the tantrum happens to be, the more this is true. A tantrum cannot go on for very long until the kid has to pause to catch his breath. Tantrums burn a energy, and kids cannot sustain them for very long without a brief break – regardless of how fleeting this respite seems.

Now, the first rule of treating a tantrum is that the kids cannot hurt themselves. Once that has been satisfied, we move into the treatment phase. For this, I remind moms that we remove *all* reinforcement from the environment. For example, if you have to move your child, pick them up side saddle, like a log instead of in an embrace. Don't make the contact reinforcing. Even remove eye contact. If this will be hard for you, grab a newspaper or magazine to hold your gaze.

Now, as soon as the kid pauses to catch his breath, swoop in and reinforce the heck out of his ability to stop himself. This maneuver will invariably kick off another round of tantrums because now he has the attention, but that's okay – remove again all forms of reinforcement, and await the eye of the storm. Then repeat the treatment phase.

This method of weaning temper tantrums emphasizes an opportunity to feel reinforcement during times of controlling and containing. It parallels your warnings system in the classroom. With warnings, you give your students a chance to have their capabilities reinforced, and will begin to turn that oil tanker around by giving them another option when it comes to seeking reinforcement, and controlling and containing their own behavior.

If you are searching for a warning system that will work well, or perhaps you are ready for a change, I recommend one that may seem a bit medieval on the front end, but will have some staying power.

To accomplish this warning system, go on down to PetSmart® or PetCo®, or your local pet supply shop, and get yourself one of those clickers that animal trainers use. (For those of you who were rooting for me to instruct you to get a shock collar, *shame on you!*) The clickers are small, easy to use, and make a very sharp, distinctive noise when you press the button.

Using a clicker has several advantages: first, they are small enough to fit right into the palm of your hand. Therefore, you can be tooling along with your lecture, and if there are a couple of students messing around in the back of the room, you can hit the "click" button without missing a step. In fact, some even with a gizmo that wraps loosely around your wrist, so you can't drop it by accident!

Second, the noise is truly unique, which makes it difficult for kids to *not* hear it. Think about this: if you use your voice for a warning, students may get very skilled at tuning you out. Or think about how easy it is for your own children or your own *spouse* to tune out your voice! You can't tune out the clicker.

By the same token, while the noise is unique, it is not overbearing. Thus, it acts as a more subtle reminder than the bell on your desk or the whistle you have been thinking about utilizing. You hit the clicker, and the teacher next door doesn't poke her head in your door to make sure everything is okay!

Lastly, using any auditory warning has a couple advantages over a visual warning. The first is that when you hit the clicker, you put the whole class on notice. For this first warning, you are not singling anybody out and either embarrassing them or giving them the attention they may be seeking. You give them a chance to pull it together without having the glare of the spotlight hit them between the eyes. And don't worry about the students being confused about what just happened – most kids know the score of the game. They know who the warning has been issued for. And even if they don't, a hint of ambiguity may make them *all* sit up a little straighter and pull it together for themselves!

Secondly, we have to remember a quality of our boys; if you have a couple boys messing around in the back of the room and you do something that is solely visual, they may not have any idea that they have been warned. But, when you hit the clicker they will hear know that they have been duly warned.

You can work out the remaining details to fit your particular room. One warning, maybe two or three – whatever the system happens to be – go over the rules of engagement before you begin the program. Then institute the rule with as much consistency as you are able to manage.

5. *When misbehavior occurs, stay calm and be concise*

Here's an easy one: when the world seems to be crashing down around you like the Four Horsemen of the Apocalypse galloping at full gait through your classroom... *stay calm!*

I'm sure you have heard this little pearl of wisdom in just about every training and staff development you have attended since you were a student at the university. As trainers, we love to blow hard about all the "shoulda's" and "oughta's" out there. These universal truths are pretty easy for us to say, but difficult (at best!) to actually pull off in the heat of battle. But let's say you begin to recite this mantra while the tectonic plates are mounting tension... what's the point?

The point has to do with *energy.* In most escalating situations, your goal should be to remove energy rather than create or add to it. If you begin to get hyped up, you are actually adding energy to an already out-of-control situation, and that emotion will act as jet fuel – and will lead to a hotter flare-up.

In fact, we always advise school personnel to remember one of the issues that we discussed earlier in this book. That was the one that had to do with the parasympathetic nervous system: control your breathing and model deep breaths (Benson & Klipper, 1975) for the students who are in a state of distress.

This is important not only to little kids who, when they get amped up, sometimes push themselves past the point that they are unable to even *speak.* You ever get around a younger child who is that upset? He or she will be breathing rapidly (almost hyperventilating), probably with the bottom lip stuck out, and almost invariably with tears pushing out of their ducts! These are kids who are almost wild-eyed with emotion. With these kids, set them down, make physical contact (like hands on the shoulders), keep good eye contact, and begin to *breathe* while you are addressing them.

The goal here is to have them – even on a subconscious level – recognize the breathing pattern you are modeling, and eventually start to reflect or mirror that same pattern. They cannot get themselves calmed without controlling the breathing. And to reiterate, you will not be able to accomplish this feat if you are also beginning to escalate.

Shifting over to big kids for a minute, the same principal applies. Let's say you have a couple high school kids going at it like prizefighters in the hallway. As you step in to break things up, they will invariably be in a state of sympathetic arousal – with adrenaline flowing full bore, open throttle. As you spilt them up and take one of the offenders over to the penalty box, make a conscious effort to control your own breathing. Model calming down and they will have a better shot at grabbing control.

Some folks call this meditation, some call it relaxation... whatever the moniker, and your goal is to suck the propane out of the grill rather than open the valve to its maximum.

The last part of number 5 has to do with being concise. To illustrate what I mean by this point, we will again go back in time in this book. Remember the "talkin' lickin'!" In moments of crisis or high emotion – there's not an opportunity for a teachable moment.

All of us look for those rare opportunities to impart a life lesson in the face of some mini-disaster. We do this because, as it ought to be, we are trying to give wisdom to our students. A wisdom that transcends the fundamentals of the daily lesson plans. We try to help teach our students how to *think*, and these teachable moments are incredibly powerful to pull this off, because the student relates instantly to whatever situation is immediately before him or her!

The art of delivering a solid teachable moment lies in its timing, however. And think about this example to drive home my point: have you ever had a really good argument with your spouse or partner? I mean a *good* one. The kind of argument that doesn't lead to physical acts of violence, but still one where the neighbors are pulling their kids in off the streets.

Now, let me ask you this: do you really *hear* what your partner is saying during the heat of battle? My guess is that you probably don't.

Resolution in marriage or any intimate relationship lies in moments of calm, not moments of distress. Same with our kids: teachable moments lie in moments of quiet, not in moments of intensity. Once kids pass a point of emotional arousal, their capacity to process logic takes a back seat to survival mode.

Thus, the best bet is to get them separated from the herd, and out of whatever situation is over-stimulating them right now. Give them a chance to get themselves together, and *then* launch your teachable moment. Give the students the best opportunity to hear and retain what you are saying before you even try to say it.

Being calm and concise will accomplish this in the most efficient manner.

6. *Empathy*

Does everyone know what empathy is? We touched on it during the discussion of conduct disorder in Chapter 4. Empathy is the ability to understand how the other person feels or the ability to put yourself in their shoes.

I bring up empathy for two reasons. The first is to remind you to be careful with the *how* you deliver a consequence. Do your best to deliver a consequence in a manner that builds rather than destroys the relationship you are forging with the student.

For example, let's say you have to send a student off – either to time out or to the principal's office or wherever. There is a big difference between phrasing it in this way: "Get out of my room... I'm sick of looking at you," and putting it this way, "Jeremy, you are getting way out of control and need to cool yourself down. Let's go down to Mrs. Mitchell's office to get it back under control."

One says, "I can't stand you!" and the other says, "I am looking out for you." Remember, the goal is not only behaviorism, but also relationship.

The other issue salient in the empathy section deals with how you react when a student returns to civilization after serving a consequence. To illustrate this point, let me ask you another question about your past: when you were growing up, did any of you have a parent who would give you the *silent treatment* if you did something wrong? Or perhaps, did you have a friend or acquaintance whose parent would give them the silent treatment?

The silent treatment creates an almost unmanageable state of anxiety in children because they have a hard time dealing with feeling like mom doesn't love them anymore because of something they've done. Or they have difficulty dealing with thinking they have somehow "damaged" their relationship with Dad because of their behavior.

Take this same concept and bring it into the classroom. When you send a student off (again, time out, principal's office, have them sit out recess or lunch period, whatever), they serve their punishment. When they return to your classroom (or wherever you happen to be), they bring themselves back into the fold. And it doesn't matter how angry or tough of a kid he is, he will be looking either dead on or out of the corner of his eye at you to see what exactly the temperature is now.

In other words, he is feeling tension, wondering if you guys are going to be good now, or if you are going to be holding a grudge and perhaps taking it out on him further on down the line.

This will be particularly true for kids who come from a home where the silent treatment is employed as a parenting technique by caregivers.

So my recommendation is to take a half of a second and let that student off the hook when he re-emerges. You don't have to sing *Kumbaya* and hold hands whilst dancing around a campfire, but take a minute to convey a message something like, "You did the crime and you did the time, now welcome back. If you're good, we're good."

Remove the anxiety he may be feeling by creating an atmosphere where he can bring it back together without ill will hanging in the air.

7. *Make effective discipline a team approach*

I'll be brief in the last two points of this section, as they do not require a lot of explanation. The first is to problem-solve together, particularly in times of extreme frustration for you. This speaks especially well to the students who are like the good hunting dogs, as it gives them a sense that they are not being "forced" into any one direction, or that your consequences are arbitrary in nature.

Now, I will begin with a caution about how to begin a conversation in this direction: be very careful to maintain your power position when problem solving together with a student. At no point should it seem like you are putting the ball into his court, as that is not his role. Remember that *you* are the bottom line in this equation, not the student.

Having said that, here is a good opening to use when speaking privately to a repeat offender in your room; "Listen, Zach... we've been around this tree a hundred times this year, you know? What can we do to better manage this situation?"

He will probably respond with a shrug and a sullen, "I don't know." But, seize the day! Respond with firmness, but empathy, "Yeah, it's rough. There's got to be a better way though... this way is getting pretty ugly, you know."

You can even appeal to his sense of loyalty with something like, "I hate to keep calling you out in front of your buddies, so what needs to happen here?"

If you continue down this path and he continues to disengage, you will have to wrap up with a bottom line of your own. If, on the other hand, he begins to open up and participate, ask what is going on with him, or even what his opinion is as to what we can do from here. Guide him rather than acquiesce to him. Allow him to feel he has some say in the direction without giving him the authority to undermine you.

This technique is especially important when dealing with leaders in your classroom. Again, aligning yourself with the leader will require one-on-one conversations at times, and gaining his or her insight may give you a valuable perspective that you wouldn't otherwise be privy to. Plus, you have the added bonus of reinforcing his or her "leader" status in the room.

On a whole classroom level, you may want to hold a "Town Hall" meeting once in awhile to air some difficulties in the group. Even if this does not evolve into a two-way conversation, you can still bring about the desired effect with a "State of the Union Address" to the room!

8. *Leave the door open to deeper discussions*

This point naturally evolves out of number 7 above, but it also goes a bit deeper. And before I start, I want to point out that I completely understand you are not a therapist, a parent, a minister, or any other in a more intimate relationship with your students, but I do want to pay some homage to the position of importance you hold in their universe. Do not underestimate how important you may be to them. The kids may never let on that they respect or even *like* you, but there may be a current beneath the surface (that is heavily protected) which holds regard for you.

Having said that, tread cautiously but confidently into the inner-lives of your students. But beware! You may uncork some issues that are pretty heavy. Some kids really come from a place that is pretty awful. In these cases, just keep in mind that you are not there to save the kids, but can give them support and understanding outside of their world.

I would be remiss to not also remind you that legally, you are in a position whereby you are obligated to report incidences of abuse or neglect – even *perceived* abuse or neglect. If you are trying to build relationships, this too must be done with finesse. I recommend bringing in another professional to help talk you through the manner by which the reporting is conducted. Not only to help you think through the procedure, but perhaps even to "take the heat" so as to maintain the trust in the relationship you have with the student and to protect it.

But back to the talking about feelings, as even the students from great homes may need this platform. Some teachers open the day or the period by having an "open forum," whereby students are afforded an opportunity to talk about whatever happens to be on their mind. Encouraging an honest exchange and an atmosphere of acceptance can build trust and will give your behavioral plan more power.

If this method is not in line with your personality or not possible given your specific circumstances, I encourage teachers to, at the very least, identify feelings when they happen in a non-threatening way.

For example, you see Jackson embarrass William, so William slugs him. He has to go down to the principal's office. At some point during that journey you could drop in, "Geez, that had to be embarrassing. Sorry about that." Then, let it drop completely.

The point in doing that is to not further embarrass William. Rather, it is designed to do two things; first, it lets him know that you get it. You understand what is going on behind his eyes, and that understanding may be unique in his world. Remember your favorite teacher growing up? Did he or she understand you? Sure! That's part of why they were your favorite! But as always with some of the angry kids, hit it and let it go. Just state you case. Drop it so he does not feel pressed into responding in a way that takes him totally out of his protected comfort zone.

The second thing you accomplish by identifying the emotion is that you allow William to understand he is able to have an emotion *other than* anger. Particularly with the "Bad Kids," they are good at anger. They are angry a lot, and probably have that rap mastered by now. Particularly with the boys, helping them to differentiate or identify emotions will give them options in the future. He may never act on those options, but at least you are bringing it into the realm of a choice he is making rather than reacting in the only way he knows how.

Bottom line: trust, as established throughout the first section of the book, will give more power to the structure you impose via your behavioral plan. Trust will calm some of those hunting dogs… it will put some slack in the tug toy… it will give the mean girl some pause… it will relax the class as a whole. This trust will then allow a behavioral plan to be more effective because the students are more likely to buy into it if it comes from a grown-up they know has their best interest in mind. Give the students a chance to practice control and contain, and be an ally rather than an enemy!

Help the kids learn to trust. It is amazing, really, when you think about all the trust we need to place in the hands of fate (and of others!) while we live as grown-ups. We trust our spouses and lovers to keep the relationship sacred. We trust that, without the gold standard, the dollar bill in our pocket will still be worth a dollar tomorrow. We trust the other drivers on the highway to not swerve across the center line. We trust that, if we close our eyes real tight, the world will stay the same when we re-open them. The fabric of civilized society is stitched together with tenuous threads of trust in each other!

Chapter 11

Functionalizing Behavior

Making it Easier on You ... How About That!

Let's keep plowing ahead with the behavioral part of the program, and talk about another big word that means a simple concept: *functionalizing* behavior. Functionalizing merely means *operationalizing*

Functionalizing (or operationalizing) refers to the idea that in order to attack any targeted behavior with a behavioral plan, the behavior you are going after must be *concrete, observable, and measurable* (or .com as the acronym).

The reason we do this is twofold: First, and perhaps most clearly, it is so that you are able to achieve success. If you have a more ambiguous goal – one that is not founded upon specific behaviors – it will be very difficult to ascertain if you have ever achieved the goal. If we follow this through to its logical conclusion, then the goal would therefore be impossible to achieve.

For example, if your goal is just for Little Johnny to "be good," you are set up for failure. He will have good days and bad days. You will have good days and bad days. Pretty soon, you are back to the drawing board and feel rolled over by Little Johnny. Unless he suddenly becomes a model student, his improvement will be fleeting – a carrot on a stick that you will never fully catch.

Secondly, we functionalize because it helps us from feeling frustrated and defeated if the results do not cross home plate immediately. And I'll tell you where I hear this defeat and frustration most often – it is when a parent comes into my office, plops down on my couch, and opens the intake with some form of the following line: "I've tried everything, but nothing works."

You ever hear a mom or a dad say that? You ever hear yourself saying that? Sure! By the time a parent gets to my office, they have been through the ringer with behavioral stuff. But let me mention what my ear hears when I hear a parent say, "I've tried everything but nothing works." Almost without exception, this is what it implies (and we'll use mom as the lead parent in the example): mom got some advice on a cool behavioral plan to try at home. So, she tried it for awhile, but it did not work all the way, so she shifted over and tried something else. Then, she tried that plan, but it did not work all the way, so she shifted over and tried something else. She tried that one for awhile, and then tried something else, etc., etc., etc...

And believe me, there is no shortage of "Other Things to Try" out there for worried moms and dads. Those of you with kids of your own... think how many people give you parenting advice when you have those children? Everyone?

Sure – everyone you meet, from your own mom or dad all the way down to the friendly (but somewhat meddling) stranger in line ahead of you at the post office. Everyone is an expert in parenting their own kids, and they are not shy to share with you the miraculous cures they effected with their own kids – who, by the way, must be *exactly* like your kids.

Add to the kindly words of every parent in your life the number of audacious Parenting magazines, boasting headlines such as "Turn Your Child from Devil to Angel in Three Easy Minutes" or "Get Control of Your Wolf-Boy by using nothing but a Spatula and a 16-oz. Bottle of Yoo-Hoo" or "Last Week, Our Home was a Bowery; Thoughts from Our New Garden of Tranquil Paradise."

Plus, for good measure, we have about fifteen bazillion internet sites for parents; the professional words of pediatricians, teachers, and seminar speakers; overzealous journalists writing for the local newspapers, and the jabber of popular talk show experts on

TV and radio. Mix them all together in the already overwhelmed brain of a frazzled parent, and you have the recipe for failure.

Why? Because typically, parents are trying to do the best they can and feel that if success is not realized quickly, they must be doing something wrong. So, they grab onto the next life raft that floats by, and tries that one for a while. See the problem in this pattern?

The behavior programs the parents choose may or may not be good ones, but that is irrelevant because the plans aren't given a chance to gain any traction with the kids. Parents may have the rich loam of intent, but a plan cannot grow roots without the sun and water of time and opportunity. When they feel like there must be a "next something better" out there, they jump on and off bandwagons. In the end, their kids aren't able to develop past a certain point.

Teachers can get caught on the exact same treadmill, so that's why we recommend that they *functionalize* behavior. This can keep you from growing frustrated because you won't be caught chasing your tail around the "next great idea" tree. A well-functionalized behavior plan will *change your perspective*! We need an example to make this clearer.

Okay, here's how we go through the exercise. And feel free to extrapolate this example to fit your particular set of circumstances. Now, let's say you have a child in your room named Martin. Martin does about seventy-four things that drive you absolutely insane, but pare those down to one or two concrete, observable, and measurable (.COM) behaviors to target for intervention. If you try to create a behavior plan to address all seventy-four you are going to truly go batty, as there are not enough hours in the day. Plus, let's face it, you do not have enough energy to keep up.

Pick one or two that you can have some semblance of control over in a COM sense. For the sake of argument, let's say you choose to modify his "getting out of his seat" behavior.

The initial step in developing any behavior plan is to develop a baseline. To pull this one off, you must obtain the expensive and hard-to-find tools... 1) a pencil, and 2) a pad of sticky notes. For the next two or three days, let Martin do whatever it is that he does. Allow him to exist unabated in his natural habitat. You do this because you want to know what kind of behaviors (or more specifically – what kind of *numbers*) we are dealing with here.

You set a certain period of time within which you will conduct your data collection. For this example, let's say you are interested in marking the period between opening bell and the first recess. Now, every time he jumps up out of his seat during this time frame, you nail the sticky pad with a tally mark. No intervention yet, just observation and recording.

After you collect your data, you find that on average, Martin gets out of his seat about 19 times in the allotted period. Next, you start the treatment phase. Whenever Martin is sitting still in *his own seat* and marginally paying attention, you reinforce the heck out of him. You make it better to be good than to not be good. You make eye contact, you give a verbal "atta boy," you nod, you smile, you give a token... whatever it is that you decide to do behaviorally.

After seven or eight days of the reinforcement, you take another baseline. Now, you find that, on average, Martin is getting out of his seat fourteen times during the allotted time period. Is fourteen still a lot? You better believe it is!

But here's the rub: if you are not paying attention, fourteen and nineteen feel *exactly the same*! They would be precisely the same number – and that would be, "the number of failures." They are both too much, and they both make you wonder if the orange aprons at The Home Depot® will make your hips look slimmer.

However, if you *are* paying attention, we suddenly have a different frame (or different *perspective*) around the number 14: it would otherwise have been failure, but now becomes progress. Martin does not go from nineteen to zero without passing through fourteen. And by the way, Martin will never be a "zero" kid – we may get him down to three or four, and that is very much manageable; particularly compared to where we are today.

You renew your resolve because rather than feeling defeated ("I've tried everything, but nothing works"), you now feel effective. After another week or two, Martin may be down to eleven... or nine... or twelve... but as long as you are moving toward the finish line, you still have forward momentum.

Lastly, here's the other secret about Mr. Martin: when you begin to get the one or two behaviors under control, others in the big gloopy glob of seventy-four will start to follow suit. Perhaps not all, but Martin's oil tanker will start to swing around to the positive.

The reason is that you have now effectively begun to change the rules of engagement with Martin. Too often, teachers get caught up in the negative spiral of only paying attention to the student when he or she is being bad. Now that you are making an effort to create positive reinforcement, and now that you are forcing yourself (for lack of a better word) to look for moments of good behavior, Martin and you have a different level to interact upon.

In other words, you set up a scenario whereby Martin can behave in a manner designed to *achieve positives* rather than to *avoid negatives*. That may seem to be a subtle difference, but that shift in philosophy can be very powerful. And that shift is made possible when you functionalize behavior.

Once the problem has been adequately defined, we shift focus and become much like a private investigator as we possibly can. By doing this, we train ourselves to pay close attention to context as the context unlocks the keys to understanding and controlling the behavior.

Simply put, we are trying to intervene at the 'A' as much as possible so we can diffuse that bomb before we have to clean up the room afterwards. So, answer some key questions about the lead-in to the bad behavior. Questions such as:

a. *Who* is present when the behavior tends to occur or does not occur?

b. *What* is going on when the behavior tends to occur or not occur?

c. *When* does the behavior tend to occur or not occur?

d. *Where* does the behavior tend to occur or not occur?

e. *How often* does the behavior occur: per hour _____, per day _____, per week _____?

f. *How long* does the behavior occur per episode_____?

This is a simplistic way of looking at it, to be sure. But once again, as teachers we are not always privy to the lead-in. We hear the explosion, and are then forced to react. And, while we feel as though the explosion happened at random, remember again that all kids are trying to get a need met when they act out. Attention, power, revenge, etc… these are students who – at their very worst – have been shaped into the bad behavior machines you see before you.

Next, continue down this path and work backwards to figure out more specific details about the 'A'. Ask yourself questions such as:

a. When? (Time, day, date)

b. What happened before the behavior occurred?

c. Describe the behavior. Include how intense, how long, how many.

d. What happened after the behavior occurred?

Noting again that question "a" above deals with the lead-in (i.e., the "A"), but question "d" moves you beyond the "A," and deals specifically with potential re-enforcers or consequences (i.e., intervening at the "C").

I'll give some easy examples of how context can be understood when playing private investigator. Perhaps the simplest example is one which I am sure many of you face in your classrooms. You have Richard, who is fantastic one-on-one and you also have Kenny, who is great one-on-one. But, you get the two of them together and look out! You've got vinegar and baking soda – a made-for-TV third grade science fair project!

In this example, arranging the physical proximity of Richard and Kenny to each other (or away form each other!) can have an impact.

We'll get to more specific behavioral interventions later in the book. Here are a couple other clear examples of how context can play a role in behavior. These may not bring any dazzling insight into your life, but these are easy to follow to illustrate how the "A" can wield a certain power.

Sometimes with kids you have a "time of day" issue when it comes to bad behavior, and this can be driven by one of a couple factors. First, you might have students who get cranky and start acting out with greater frequency and intensity if they have gone too long without food. In the period of time leading into lunch or snack, their blood sugar may be dropping, and they may get harder to manage (both for you and for themselves). If this is the case, offering a quick snack may even them out to help them maintain until a more formal meal is granted.

Time of day is also the culprit of some students who come from a place of high stress at home. These kids may start to spin out toward the end of the day as they look ahead to a brutal evening (or maybe a tough walk home if it is through a neighborhood they abhor). This conceptually also wreaks some havoc during the period as vacations and school holidays come up. As the time of separation draws nearer, these kids feel their internal stress ratcheting up, and they spin out.

Something you may want to try with these students – particularly younger ones – is to help bridge the gap between today and tomorrow by using a transitional object. A transitional object is a small, concrete representation of you that the student can take with them.

To accomplish this, simply grab a knick knack off of your desk, hand it (on the down low) to the student, and say something like this, "Listen, I need somebody to look after this tonight. Do you think you can help me out with that?"

If that student likes you, this will be very meaningful, and he or she will probably agree. That knick knack may be a hokey intervention, but it's a little piece of you that they can have with them and may rely upon it during times of stress. An object is easier to identify with for kids, as they have a harder time with abstract memories or thoughts of you.

We use this same concept to teach parents how to help their kids deal with divorce or separation. Usually, when parents split up, it is the dad who leaves the home. Kids have a tremendously difficult time wrapping their brains around losing one of their parent figures. And surprisingly, it doesn't seem to matter a whole lot the sex of the child, or the amount of stress in the house prior to the split-up. Kids (generally speaking – there are some truly remarkable exceptions to this rule) will put up with a bad situation forever if it means having both parents in the house. In fact, how many times do you see or hear about kids falling on their sword just to save an awful union between their folks?

As the fathers leave the home, we recommend that they help with a transitional object. For this scenario, if there is not a good visual representation (i.e., photos, trinkets, etc.) we go after olfactory objects. In other words, we have the dad dab a bit of his cologne or some of his deodorant or shampoo on a stuffed animal, or a pillowcase, or something absorbent that the kids has around them during quiet times. The scent of the father will hold a position of power in the mind of the child, and will work to soothe in the absence of the real person.

Timing can also play a role in bad behavior toward the end of the school year. This is particularly so with kids who have had to deal with caregiver separation, either due to divorce or death or abandonment. These kids feel their old wounds getting torn at when they look ahead to an impending separation from you. In other words, the feeling of loss will re-ignite the trauma of past losses.

With these kids, bridging the gap is also important. But rather than exclusively using you as the bridge, it may also be important for that student to spend some time with next year's teacher so they have a more concrete representation of what to expect when they return. That student can leave knowing that there is a real person at the other end of the long summer.

Have the next teacher come into your room and play checkers with the student or engage in some sort of interactive activity to ease the transition.

And by the way, here is another great example of why teacher turnover is troubling for the students. For the kids we are talking about – those who are feeling the pain of missing you before the year is even ended – they need to know that, even though they will not be in your particular classroom, that you are *still going to be here*. That student may fall into stride and never come see you next year, but knowing he or she has that option can calm their anxieties, and, yes, can curb some bad behavior.

Those are just a few examples of how understanding the 'A' can help you cut bad behavior off at the pass. A great way to encapsulate this data into a quick and easy-to-read form is to put it onto a FBA (Functional Behavior Assessment) form.

I'm going to hit you with an example of an FBA form to help you picture what it is I am talking about. Now, for those of you who work in Special Education, already, you probably see these things in your sleep. After combing over 147,000 of these over the years, you may not be able to close your eyes without seeing one pop up! I put this in the book more for those of you who may teach in a regular education room, and only see one of these every so often. For those of you who work in private schools (or maybe even for some parents out there who do not work within the school system), you may have *never* seen one of these!

Every individual state or school district will have its own version of this form, so check with your Special Education Coordinator to see what your school-specific form looks like. If you are interested in pursuing ideas from around the country, there are literally over one hundred of these forms available on the Internet if you do a quick Google search. I pulled this one out of the public domain and off of the Sevier County School District (Tennessee) web page. I am using it because it is comprehensive, easy to read and understand. Without further ado, here is how we think about conceptualizing problematic behavior.

Sevier County School System
Functional Behavior Assessment Worksheet

Student Name: _____   Date: _____

Teacher Name: _____

Classroom Intervention Components

I. Preventative/Proactive Components (check all that apply)
___ Clearly posted rules; frequently revisited.
___ Instructional level/methods appropriate for the child.
___ Predictable routine -posted and reviewed each day.
___ Classroom setting/schedule set up to promote positive behavior
___ Behavior monitoring system in place; frequent feedback given to all students for positive and negative behavior.
___ Other _____

- List or attach classroom rules/expectations posted in the classroom

- List motivators/incentives for positive behavior (free time, privileges, etc.)

II. Consequences: What Is the teacher's consistent response to the following negative behaviors?

- Non-compliance (failure to follow a reasonable request):

- Physical aggression (hitting, kicking, etc.)

- Other:

Pro-Social Behaviors:

What does the student do well?	Where does it occur?	What is/or can be done to reinforce this behavior?

Dr. Steven T. Olivas

Prioritize up to **two target behaviors** that most interfere with the child's functioning in the classroom. Estimate or directly observe the frequency (how often), intensity (hi, med., low), and duration of each:

Behavior: (baseline levels)	Frequency	Intensity	Duration

From the list below indicate the triggers (antecedents), concurrent events, and consequences that seem to support the current behavior

Triggers
- [ ] Lack of social attention
- [ ] Demand/Request
- [ ] Difficult Task
- [ ] Transition (task)
- [ ] Interruption in routine
- [ ] Negative social interaction
- [ ] Consequences imposed for negative behavior

Concurrent Events
- [ ] Independent seat work
- [ ] Group Instruction
- [ ] Crowded setting
- [ ] Unstructured activity
- [ ] Unstructured setting
- [ ] Peer attention
- [ ] Adult attention

Consequences
- [ ] Behavior ignored
- [ ] Reprimand/Warning
- [ ] Time-out
- [ ] Loss of privileges
- [ ] Communicate w/home
- [ ] Sent to office
- [ ] Out/school suspension
- [ ] In -School suspension

What function(s) does the identified behavior(s) seem to serve for the child?

Escape
- [ ] Avoid a demand or request
- [ ] Avoid an activity/task (if known)
- [ ] Avoid a person
- [ ] Escape the classroom/setting_
- [ ] Escape the school_
- [ ] Other

Attention/Control
- [ ] Get desired item/activity
- [ ] Gain adult attention
- [ ] Gain peer attention
- [ ] Get sent to preferred adult
- [ ] Other

Was this information collected through? [ ] Teacher interview _ *or* [ ] Direct observation?
Other Comments:
_____

Suggest any preferred items, activities, or people that could be used as incentives in an intervention for this child (what can be used to increase positive student behaviors).

2

- 188 -

Once we have gathered all of this data, we can launch into the scientific method of putting it into practice. You all remember the scientific method, right? You form a plan, you test the plan, you evaluate the plan, and then you re-form the plan consistent with the data you have gathered. For the most part, there is another way to encapsulate this process into a form, and that form is a BIP (Behavioral Intervention Plan).

As a quick aside, the other means by which we use these forms through my private practice office is to help parents prepare for the planning and/or IEP meetings. And let's face it; parents are usually pretty defensive during those meetings. Parents are pretty consistent in that they feel outgunned in the conference room. After all, how many school people are in a meeting like that? Quite a few, is my guess. The Vice Principal is there and sometimes the Principal; every teacher who touches the student's life is rounded up. If there is testing to interpret, the School Psychologist makes an appearance and the Special Education Coordinator sits in the meeting... wow! The parents feel overwhelmed, especially if it's a single mom in there! Now, she feels like she is on a folding chair at the end of the gymnasium, with white hot spotlights blaring down on her!

We use these forms to help parents understand what is going to happen in the meeting. It helps grease the skids some so that we take the "unknown" out of the equation. Helping parents know what to expect takes a lot of anxiety out of the situation. And remember, it is about diffusing energy, right?

Here is an example of a BIP borrowed from the State of Illinois off of their website. There are, like with the FBAs, a gaggle of these in the public domain to peruse and evaluate. Some are more complicated, some are less complicated. I chose this one because it walks down the middle of that road, combining ease of use with detail.

BEHAVIORAL INTERVENTION PLAN (AS APPROPRIATE)

Complete when the team has determined a Behavioral Intervention Plan is needed.

Student's Strengths – Describe student's behavioral strengths

Target Behavior

Is this behavior a ☐ Skill Deficit or a ☐ Performance Deficit

Skill Deficit: The student does not know how to perform the desired behavior.
Performance Deficit: The student knows how to perform the desired behavior, but does not consistently do so.

Hypothesis of Behavioral Function – Include hypothesis developed through the Functional Behavioral Assessment (attach completed form).
What desired thing(s) is the student trying to **get**? OR What undesired thing(s) is the student trying to **avoid**?

Summary of Previous Interventions Attempted – Describe any environmental changes made, evaluations conducted, instructional strategy or curriculum changes made or replacement behaviors taught.

Replacement Behaviors – Describe which new behaviors or skills will be taught to meet the identified function of the target behavior (e.g. student will slap his desk to replace striking out at others). Include description of how these behaviors/skills will be taught.

Behavioral Intervention Strategies and Supports
Environment – How can the environment or circumstances that trigger the target behavior be adjusted?
Instruction and/or Curriculum – What changes in instructional strategies or curriculum would be helpful?
Positive Supports – Describe all additional services or supports needed to address the student's identified needs that contribute to the target behavior.

Motivators and/or Rewards – Describe how the student will be reinforced to ensure that replacement behaviors are more motivating than the target behavior.

Restrictive Disciplinary Measures – Describe any restrictive disciplinary measures that may be used with the student and any conditions under which such measures may be used (include necessary documentation and timeline for evaluation.)

Crisis Plan – Describe how an emergency situation or behavior crisis will be handled.

Data Collection Procedures and Methods – Describe expected outcomes of the interventions, how data will be collected and measured, timelines for and criteria to determine success or lack of success of the interventions.

Provisions For Coordination with Caregivers – Describe how the school will work with the caregivers to share information, provide training to caregivers if needed, and how often this communication will take place.

Chapter 12

Rate Your Teaching Style

Gaining Insight About You

Let's take a brief sojourn into an area that will be used a bit in Part IV of the book. We spent a lot of time addressing leadership in Chapter 7; now let's put you to the test. Take a few moments and complete this brief questionnaire (Ingersoll & Bosworth, 1996; reprinted with permission) assessing your teaching style. I will provide explanations of each subscale below, and then add my own commentary.

As mentioned, we will be using these results a bit in Part IV of the book. I will also make the results pertinent to your management of bad behavior in my commentaries of each subscale/teaching style. From there, we will get directly into different strategies for specific management techniques.

The subscale with the highest score can be considered your predominant style, although you can certainly have features of each in your general approach. Still, we are looking for the highest score to determine what your "go to" style is – particularly when stress is applied in the classroom setting!

This quiz is designed to identify teachers' leadership style in relationship to relating and expressing authority. I use it in my seminars, and have been granted permission by the original author to recreate it.

Answer the following twelve questions and learn more about your classroom management profile. Using the scale provided below, please indicate your perception of the following statements. Read each statement carefully and respond to each statement based upon either actual or imagined classroom experience.

Please put the *number* value of your agreement in each blank, as you will have to add them according to subscales to achieve a scaled score for each.

1 = Strongly Disagree

2 = Disagree

3 = Neutral

4 = Agree

5 = Strongly Agree

1. _____ If a student is disruptive during class, I assign him or her detention without further discussion.

2. _____ I don't want to impose any rules on my students.

3. _____ The classroom must be quiet in order for students to learn.

4. _____ I am concerned about what my students learn and how they learn.

5. _____ If a student turns in a late homework assignment, it is not my problem.

6. _____ I don't want to reprimand a student because it might hurt his or her feelings.

7. _____ Class preparation isn't worth the effort.

8. _____ I always try to explain the reasons behind my rules and decisions.

9. _____ I will not accept excuses from a student who is tardy.

10._____ The emotional well-being of my students is more important than classroom control.

11. _____ My students understand that they can interrupt my lecture if they have a relevant question.

12. _____ If a student requests a hall pass, I always honor the request.

To score your quiz, add your responses to statements:

Statements 1, 3, and 9 refer to the authoritarian style.

Statements 4, 8, and 11 refer to the authoritative style.

Statements 6, 10, and 12 refer to the laissez-faire style.

Statements 2, 5, and 7 refer to the indifferent style

The result is your classroom management profile. Your score for each management style can range from 3 to 15. A high score indicates a strong preference for that particular style. After you have scored your quiz, and determined your profile, read the descriptions of each management style. You may see a little bit of yourself in each one.

The first two paragraphs of each subscale description are re-printed from the original text version of the quiz (Ingersoll & Benson, 1996). The remaining commentary represents my own thoughts.

1. Authoritarian

The authoritarian teacher places firm limits and controls on the students. Students will often have assigned seats for the entire school year. Desks are usually arranged in straight rows and no deviations are allowed. Students must be seated at the beginning of class and they frequently remain there throughout the period.

In this environment the room is usually quiet and mutual exchange of ideas are infrequently allowed. Students know they should not interrupt the teacher. Since little verbal communication is allowed, students do not have the opportunity to develop problem solving skills and may become dependent and irresponsible.

At times, "Authoritarian" gets a bad rap, as it is lumped together with being punitive, dictatorial, or at the very worst, abusive. These conditions can certainly evolve out of an authoritarian mind-set, but in general, this style refers to folks who tend to be pretty rigid, extremely structured, and black-and-white with regard to rules, consequences, and right and wrong. They tend not to give kids wiggle room when it comes to punishment, and are sometimes called, "My way or the highway" managers.

Here is the rub with leaning toward an Authoritarian style; with some of the worst students in our systems, this style *can actually work* – but not typically in a setting many schools offer in the traditional classroom. In other words, some of the "bad kids" will respond favorably to tight structure and hard-and-fast rules. The predictability of the routine and the reward/consequence system can be a welcome change from feeling out of control.

But alas, kids who respond well to this type of structure require a *lot* of exposure in order to break past the steadfast anger and rebellion this style tends to elicit from the *hunting dog* kids! Hence, if you've got them in a wilderness/survival setting, or perhaps a boot camp, you can truly do wonders to turn trouble-makers around and affect long term, dramatic change in their lives.

If, on the other hand, you only have a kid for fifty-two minutes, five days a week, it is going to be a difficult task to break him down to the point that he accepts the rigidity over the rebellion he is (without much exception) going to feel toward you.

Plus, that is not to mention the tendency of authoritarian teachers to bear down harder once they begin to sense that rebellion. This will, as you can predict, force the hand of the ODD student, who will dig his heels in deeper in response to the increased rigidity. This will make the teacher bear down more, etc. You can see how that bad spiral can slip out of control, and lead to a lot of frustration.

And think about it in the context of your own life; have you ever had a "rule with an iron fist" parent? Did one of your buddies, perhaps? Or, have you ever had a boss who was constantly on you, looking over your shoulder? If so, you may have felt a tickle of that same rebellion.

So, if your teaching style leans in this direction and you find yourself often getting into power struggles with the hunting dog students, you may want to take a step back and breathe. Without that breath, you and the student are going to end up like a couple of mountain goats with your horns stuck together. You will not be able to break free of the other's gravitational pull and you will both eventually topple over the edge of a cliff because you can't back off enough to see it coming.

The point is, in the midst of a standoff like that one, one of you has to blink. You are the grown-up, so give the tug toy a little slack, and help the hunting dog relax. You will be in better control in that scenario.

2. *Indifferent*

The indifferent teacher is not very involved in the classroom. This teacher places few demands on students and appears generally uninterested. The indifferent teacher just doesn't want to impose on the students. As such, he/she often feels that class preparation is not worth the effort. Things like field trips and special projects are out of the question. This teacher may fail to be prepared to teach and may even use the same teaching outline year after year.

In such classrooms discipline is often lacking because the teacher may lack the skills, confidence, or courage to discipline students. Students often sense and reflect this teacher's indifferent attitude. In the "indifferent" classroom students have very few opportunities to observe or practice effective communication skills or self-discipline. With few demands placed on students and very little discipline, classroom achievement motivation is low.

Actually, for teachers, I tend to lump this style in with style number 3 below, so I will reserve my commentary until that time.

3. *Laissez-faire*

The laissez-faire teacher places few demand or controls on students. "Do your own thing" describes this classroom. This teacher accepts the student's impulses and actions and is less likely to monitor their behavior.

However, this overindulgent style is most often associated with students' lack of social competence and self-control. It is difficult for students to learn socially acceptable behavior when the teacher is so permissive. With few demands placed upon them, these students frequently have lower motivation to achieve.

As noted a bit earlier, I tend to combine Indifferent and Laissez-faire into one grouping, which I will label as "Passive." Passive teachers are, in my experience, typically either burnt out or they have a hard time differentiating between "assertive" and "aggressive." This may be due to anxiety, or personality variables, or even unrealistic expectations of their current class. Whatever the reason, teachers in these categories are not effective at setting rules, holding fast to boundaries, or sticking to limits. Thus, they tend to avoid conflict with the students at all costs – it is easier to give in than it is to hold the boundary or rule and assert themselves as the manager of the room.

Now, it may feel like I am ripping on these folks a bit; but I do understand that there are a host of legitimate reasons for a person to have this teaching style. Still, to avoid further complications with some of your more difficult students, here are a couple things to keep in mind.

First, if you find yourself in this position and are reluctant to change, you can (if possible) team yourself up with a teaching assistant, aide, or even team-teach with another professional who tends to lean toward authoritarian. As odd as that may sound, you two can actually maximize the strength of each to help your class. In other words, the other professional can feel as though they can come in and impose rules and restrictions – while knowing that you can provide balance in the resulting atmosphere.

You, then, can be softer and can play the role of "good cop" when dealing with the students. They can use you as a resource or a mediator. Having said that, however, a cautionary comment here: make very clear between you and the other professional what your roles are going to be. Neither of you need to feel undermined by the other, so keep your eyes on working together rather in competition with each other.

The other option for you, and this is one that is going to take more courage on your part, is to work hard the first couple weeks of each school year to be as assertive (mean?) as you possibly can. The rationale here is simple: it is a *lot* easier to start off tough, and then back off over time, than it is to start off soft, and then try to toughen up over time.

In fact, once the class figures out your reluctance to be the "bad cop," they will start to run right over you if and when you actually make attempts to assert yourself. In other words, they have always known you to be the soft touch, so they will just figure (and with some degree of accuracy) that if they just wait you out, you will return to the more fearful, or more un-assertive teacher they understand you to be.

Remember too, that being too nice all the time does *not* create an atmosphere if respect among the students. Kids respond to teachers who have good, well-defined boundaries much more positively than teachers who are not as capable of towing the line. It pays off to say "no" when necessary!

To bring this concept into better focus, think about it like a challenge of parenting. Think about a fully functioning, very healthy family system. If you did not come from a family who modeled that concept, think about a friend who may have had a healthy family system. In every healthy family, there is a very strong bond between parents and kids, right? Sure... that is the beginning of health. The other part of it, though, is that there is no role confusion. The parents are always the parents and in charge; the kids are always the kids and settle into a role of lesser power than the parents.

In other words, the best systems to create are ones whereby there is clearly defined power, yet there are relationships based upon trust and mutual respect. Giving into a child all the time creates role confusion because now he or she has way too much power!

As Dr. Fred Johnson (Johnson, 2006), likes to say, "Structure creates safety." When your moves and reactions are predictable, children can feel safer and more trusting because they are not called upon to be surprised or caught off guard by a maneuver you make.

Let's get back to passive teachers. If it is deep into the school year, and you have lost the control or respect of your room, you are going to have to be assertive or mean for a longer amount of time. You will have to go out of your way to re-boot the hard drive of the classroom. Once again, the kids will still try to run over, or perhaps wait out, your infrequent attempts at gaining control, so you will have to re-set the rules.

Get medieval on the room for a good three weeks! I'm not saying that punishment has to now be random, severe, or arbitrary just to impose your will upon them. No! But establish a relationship with a mentor who can coach you through appropriate assertiveness, rules, and consequences. Then launch your sinister plot to wrestle control away from the students and enjoy the fruits of your labor once the general atmosphere has been re-set. Again, you don't have to stay with this program forever. Frankly, you are probably best serving the students when you can be "the good cop," but they need to understand that you *can* go both ways when you need to.

4. *Authoritative*

The authoritative teacher places limits and controls on students but simultaneously encourages independence. This teacher often explains the reasons behind the rules and decisions. If students are disruptive, the teacher offers a polite, but firm, reprimand. This teacher may respond with a consequence, but only after careful consideration of the circumstances.

The authoritative teacher is also open to considerable verbal interaction, including critical debates. Students know that they can interrupt the teacher if they have a relevant question or comment. This environment offers the students the opportunity to learn and practice effective communication skills and will become responsible and independent; practicing self-discipline.

Obviously, this bears out to be the best situation for teachers. These are folks who are firm, but flexible. They have a well-defined set of rules, but also understand that students need a *mulligan* once in awhile. There is some wiggle room for if the kids (or you!) are having a tough day.

When we deal with parents in therapy, we always try to help them achieve some aspects of authoritativeness, as often times, parents get into corners of being either too strict or too easy on their kids. This then becomes the root cause of some of the acting out they see from the children!

Part IV: Ideas for the Classroom Teacher

Chapter 13

Less Involved Strategies
Things You Probably Already Do

In this Chapter, we are going to discuss some specific behavioral techniques to use as you manage your classroom. We will be moving from a few simple interventions that are probably no stranger to anyone. These will be less involved (time, attention, etc.), and as I mentioned, are probably things you are already doing as a matter of course in your room.

From there, we will move to some strategies that are a bit more involved. I will take this opportunity to help you set up behavioral programming for either the entire class or for individual students. As always, we will bear in mind that we try to hold to some of the basic rules of making target behaviors be "concrete, observable, and measurable" (again, COM for short). In this portion of the book, I will take special note of the Token Economy and go through a step-by-step method of creating and implementing this program for a variety of developmental levels.

Finally, I will take you through a few strategies to help in dealing with the students who truly are bent on giving you grey hairs. These are the ones who will fight you all the way to the finish line, because that seems to be somehow written right into their DNA. These are not going to be strategies that will guarantee success overnight, but will help to get you moving them in the right direction.

Oh, and before I begin with the Less Involved strategies, I do want to step over for a sidebar with you: I am going to deliver here a disclaimer that you are not going to like – in the following sections, *I am not going to give you what you want.*

Here's what I mean; you have picked up this book because you, in some form or fashion, have an "if, then" question or scenario in your mind. Each of you has a specific student, group of students, or classroom *full* of students who are making you nutty, and subsequently start you looking for answers. You want to push this book forward by asking your specific "If this... then what" question... right?

But here's the deal. If I were to tabulate every single specific scenario or situation your readers are currently experiencing in your schools, I would have to come up with finely differentiated responses to about 2,453,678 questions! In other words, every single one of you is in a unique constellation of students, group dynamics, parents, administration, physical surroundings, region, and even variables in your own personalities... I cannot – nor would I – address each and every one in a book of this size.

What I am offering to you is a general overview of some of the best tried and true methods of implementing behavioral strategies. I am not saying these are *The Answer*, nor are these anything that Moses may have brought down from the mountain with him and handed right into my waiting arms. Rather, what follows in the remainder of this book are more like pliable pieces of warm plastic – they have a shape and a form of their own, but they are adaptable across numerous situations; they can expand, contract, be painted, cut up, added to... or loaded into a cannon and shot toward the sun! In other words, take these ideas and make them your own.

Not all teachers have the exact personality that their neighbor may have. Not all share the same set of strengths and weaknesses, have identical delivery methods, or similar management styles. Mold the ideas to fit *yourself...* take the ones you like, and leave the ones you don't.

1. Planned ignoring

I think I may have already alluded to "planned ignoring" in Chapter 9, but very simply put, you are intervening at the "C" by removing all re-enforcers from a bad, attention-seeking behavior. You choke off the fruit by no longer feeding it, thereby allowing it to die on the vine. The proper psychology word for this act is *extinction*, and for the most part, a "planned ignore" will work over the long-run (Haley, 1993).

But, as you can imagine, there is a catch. Planned ignoring is extremely difficult to accomplish! Now, that's not to say that the idea should be scrapped entirely... rather, I would recommend using the planned ignore for situations that are more individualized, and lean away from the planned ignore when the entire class is involved. I'll explain a little further.

A planned ignore is almost impossible to pull off on a class-wide basis for a few good reasons. And believe me, I know that you are always told to do the planned ignore when you read behavior modification books, or attend seminars on classroom management... what they don't tend to tell you, though, is that it is a lot harder to accomplish than you may think!

The first pitfall; bad behavior is extremely difficult to ignore. In Psychology, we call this phenomenon "The Cocktail Party Effect" (Cherry, 1953). Simply put, let's say you are around a large group of people. Everyone is chatting, laughing, or buzzing... if you hear your name mentioned in any of the conversations, you will automatically orient your attention toward the name. You will have this happen, because attending to your name or hearing it above the din is an over-learned response.

The novelty of bad behavior grabs onto you in a very similar manner. If you look out over a sea of heads, and one starts bouncing up and down in the back, it pulls you in. It is the "Shiny Ball" phenomenon. Novelty forces attention unless you really take a moment and psych yourself up to not give in to the tendency to orient toward the bad behavior.

Because of the Cocktail Party Effect, even if *you* withdraw your attention, the rest of the class may feed the fruit by offering the sweet nectar of their own delightful attention. The acting out student, therefore, may shift his or her focus away from you and onto the rest of the folks in the room with you. After all, attention is attention, right?

The second pitfall; despite eventual extinction, the bad behavior invariably *will* get worse before it gets better in a planned ignore. And the reason is fairly obvious: the student figures to himself, "Well, I've had the volume on a six and the teacher has been ignoring me... let's see what she does with an eight..." And believe me, the volume knob on some goes well up into the seventies!

So don't throw planned ignoring onto the scrap heap in its entirety, but utilize it to extinguish minor nuisance behaviors, or behaviors that are demonstrated in a more personalized setting (i.e., when it is just you and the student, or if there are just a few people around).

A practical example would be if you were trying to help one student, and another is trying to horn in on the conversation, or trying to snatch your attention from your charge. In this instance, you have most of the external variables covered and will be able to – without eye contact if possible – hold out a hand in a gesture to let the interrupting student know he has been acknowledged, then continue your engagement with the first student. If the interrupter persists past the yellow light, maybe placing a hand on his shoulder will give the message. In the end, even if you have to take a beat to let him know that you will be with him in a moment, be sure to debrief and let him know the most appropriate way to approach you in that situation. Provide an alternate behavior in a non-punitive manner to facilitate learning.

2. *Humor*

I'm not going to write a whole bunch about how to use humor, as each of you has to assess how comfortable you are in using humor. Too, it is hard to write about specific humor techniques, because everyone is so different in their style, content, and delivery of humor.

So, a few guiding principals;

a) Use humor to deflect tension, to quell the building storm clouds, and to diffuse anxiety. Allow the students an "out" if there is a standoff situation and they feel painted into a corner. Humor can ease de-escalation.

b) Use humor to build relationships with your students. Humor is like the loop ends of Velcro, and the students' personalities are like the hook ends – with a good sense of humor, you offer them a place (or an opportunity) to connect with you.

c) Any relationship has to have a good balance of humor and seriousness to it. If you overuse humor, you lose respect because students will not trust you to take them or their situations seriously. A jokester is just about the last person on earth you would ever confide in, right? A lot of fun to hang out with, but not somebody you can get close to. So walk the line, and feel out the best way to use the sense of humor you carry.

d) If humor is not your forte then don't try to use it! Nothing is more painful to watch than a person who is totally uncomfortable with humor, but insists upon awkwardly stumbling through a joke or a witty come-on. In essence, they *become* the punch line! Use what you got, and stick with your strengths.

3. Non-verbal

This section will fall a bit under the "self explanatory" umbrella, as I am sure you all have the "Stink-eye" honed to a science. In fact, if you wear glasses (as do I), you can underscore The Stink-eye by first snaring the upper corner of your glasses with one hand, then forcefully removing them whilst maintaining Stink-eye contact with the student in question! But non-verbals can also take on a couple other meaningful implications for the classroom.

First, you can use physical proximity as either a part of your warning system or even to quell uprisings or misbehavior in certain sectors of the classroom.

To use it as an indicator of a warning, you can stroll casually past a student who may be misbehaving, and lay a hand on his shoulder (or maybe a gentle tap) as a warning or even tap your forefinger on his desk to indicate that he has been served. Incidentally, using the finger tap is a wonderfully subtle means to issue a warning, as it can be done in an unobtrusive way, thereby not alerting the rest of the class to this student's plight. The finger tap can also re-direct, as it can draw the student's attention away from the fascinating bug crawling across the floor and back to the surface of his desk – where it belongs.

You can utilize proximity to be subtle, yet strong. If there are students misbehaving in a sector of the classroom, you can adjust your position to be nearer the action while you are teaching or lecturing. The students will hopefully be less inclined to feel "invisible" if you are standing close by!

Alas, I have had to do just that in a few of my seminars with adults! I typically stand to the same side of the room to deliver my show. It is my right, your left. Unfortunately, I have had a couple instances whereby the teachers on the opposite side of the room have felt the incessant need to talk – at times somewhat loudly – amongst each other during the show. As I said, this has happened a couple of times to me, but it was handled with no embarrassment or accusations to an individual by merely having me switch sides at break or lunch time. That way, it looked as though I was adjusting simply as a matter of course, and not because of any one person or group of people. Nobody got "called out," but all of the teachers around them breathed a sigh of relief as the chatting was halted.

Lastly, a non-verbal can be a powerful "signal" to students who are either non-verbal themselves, with little kids in general, or perhaps in a situation when the cacophony reaches a fever pitch, and you do not feel the energy to shout above the din! Many preschool and elementary teachers try to capture the attention of the class as a whole by clapping a rhythm. Either the front end of shave-and-a-haircut (the students respond with: two bits), or a cadence that the rest of the room is asked to clap along with. It is light, engages all students, and gets everyone focused on you.

You can work out a non-verbal with your students – not unlike how a third base coach would work out a series of signals with the batters on the team. For example, you can say that when you pat your head, the rest of the room must return to their seats and pat their heads. An example of re-direction that has a little air of levity to it, this may be more easily followed by the class than a more punitive measure.

You can have a signal with just one of the students. You can work out with Matthew that when you put your finger on your nose, he is doing a great job... if you tug at your earlobe he is getting out of hand, and needs to pull it back together. The rest of the class does not have to know these signals, thus protecting Matthew some from repeatedly being called out in front of his peers. And, just like the opposing manager in a baseball game, if the class "steals your signals," and starts to figure out the system, you and Matthew can change up, thereby establishing a rotating series of signals that may stay one step ahead of the class. One or two hands in your pockets, crossing your arms, pushing up your glasses on the bridge of your nose, or even a good old fashioned wink of the eye can be powerfully subtle signals to help Matthew feel connected and on track.

The other benefit of a private non-verbal communication with a student is that the protected nature of the signals establishes a bond with you that Mathew may thrive under. This is an exceptionally powerful intervention technique for male teachers with their male students.

4. Behavior shaping

There is not a whole lot to this concept, as it means literally, to work on reinforcing a complicated set of behaviors one step at a time. Or, as in the movie "What About Bob?" we have to move in "Baby Steps." In psycho-babble, we use the term *successive approximations* (Peterson, 2004) to describe this process.

In other words, remember the oil tanker, or the freight train metaphors. Rome was not built in a day and neither were these troublesome students. They have been shaped by their world to behave in this manner to get their needs met, and they will continue to struggle with changing their strategy as you work toward a different solution. So it will take time, energy, and patience on your part – but hang in there! Making progress with students who feel like a heavy load will always feel more satisfying that moving along the kids who are a joy to have in the room!

5. Catch kids doing well

Here is another one of those idioms you end up hearing in every seminar you attend as an educator, in every fireside chat about parenting techniques, and in many other "rah-rah" venues. The problem is that this is a concept we all *know*, but a very difficult one to actually put into motion!

Often, as I am consulting with a teacher, I throw out the old "Catch 'em being good" stand-by. Typically, this elicits a reaction of thinly-contained frustration, as the teacher fires back with some version of, "Are you *nuts?* If that bear is hibernating, I'm not going to go over and kick it in the head!"

In other words, when the student happens to be quiet or working or just – by pure happenstance – has randomly decided to sit still and face front, the teacher tip-toes in the other direction. We have all done this, as we embrace the warm tranquility that ensues. That moment or two of peace and quiet becomes a brief port in our stormy day or raging classroom, for sure.

But think about what you are teaching the student when you do this – that when he is being appropriate, you leave him about as alone as possible, as you don't want to irritate the coiled snake. But if he begins to misbehave again, you are probably back on top of him – and maybe with added vigor because he stepped all over your brief Nirvana.

So, remember, *the worst student in your classroom is not bad 100% of the time.* It just doesn't work that way. Yes, he is misbehaving at a greater pace than perhaps any student in the history of organized education... but there are times of peace throughout the day, or throughout the class period. Find those times, and reinforce rather than leave alone. Make it better for that student to be good than to not be good.

And remember too, if attention-seeking is the goal of the bulk of his misbehavior, see if you can make attention be the reward he works toward (i.e., lunch with you, a brief sit-down with you, time to entertain the class, etc.). If it is power, then give a little power (special helper, doing work in the principal's office, playground monitor, etc.). In other words;: using M&M's®, stickers, homework passes, etc., may be effective, but tailoring a reinforcement system to the specific needs of the student can have a more powerful hold on him. Remember diplomacy? Reach behind the misbehavior and tend to the issue that is breathing life into it.

6. The "Premack Principle"

The "Premack Principle" (Premack, 1959) is a term that you probably recognize on some level. It seems to ring a distant bell from somewhere buried deep within in your Intro-Psych-curriculum unconscious. Again, this is one you memorized for the midterm, and then promptly replaced it in your memory with some sort of sports statistic, bundt cake recipe, or uncanny ability to tell the difference between "kind of dirty," "still wearable," and "torch this thing with Napalm" when sifting through the clothes on your dorm room floor (I have a feeling I am only talking to the guys here)...

But, to refresh your memory, this principle refers to the idea of placing a low priority behavior before a high priority behavior. In other words, you earn the right to do what you want to do AFTER you do something that you don't want to do. The high priority behavior becomes the re-enforcer to the low priority one (e.g., "The class can earn five minutes of extra recess if you can *all* get the math worksheet done by 10:15"). As Pink Floyd said (about a hundred years ago, I'm afraid), "How can you have any pudding if you don't eat your meat?"

If you can set up similar contingency-based plans with your students, you may find that this works. These plans can be set up on a classroom-wide basis, as was the example I cited above, or they can be forged toward an individual student. In the end, the students are not working to avoid a negative consequence, but rather are working to earn a good one. If they do not all get the math worksheet in on time, they do not earn the re-enforcer no harm, no foul. We'll try again tomorrow.

7. *Contracting*

This is an interesting one, because on the surface, it does not seem to carry a lot of weight. When I bring this up in seminars, many of the participants raise an eyebrow, and then check to see if I had actually drank my lunch.

But I am here to say that signing a contract does seem to carry a lot of weight with students – especially with males and particularly in upper grades. There is still some "honor among thieves," as agreeing to a behavioral contract can add a dimension of self-control that just discussing may not. But don't limit your usage of contracting to older males; this technique can work with boys and girls of all ages.

In fact, this is so powerful of a tool, we therapists often draft "suicide contracts" with clients who are feeling inclined to end their lives. Legally, we cannot let them leave our office if we feel strongly that they are intent upon attempting suicide (i.e., they have a desire, a plan, and an available means). We often squawk about this responsibility, as that implies to some extent that we should be able to read minds and predict the future accurately, but that is currently the burden we shoulder in our profession.

If a client talks through a desire to end their life, but arrives at a tentative conclusion that they will *not* attempt suicide, we can satisfy our legal obligation, and give the client a good-faith vote of confidence. We do this by allowing them to go home, and then to return in a day or two to continue working through their painful process – but only after we each sign a suicide contract. The contract basically says that the client agrees not to do harm unto themselves without first following a set of clearly defined steps (like calling the therapist, going to the Emergency Room, calling a specific friend or family member, etc.). It will also spell out the date and time of the next scheduled appointment, and that they agree to attend this session without exception.

In the end, both parties sign on the dotted line, a copy is made for client and therapist, and we agree to move forward.

Again, on the surface this may seem to lack any bite, as the client can certainly walk out the door to my office, and kill himself in the parking lot – but that is not usually how it works. That consenting signature carries lot of weight for a couple of reasons: first, despite the attorneys in our world working over-time to mess everything up, with most people, their word and reputation is important to honor. Second, the fact that I cared enough to; 1) go through the process of talking them through their remarkably uncomfortable thoughts and desires and 2) drafting the actual contract speaking to these thoughts, sends a message of commitment that the client may not feel in other areas of his life. And third, the contract offers a valuable incentive, *hope*.

To bring this back into the classroom, utilize contracting with your junior high or high school students to make concrete the agreement you are willing to forge with them. Of course, you sticking to your end of the bargain is of utmost importance, but creating a tangible record of the deal gives you a document to return to should the student ever cry foul, plus it gives them a feeling of respect from you that you felt they had the dignity to honor a contract.

Contracting can be powerful. And to be frank, if they don't sign an informal contract with you in the classroom, there could be other, more seriously binding contracts that are set into motion in their lives with breaches of said contract (i.e., suspensions, legal action, failure, etc.).

8. *Opportunities to serve others*

As I mentioned in the section regarding bullies, creating situations whereby students can earn respect from others in situations that are extraordinary are powerfully incentive-laden scenarios. And think about it this way: some of the students who drive you bananas are ones who have learned to get their 'respect' needs met in a variety of misguided ways. The respect they garner in these negative scenarios may not always be exceptionally gratifying, but in the mind of the "Bad Kid," it's all he or she has got to get that need met. The behaviors are always hooked with stress though, as the 'respect' is somewhat ill-gotten.

For example, a high school sophomore may suddenly get into Satan-worship because it elicits a shock or a fear reaction from peers and/or adults. You add to this a delightful array of piercings, black fingernail polish, outrageous clothing, and other assorted body art, and now he elicits a similar repulsion response from strangers who may not know about the Satan worship. This reaction will give the kid a brief, intense, sense of satisfaction, but it is inadequate when compared to other behaviors which may not have the stress or negative consequences associated to them.

Opening up new opportunities for respect to be earned in conventional (read as: HEALTHIER) situations can begin to turn the oil-tanker, because once the kids choose the ill-gotten path, they are probably exceedingly pessimistic that the usual way will work at all for them.

I am being a bit wordy in this section, but suffice it to say that true respect will strike a different chord in these kids than fear, shock, or other fleeting forms.

By the way, some kids who have been on a bad path for a long time may actually behave worse once they are put into a healthy situation, as they begin to feel either 1) pressure to keep behaving well – something they do not believe they are capable of doing, or 2) angry at whatever hand of fate dealt them the hand they have been given.

So, while misbehavior may spike temporarily in this instances, stick with the student, and offer as much support and guidance as you are able.

All right… we're in the middle of the 7th inning here, and we have yet to get to any plans that are more structured and systematic in their approach. The next couple chapters will do exactly that, so fear not! I'll get the relief core warming up in the bullpen, and we will grab a hot dog and a beer while we embark upon the seventh-inning S-T-R-E-T-C-H… Anyone care to sing "Take Me Out to the Ballgame" in the voice of Harray Caray? Let's go, Cubbies!

Chapter 14

A Bit More Involved

Teaching Old Dogs New Tricks

Moving forward, we transition our ballgame into later innings by thinking about some strategies that involve a bit more in terms of time and attention from the teacher. Still, while these strategies may ratchet up the level of commitment on your part, they may also ratchet up the impact on the classroom. We are going to cover a few old standbys, but put a different spin on them to facilitate user-friendliness!

In this section, we will cover The Good-Behavior Game, Time-Out, and perhaps the senior member of our eldest dogs club; Taking Away of Privileges. I will then reserve an entire chapter to cover Token Economies (see Chapter 15), as this technique, when properly applied, can reap enormous benefits... I will explain further and offer ideas for adaptation to different situations in just a little bit.

For now, lower the protective eyewear, snap the rubber gloves into place, and get ready to get down and dirty with me!

1. The Good behavior game

Versions of the Good Behavior Game have been around since the days of Cro-Magnon Man. This is evidenced by recently discovered ancient cave drawings depicting classrooms whereby teachers, clad in stylish yet comfortable Mammoth skins, are seen doling out Skittles® and Tootsie Rolls® to third grade students with thick, slanted foreheads and hairy, muscled forearms (the students that is... not the teachers). On the board in the backdrop of the scene we can make out the outline of a crudely drawn Jon Bon Jovi (popular even before music was invented) stickman – he is missing both legs and one arm. The missing appendages were cause for initial concern to the archaeologists who unearthed this particular cave painting, but when they put the scene into the context of the Good Behavior Game, it all suddenly became perfectly clear.

The power of the Good Behavior Game is not in the name, but in the opportunity to incorporate a warning system (or, some "Mulligans") directly into your behavioral strategy. Plus, you can also build a sense of community and accomplishment class-wide, as the system relies on social monitoring for success. Everyone pulls on the same rope, so to speak.

This is also the standard recommendation for classrooms with two or three or four (or so) acting out students in the room. For the sake of argument at first, let's assume we only have one student acting out, then will expand into more. In describing the game, I will be using a lot of words and a number of pages, but bear in mind that this is actually a very simple strategy to implement. I will explain the pieces involved, and also sprinkle in a couple real-life examples to draw the pieces together, and to illustrate how the pieces work in perfect harmony. Here's how the game works (loosely adapted from its original creators, Barrish, Saunders, & Wold, 1969):

First, you make a drawing on the board. I will talk about situations involving older students later on in this section, but will open the discussion with a room of younger students. In this case, the drawing on the board can be somewhat rudimentary: a thermometer, for example. There are countless other possibilities, limited only by the imagination of the teacher and/or students. But I will stick with the thermometer example for the sake of continuity and clarity.

You draw the thermometer on the board with a reservoir at the bottom, then five graduations of temperature running up the side of the tube. Each graduation (i.e., temperature, or "degree") is clearly marked as counting down to the "zero" point, which will be the reservoir itself.

For the rules of the game, take your target behavior – let's say it is yelling out in class without raising your hand first. Explain to the class that, when you hear a student yell out, you will either:

a) Issue a warning

After the warning, you will then either proceed directly to step 'b', or issue a second warning. And to repeat, the number of warnings will depend on the general nature of your room. With students who are overall well-behaved, you may issue a single warning to give them a chance to pull it together. For rooms that tend to be more on the rambunctious side, you may give a couple warnings. In any case, you will either issue a warning, or proceed directly to:

b) Erase the "5 degrees" mark off of the thermometer

By the way, when you erase the "5 degrees" mark, you can either lop off the number alone, or obliterate the entire part of the tube that sticks up past the "4 degrees" graduation. And, as you can probably anticipate, with each repeated transgression, you erase another and another graduation, until finally the reservoir at the bottom gets erased, and the prize is not granted for that period of time. If there is still mercury in the reservoir at the end of the pre-determined length of time, the class earns the prize, or the reward.

A couple of variables free to adjust to your situation are; *1) the latency of re-set* and *2) the number of degrees*. These two variables play off of each other, and need to be considered in tandem to maximize the potential of the game. The level of variation will (again) depend on the general nature of your class, as you will eventually settle onto a point of *equilibrium* with them. In this instance, equilibrium means that you hit a point whereby your students have the right combination of *latency* and *degrees* to be able to earn the reward. This equilibrium will give the game some traction, as it will allow the students to reap benefit, and 'get it.' Over time, the goal will be to push that wall back, but I'll explain that in a moment as well. Lots of big words and complicated sounding concepts and rules! Here is how to think about each of these concepts, and then to put them into motion:

Regarding *1) the latency of re-set*, this refers to the amount of time the game goes on before the clock gets re-set; the thermometer goes back to five degrees. It is also the amount of time required for the students to either earn or not earn the pot of gold at the end of the rainbow. Thus, if you have the students for only a set amount of time (like, fifty-two minutes per day if you teach a course in middle or high school), then your time is pretty much determined for you. No need to mess with the natural schedule of the day, unless you have a room that is remarkably out of control, in which case you will work to re-set the clock more frequently – again, the goal is to reach equilibrium.

If you have your class all day, you can either go the entire day on one thermometer, split the day into "pre-lunch" and "post-lunch," or move to re-set after each subject is taught – or, even "hourly" if that is an easier method for the kids to digest. The determining factor will be how well they are able to wrap their brains around the concept, and also how well they are able to succeed. Plus, keep in mind that smaller, shorter term goals are generally more effective than longer-term, bigger ones. This is particularly true with younger kids who are not as accurate of envisioning longer time frames.

While we are on that point, let me take a brief sidebar here. And I know I left our last concept a bit fuzzy, but I will return and clean it up for you.

If you would like to use a bigger goal as the carrot on the stick, you will need to help the students move toward it slowly. For a step-wise progression toward a bigger goal (like a field trip or a pizza party – something remarkable in being special, both in terms of time and expense), then work to have the students earn points along the way. This way, they can feel as though the immediate goals are well within reach. But too, this system can allow some flexibility to allow for bad days to take place without sinking the ship of the entire operation. For example, make each day that they have mercury left in the reservoir will be worth ten points, but make the trip to the Science Museum to be worth two hundred points. Then, you can use a graphic representation of a *big* thermometer, with graduations of ten that you can slowly fill all the way up to two hundred. This system maintains hope even through some poorly behaved days. Plus, if you can keep the date of the trip flexible, it can depend solely on the behavior in your room. The better behaved they are, the quicker we can earn the field trip. The whole class is involved in the toil and in the reward... everyone pulls on the same rope.

In the above example, I made the successful completion of the short-term game (i.e., keep the reservoir until the end of the class period) worth ten points for a reason. If it is worth one point and the field trip is worth twenty points, you limit your own flexibility. If the mercury is worth ten per day, you have the capability to throw in some bonus points along the way for exemplary behavior, or for other class projects that may be fun to add to the mix. You can now throw in three, five, or seven points at random intervals to drive home the point that good behavior is *always* going to be more beneficial than bad behavior.

So, that was number 1), and we learned how to determine re-set time. In explaining 2), the number of degrees, we have to again consider the general behavior of the room. If the room behaves well, you may only need three, or maybe even two, degrees. A room that is more ill-behaved may need six or seven... again the whole time keeping an eye toward helping the students achieve the goal to help you set the hook. In a nutshell, fewer Mulligans for better-behaved rooms, more for rooms that need a little extra help to reach their goals.

How these two concepts play out together requires a little ingenuity on your part. With a room that feels more out of control to the teacher, you can either add more degrees, or you may wish to shorten the latency to help students get some grip in the game. In the end, you want the right combination of degrees and latency to ensure success of your students.

And before I go on, I know I keep emphasizing that the class has to feel successful, so it is imperative that the game find that equilibrium point. The reason that success in the short run is so important lies in some of the "bad kids" in your room. These are kids who have generally been perceived as the "Bad Kids" throughout their days in school, and may not realize that success is even within their grasp. They get good at losing, and of course, perception is reality. Getting the oil tanker turned requires that they begin to re-define the opportunity as "possible" rather than "impossible."

Once you have reached that point of equilibrium, and your class begins to earn the pot of gold, you can begin to tinker with degrees and latency to push the class to maintain good behavior for longer period of time, and with fewer warnings or, "push the wall back."

For example, you may, after two weeks, decide to make the latency ninety minutes instead of sixty. The number of degrees will remain the same, but they will be required now to hold it together for a longer period of time with the same five degrees. Or, you can keep the latency at sixty minutes, but shorten the number of degrees to four or three instead of five – thereby requiring that the students have fewer "yelling outs" within the same period of time to earn the pot of gold.

Another way to monitor this "pushing the wall back" will be to reward better behavior with higher point values of keeping some mercury in the reservoir. Thus, it used to be ten points for not burning through five degrees in a fifty-two minute class period. Now that you have lowered the number of initial degrees to four (from five) you can make the successful completion of the class period to be worth twelve points instead of ten. You create a system of greater reward for greater behavior.

This system will keep its grip if you follow through on the longer term payoff, then immediately establish a new one. Sort of a quid pro quo: if they let you do your job as a great teacher, you will let them do their job of being screwball students!

If you teach high school, a thermometer on the board may seem a bit hokey, which may de-rail your attempt to establish roots with the game. Here is how I used the Good Behavior Game to help a high school Chemistry teacher in a pretty rough inner-city school begin to regain control of her classroom. In her case, the kids would begin to shout insults to one another, which would (of course) escalate until a fight would break out. And in general, we tend to frown upon fights breaking out in a fully-stocked Chemistry lab… know what I mean?

Same rules apply, but with a twist: I told her to ask the students to come up with an icon who could, in essence, represent the thermometer. In her case, the class liked a rapper named L'il Wayne. So, fine… let's use L'il Wayne…

So, she drew a picture of L'il Wayne on the board – but in a particular manner. I told her to draw him with a full face (eyes, ears, nose, smiley mouth, hair), then the rest of him as a stick-figure. The stick-figure had a trunk, two legs and two arms – in other words, five appendages ("Degrees") and one smiling face ("Reservoir"). Now, the system was set up whereby she would erase one body part of L'il Wayne each time she heard an insult, with his face being the last part to go. Thus, if L'il Wayne was still smiling at her at the end of the class period (i.e., there was still mercury left in the reservoir), she gave the class a tally on the board. And for the first wave of the game, three tallies would equal a reward the class could work out amongst themselves.

Over time, I advised her to increase the number of tallies required to earn the reward, but to also work with the class to increase the value of the rewards. Better behavior for better rewards, right?

Also, she had flexibility to add hands and/or feet to L'il Wayne in her attempt to find the point of equilibrium. If the class could not initially manage to get through chemistry with five body parts, we would add a couple or a few – until we found the point whereby they could hold it together and start forward progress in the game.

Before moving on, I'll again state that the success of the entire class rests on their ability to pull the trouble-makers under control. This system gets difficult when there are four or five students acting out, as they may (de facto) band together to make their bad behavior nearly impervious to the efforts of the rest of the room to contain them. If this is happening in your classroom, then divide the class into, say, four teams (based on the number of troublesome students). Then, put one of the behavior-problem students on each of the teams. This will eliminate the cumulative effect of the four together, and thereby make each team responsible for reigning in only one of the acting out peers rather than all four.

You can then reward each team individually for keeping mercury in their reservoir, or have each feed into the BIG thermometer, or some combo of both. The beauty of any good behavior plan for classroom management is in its ability to be adaptable across a number of developmental levels and classroom situations!

Incidentally, the only way that the good behavior game will not work is if you have a student who enjoys the power of being able to derail the train of the entire classroom (or team). If this happens, you can try to put him on a team with some of the stronger-willed classmates in an effort to give them a chance to rein him in, or else you may have to set up a plan to deal with him individually. More examples to follow!

2. Time-Out

Ah, perhaps the most ubiquitous of the behavior programs with a specific name. "Time Out" has almost created its own wing in the Parenting Hall of Fame. I have been sitting here for several minutes, drinking a Dr. Pepper, trying to think of any other behavior plan that has reached such widespread acclaim… needless to say, I can't. Pretty much anyone who either; a) has kids, b) has spent a lot of time around kids, c) lives somewhere within fifty-three miles of a kid, or d) has ever been a kid themselves; has heard of Time Out.

The technique and term were first coined by a behavioral psychologist, Arthur Staats, in 1958, but really came to the forefront in 1970 (Staats, 1970). So, while this long history gives an advantage to Time Out – in that the rules of the game are generally understood without too much explanation – it also serves as a major weakness. What I mean by that is everyone has a pre-conceived notion of Time Out. And I don't just mean that they know the rules; rather, everyone also has an opinion about the utility of Time Out. They either love it or hate it, and have generally set that opinion in stone in their mind.

So, a couple issues I deal with when I consult with parents or school personnel is to first assess their mindset toward the program, and then see what rules they understand to be "The Truth" when it comes to implementing Time Out. I have to do this because the success or failure of my role as consultant seems to hinge upon my ability to break on through these pre-conceived notions, and essentially "re-teach" Time Out in a more useful way.

Having said that, I am quite certain that you, dear reader, also have your own idea of how to do Time Out, and also an idea about whether it is worth anything or not. So I implore you, please shelve these ideas for a few minutes, and read on with an open mind.

Before I wade out into the quicksand (by the way… whatever happened to 'death by quicksand' that was so popular on television in the 1970's?), let me back up a step and say a couple things. First, some of you work in an environment where you have a formalized Time Out Procedure. If you are in a self-contained classroom, or an alternative school or other structured setting, you probably have a documented, step-by-step process you must follow. If this is the case, then carry on. The bottom line in *any* employment setting is that you have to do what your boss tells you to do. And my guess is that the Procedure is in place for your safety as well as the safety of your students.

Second, I'll also say that in some settings, Time Out in any form may not work. Whenever you attend a seminar or read a book like this one, you will bump into a lot of different ideas that may or may not be applicable to your specific situation. Nothing gets more bothersome to me in a live seminar than when I introduce an idea, and then someone in the back raises their hand and says some version of, "Yeah, but... I am doing (fill in the blank), and that won't work in my room."

I am never sure what exactly they want me to say in that case, so I usually just reply with a polite, "Uh... okay." So I will say again: If it won't work, then don't do it!

Here's the deal; I am not going to teach you the nuts and bolts of Time Out. That would generally be like preaching to the choir. Plus, if you really want to know those nuts and bolts, I am sure there are volumes of text already written on the topic. Rather, I am going to help you re-think the notion of Time Out in order that it becomes a more effective tool for classroom management. I will take it out of the archaic, and move it into the slick and shiny "New and Improved!" I may even throw out the term "Space Age Polymers" to show just how unbelievably glamorous this new product is going to be. Heck, I may even get a cool celebrity endorsement to begin a groundswell of support and to lend credibility to the program!

And to begin this march, let's review the two purposes of Time Out. Or to put it another way, why do we even have it in the first place? I am sure most of you could hit this softball out of the park, but I will answer the semi-rhetorical question myself. Time Out is meant to:

a) Separate from the herd. Remove the student from whatever the situation is that is causing over-stimulation, distress, or anxiety.

b) Give the student a time and a space to cool off. And I really meant to write it that way – practicing that "gaining of control" is an important skill for kids to get a handle on.

Most everyone knows that already, but the most pressing problem (as I see it) evolving with Time Out is that it becomes another venue for a power struggle to develop between student and teacher. If there was a way to take some of the sting out of Time Out, we may be in a position to encourage higher levels of compliance, and thereby remove some of the fight when the Time Out situations arise. In other words, I want to help you make 'calming down' NOT be viewed as a punishment all the time; rather, re-tool the students' thinking into viewing it as an opportunity to get settled back down to earth. Heck, most adults will joke, "I wish **I** could get a time out once in awhile!"

You know why grown-ups say this? It's because time to *chill* is not seen as a bad thing to us! We have the ability to self-select, and thereby we interpret 'time away' as a positive rather than a constantly noxious event. Here are a few ideas to tweak to Time Out concept, to take out some of the punch, and to make it more user-friendly.

a) Name Change

The first order of business is to change the name. "Time Out" tends to be a loaded – if not somewhat antiquated – moniker. As I said, everyone has an opinion/attitude toward "Time Out," so let's not call it that anymore. Plus, the implication for Time Out is that the student will have to sit like a wooden soldier in some pre-ordained

Time Out spot to fulfill whatever the Time Out requirements happen to be.

That tends to be one piece of feedback I get from teachers from time to time. They ask how to 'make' the student sit in Time Out. The scenario tends to create rather than diffuse tension in the room.

So, I recommend that the name go to something with less of a toxic implication. Calling it "Quiet Time" for example, will lead to the implication that, once in Quiet Time, the student will only be allowed to engage in quiet activities. Thus, they may not necessarily have to sit still on a chair, but they certainly can if they elect to. Also, they perhaps would be able to read a book, do homework, or just chill out. Make rules such that the program slowly changes from being overtly punitive to an opportunity to calm down before getting back into the swing of things.

We can also use more 'hip' names, like calling it "Chill out Time" or "Cool out Time" or some other tag that has a positive spin. Whatever the students relate to will be what you go with, as they are the ones affected.

b) Self-selecting

Along these same lines, offering an opportunity for the students to *self select* "Chill out Time" will also take some of the punch out of situations whereby *you* select it *for them* in a negative setting (i.e., as punishment). So, if you create a space in your room designated solely for "chilling out," allow students to enter that space on their own accord, a more functional option when students begin to get out of control.

To pull this off, take a corner of the room and decorate it in a fashion that is conducive to chilling out. Or, you can call it some name that hooks onto something you are studying at the time. I have heard of teachers calling that area "Antarctica" (or somewhere similar to coincide with geography class) or "Australia." The point is, make a space that is set apart (both physically and via décor) from the rest of the classroom.

The situation that you want to eventually develop is that students are allowed to enter that space when they feel like they need to get away for a few minutes, or when they are needing to calm down some, or whatever scenario leads them to want to be alone for a while. With some students who tend to push the boundaries, you may also need to have a time limit – or an actual timer – to be in the *Chill out Zone*.

With the option of self selection, it is a less confrontational set-up when you have to direct the student into *The Zone*.

Another artifact of this idea is that the Chill Zone in your room will begin to develop a personality of its own, with its own rules for engagement! The students will know how "to act" when they enter the Chill Zone and will react accordingly. Plus, they will begin to refer to that part of the room as though it was another character in the big Broadway Play of your school year, rather than just a formerly empty corner of a cinderblock classroom.

I heard a great suggestion from a teacher at a tough private school who said he had "The Wall" in his room (an obvious tip-of-the-hat to Pink Floyd, I'm sure). When students were on The Wall, they were on penalty, and the severity of the offense determined where on The Wall they would be placed. In the end, The Wall had its own persona, and the students all knew the score of the game if one of their peers was seen at any point along The Wall. With a little buoyancy, a version of Time Out can be folded more neatly into your day rather than a diversion from it.

c) Get out of class free card

Another idea for an alternate Time Out is one that we use through our office with many of our Asperger's clients. With these students, we work out a deal with the school whereby they are allowed, once per day, to be given a "Get out of Class Free" card. With this card, they are afforded an opportunity to self-select 10 minutes to go to their Safe Place (more on this in a minute) to calm down.

This program needs to have a couple pieces in place before it can be pulled off successfully, but in general it works for these students because, once again, it affords them an opportunity to recognize escalation and then to practice de-escalation, control, and contain.

The pieces that need to be in place are as follows. First, we teach the kids how to recognize escalation. Our lesson is grounded largely in physiological reactions to stress, as these are students who are somewhat more prone to disconnecting from the emotional aspects of becoming upset. So, we teach that if you feel your fists clenching up, or your belly beginning to tighten, or your jaw clenching or any number of other reactions that the student's body may offer, then that means you are beginning to grow upset or escalate.

Next, we work out the Safe Place. Typically, this tends to be the office of a counselor we are working with It may also be the vice principal's or principal's office. Again, the location depends largely upon who has a positive working relationship both with our office and also, with the student in question.

Finally, we also arrange for an escort if the student may need some guidance in getting to the Safe Place. No need to have a little one running amok in the building if we can possibly avoid it! Usually with the younger students, they may need some assistance in getting themselves situated.

We may also help the teacher coach the rest of the class in how to address this issue, as there may be some sibling rivalry evolving in classmates who would like the same courtesy extended to them. In this situation, we can either make it a class-wide program (although the Safe Place will, for them, have to be moved to a location within the room to avoid a stampede on the poor Guidance Counselor!). Incorporating this program with the Chill Out Zone referred to above is an effective means to deal with this issue. The other option, when addressing the class, is to get them on board when it comes to helping the Asperger's student. Letting the class know they will be instrumental in helping Alan out may elicit a different reaction than being indignant.

In any case, once these moving parts are in place, we begin the program with the student. He will open with the knowledge that *any* ongoing abuse of this system will result in it being taken off the table. But to repeat, this allows a chance to practice the skill of lassoing the horse and dragging it back into the barn themselves. This has served us well in reducing the number of tantrum outbursts, as it provides an alternative to the feeling of hopeless and unbridled escalation.

d) A few final thoughts on "Time Out"

In closing this section, I thought it prudent to talk about a couple other ideas I heave heard from teachers around the country. One involves a new Time Out technique of engaging gross muscle groups to encourage calming while in the Time Out position.

I'm not sure if any of you have seen the new-fangled Time Out chairs that are being manufactured, but they essentially look like a seat on top of a half of a Pilate ball. The basic idea here is that if the students are forced to focus on *sitting*, they will be less inclined to focus their efforts on acting out further.

The way these seats work is to create an unstable base at the bottom of the seat... something akin to making the student into a life-sized website; the student has to concentrate on shifting their weight constantly in reaction to the movements of the ball base.

The other aspect of these chairs is that they are soft and squishy underneath, so they can engage the student in gross motor movement that can also detract from acting out energy. Some, not intended specifically for Time Out, will even come with little legs on the bottom to actually stabilize the ball – thus allowing some bouncing capability without the fear of falling over sideways.

Now, before you dismiss this as another flash-in-the pan idea that will fade away like other fads have, I can say that there is anecdotal evidence for the utility of these seats. I have heard from teachers around the country that they have used them with success.

The final idea is one I believe I may have alluded to briefly earlier in this book, but this is an idea that again goes back to taking a bit of the power struggle out of the Time Out situation. If you are having trouble having the students sit like wooden soldiers in their Time Out place, then back down on that requirement some. Again, adding a bit of buoyancy will help float some of the students who are regularly in very heavy situations. In these cases, maybe just put a square of masking tape down on the floor around the Time Out spot and tell them that they may not have to sit perfectly still, but that they have to; 1) be quiet and 2) remain within the square.

This will be particularly effective with younger students who may have the intention, but not the ability, to sit perfectly still for three minutes!

In a final summation of Time Out, I remind again that offering the student a replacement behavior for the offending one can; 1) build a relationship as you two take some one-on-one time to work this out and 2) give an alternative to the bad behavior. Learning takes place in times of calm – following the Time Out – not in times of distress. So, de-escalate, and then teach by subsequently reinforcing their application of the new, positive behavior option.

3. *Taking Away of Privileges*

This little nugget is so engrained in the management strategies of teachers; there is not much I can reasonably expect to add! But, I do have one thing to think about when implementing Taking Away of Privileges.

If you have a repeat offender – a student who keeps doing the same old same old to get into hot water – we can fall into a pattern whereby s/he no longer cares if you remove the privilege. In other words, if recess gets taken away over and over, the impact of the recess lessens over time. Plus, you begin to erode his hope of ever having a week of successful recesses!

With the repeat offenders, we can change up the philosophy. Because in most cases, the student does the crime, he does the time, and then the privilege gets reinstated right away. In other words, there is no further contingency. With most students, this strategy works. You yank recess for most screwball students, and they feel it. Here is what we can try with the few who *don't*:

Rather than automatically reinstate a privilege after the appropriate sentence has been served, create a contingency for reinstatement. So, let's say Gregory loses two recesses because of some transgression. He serves his time away from recess, but rather than have him go on his merry way the next day, create a system of restitution.

If you can make the restitution fit the transgression, then you have an ideal situation. For instance, if he breaks something of yours in the classroom, he serves the two recesses, and then has to "work off" his debt by cleaning the room, helping you with a project, serving others, etc. The amount of time required to reinstate recess will be dependant upon the relative value of the thing that was broken. Only after he has "undone" the offense can he return to normal recess.

If Gregory hurt another student or their property, Gregory can be required to serve that student somehow. If he wasted the class' time, he has make this up for you by doing some work equal to the time lost by his acting out. The sky is the limit to how creative you can get with restitution.

In many cases, however, there will not be a direct 1:1 correlation between transgression and ideal restitution, but you can always set up a scenario whereby the student pays back "time lost" from the class period.

The point is, value gets placed upon the return of the privilege rather than an automatic re-up. Placing a minor barrier to reinstatement can deepen the impact of the loss, can build empathy by furthering his or her understanding of the relative worth of the asset they sullied by their behavior, and continue your management plan down the path of making it better to be good than to not be good.

Those are a few ideas I have for some structured means of gaining some control over the classroom setting. As you move through them, you can begin to identify those students who are truly atypical and may not have the capability to respond to your management techniques. I will discuss those for Chapter 16. I have devoted the entire next chapter to a system that has been shown to be a very effective strategy for gaining control of the classroom, and that is Token Economy. I know many of you are already using some version of Token Economy, but I hope I can add to the ideas you carry and/or create a new avenue for those of you who are not utilizing this idea.

Chapter 15

The Token Economy

Setting the Stage for Living

Let's move into talking about a great, adaptable, flexible system called Token Economy!

I'll embark upon this discussion with a definition. I realize that most of you have at least heard of the term "Token Economy," but unless you are doing one in your classroom, you may not know exactly what one is. In a nutshell, a Token Economy is a system set up whereby the students earn tokens for good behavior (more on what tokens are in a minute) and then over time, they have options related to how they use or "spend" their tokens. It was first developed in Florida by a fellow named Teodoro Ayllon in the 1960's, but came to prominence when he published a watershed book on the topic (Ayllon & Azrin, 1968). You can get really specific ideas from his series of books on the subject, as he is still alive and hard at work writing and teaching at Georgia State University. I'll draw upon his theories and give ideas on application in a little bit as well.

So, the Token Economy works almost like currency in the classroom. You earn, you spend, and you revel in small victories. This is why I subtitled the Chapter 15 "Setting the Stage for Living." We teach the students a valuable life lesson of earning, spending, and managing their finances through this process. In fact, the lesson can be amazingly direct, but table that one for now as well. Rather than confuse matters with a cumbersome narrative on all the options available within Token Economy, I am going to set this chapter up like an FAQ (Frequently Asked Questions) page on a website. I'll keep it relatively manageable, and limit it to ten questions.

In the spirit of the Internet sites against which this section is modeled, I will list the questions first, and then get into the responses. I only wish I could make them clickable links to save your eyes the strain of actually having to read each one, but life goes that way sometimes. Here we go:

1) How do we get started?

2) What do we use for tokens?

3) What do we use for rewards?

4) How do I know what to make everything cost?

5) Can this program be adapted for older students or situations where I may have six or seven classes of thirty kids each moving through my classroom every day?

6) Can this system be used class-wide rather than for individual students?

7) I have student who get very angry because they always feel outperformed by classmates. Is there either a way to deal with this situation or perhaps a different method to dole out rewards for Token Economy?

8) Do I also take away tokens for poor behavior?

9) *What?* What is "Response Cost?"

10) Closing words of wisdom.

1. *How do we get started?*

The first step is to sit the class down and let them know the deal. You will either be implementing this program from the starting line in August or September, or you will be implementing in mid-stream. Either way, the directions/rules should be laid out in a manner by which the students can understand.

Then, you'll need to get the nuts and bolts into place. Figuring out the type of tokens you will use the goals for appropriate behavior, and the relative "cost" for each will be your task. I'll hit each of those questions separately.

And keep something else in mind as you begin this program: the power of this game with some of the students who have worn the "Bad Kid" label throughout their entire academic career is to have them *start to feel successful*. Remember a point that I brought up a chapter or two ago: that the *worst* students in your room are not bad 100% of the time. There is just no way. During those brief respites when they are sitting still and paying attention, you just have to hustle back and catch the ones being good. Change the rules of how they see themselves in the school and make it better to be good than to not be good, but also let them know that they can (at least in your room) be successful.

2. *What do we use for tokens?*

Great question! Teachers have suggested all kinds of tokens for use with this system. At times, the choice really is not up to you, as your school may have a school-wide program that tailors its tokens to either the school mascot ("Paw Prides," "Jaguar Bucks," "Happy Monkeys"), or a more generic ideology ("Catch 'Em Being Goods," "Atta Boys/Girls," etc.). If you implement this system within your room exclusively, you have options. In this case, perhaps the most common token I have heard is using the raffle tickets that you can purchase by the roll. These tend to be popular because; a) they are available at the teacher store, b) they are relatively inexpensive, and c) you get about 35 million per roll, making them plentiful enough to last you for awhile.

I have also heard of teachers using poker chips, marbles, kidney beans, pennies in a jar, and different forms of play money. Here is where it gets interesting, to tell you the truth. Monopoly-type paper money is commonly used, as it affords you some flexibility with regard to denomination. But there are many options of play money available at toy stores, or you could use faux jewels or gemstones, *Pirates of the Caribbean* Doubloons, or other play gold coins.

Occasionally, I will run into a more enterprising teacher who will make paper money on their computer with *their* face on the bills. That is a pretty cool idea, and it has the advantage of not crossing paths with any token economies used in other classrooms, as the currency is clearly specific to this particular teacher.

As I think about those situations, I tend to suggest tweaking that program some, if the teacher has the knowledge, time, and motivation to do so. In my idea, you can still make the paper money on the computer, but rather than using *your* picture, put the picture of *each student* on the money. Obviously, you would have to have a reasonable number of students to pull this off (it's not for the high school teacher who sees 135 students per day), but there are a couple benefits to doing it this way. First, the kids will feel a sense of pride because they have money with their face on it. But on an even more practical level, this method will keep the nerds from getting rolled in the bathroom for their cash – nobody can spend it except them! The cash gets personalized not only to your particular room, but also to each specific student.

And while I'm on that subject, an advantage to *not* personalizing the tokens to each student is that they can now pool their resources to perhaps show a bit of altruism to their classmates. They can offer up a few bucks to help a friend pay a classroom fine, to get a privilege they had been working toward, or even to lend an empathetic donation to a mate who was not able to earn it. I have heard some stories from teachers who were privy to these types of selfless endeavors happening in their room.

The rule of thumb, as with any program, is to keep it interesting, enjoyable, and most of all, *doable* for you! No program will bear fruit if it gets uprooted from the word "Go."

3. *What do we use for rewards?*

There are a few schools of thought when it comes to determining the rewards available to the students in return for their good-behavior tokens. Perhaps the easiest method is to just sit down with the class and ask *them* what they would like to have as "menu" items for the Token economy. Of course, that does put the wolf in charge of the henhouse just a bit, but remember that you as the teacher are not always as tuned-in to what the kids these days like or do not like!

Plus, I should also mention that the prizes (or goals, rewards, etc.) do not need to be material goods. Another of the little secrets of teaching, that I am not certain anyone outside of the teaching profession understands, is the answer to the following question; "Who *pays* for all of that stuff in your classroom?" It is *you*!

Still, for those of you that who come from districts or school systems where the teachers are *not* paid well, think also in terms of time, rights or privilege. Computer time, free time, homework passes, extra credit on a quiz, lunch with the teacher (okay – this one may not be as alluring for high school students), leading the line to the lunchroom, and "cut" passes for lines to the water fountain can all be used. Once again, the limit is only to your imagination when it comes to non-tangible rewards in a token economy.

When consulting with the class to figure out the menu items, there is a good way to pare down the laundry list that the students are sure to generate. In this case, you can create your own list of twenty or so items, then pass out a "forced choice" format checklist and ask the students to check the top five or seven things on the list. You then basically proceed as if this exercise is an 'election,' and count the votes on all of the "ballots." Then, you will have the class agree on the front end to keep, say, the "Top 10" items in terms of number of votes earned.

A twist on this idea is to personalize the menu for each individual student and just have each kid write down five or seven things that he or she would like to work toward. Obviously, this system will begin to fall apart if you have a lot of students each day, but if you maintain roughly the same class for the entirety of a school day, then you may be able to keep up with your group.

Once the menu has been created, be sure to make it visible alongside your class rules. The more there is an external system available to the students, the less you have to be thinking on your feet, and the easier your job becomes!

4. *How do I know what to make everything cost?*

While this may seem somewhat easy to tackle on the front end, you would be surprised at how often I get asked this question. As teachers, we have a strong desire to not only be effective with our classroom management system, but we also want to be fair. Of course, "fair" does not mean everyone gets treated the same, it means that everyone gets what they need! Have you heard that one too many times yet? In any case, make certain there is some wiggle room when it comes to setting price points in a Token Economy.

The starting point will be to spitball some ideas with the class, but bear in mind that you must maintain ultimate veto power with the ideas that come out of such a gathering. Your best guess at the outset is probably the best starting point, but there are two reasons why flexibility has to be present:

First, as the game evolves, you will get a better feel for how much "earning power" the students have. If the menu items are either too cheap or too expensive, work with them to adjust accordingly. Once again, this is a life lesson for the kids – small things may be easier to afford, larger things take more staying power. Talk through the process so they get a good feel for financial management.

And second, we also evoke the governing law of Supply and Demand economics. Things that everybody piles onto may go up in price! On the flip side, if there are menu items that seem to be ignored by the class at large, then either drop the price or get rid of them entirely and replace them with rewards that are a higher priority for the students.

On a related note, I have heard some very creative ways to hammer home the idea of *economy* in the Token Economies. I have heard of teachers charging students for every privilege you can think of – from renting their desk (if they miss a payment, they sit on the floor until they can afford the desk back), to being able to write with a ball point pen (for younger students), to getting a drink or going to the bathroom. They will write "tickets" for infractions, and make the students pay a fine for bad behavior.

Those teachers may take the idea to an extreme, but do demonstrate the level to which you can roll with the system to maintain order within the classroom. Try setting up a financial committee who will hear grievances about the system and work toward setting prices to avoid gouging.

Incidentally, I have often heard a question about how to deal with students who excessively have to go to the restroom or get a drink. In these cases, I recommend adopting a *hardliner* economizer's philosophy. While you cannot deny reasonable restroom breaks to the students, you *can* have one of the menu items be "Extra Restroom Pass," or "Extra Water Fountain Pass," thereby effectively putting a price tag on the privilege to go to the restroom or get a drink outside of the usual ebb and flow (pardon the pun) of the regular class-wide breaks.

5. *Can this program be adapted for older students or situations where I may have six or seven classes of thirty kids each moving through my classroom every day?*

Absolutely! I'm sure you guessed my answer on that one already. If you teach in middle school or high school, you are not just dealing with a group of twenty-three students on any given day – you may have six or seven classes of twenty-three filtering though your room. And, keeping track of a cumulative program like Token Economy for 150 or 175 students can be quite cumbersome. Further, if you try to create charts, graphs, or systems hanging around the room to aid with keeping track of all this stuff, your room is going to end up looking cluttered.

In this case, I can make a suggestion to help wipe the slate clean after each class period, thereby eliminating the chore of maintaining a cumulative system. In this system, we throw out the notion of building toward longer term, bigger goals.

For this system, get yourself a few of those one-eighth sized pads of sticky notes. They are pretty small pads that are usually available in wildly obnoxious fluorescent colors. Their colorfulness actually works to your advantage, however, because they are very visible at a glance.

So, let's say you are teaching ninth grade Earth Science. If there are a couple students in the back who talk all the time during your class period, just keep right on with your lecture on the value of igneous rocks to the ecosystem of our planet, and while you are speaking, make your way unobtrusively around the room and smack a sticky note on the desk of those students who are actually paying attention.

As an aside, this also addresses two common questions I get asked, which are; a) "Doesn't a personalized Token Economy rip off those students who always do what they're supposed to do anyway?" This system will reward everyone who is doing what they are supposed to and b) "What do I do when I have a couple of students who are talking all the time?" You reinforce around them to ease them into compliance.

Anyway, you give a sticky with the proviso that everyone is to keep them on their desk until the end of class each day. You may want to rotate the color of sticky notes so the enterprising youngsters cannot tap into the free-trade possibilities and bring their own sticky notes to confuse the issue!

Now, the strength of such a system again rests in your ability to hustle back and smack a sticky onto the desk of the students who had been talking amongst themselves once they pipe down and start to pay attention. Give them traction with the game and change the rules to reflect their ability to earn reward.

Plus, rather than have the sticky notes be worth a trip to the treasure chest, you can make them worth bonus points on the next quiz. If the class is being extra good or if you are feeling extra charitable, you can say that if anyone earns, say, five in a class period, that student gets a homework pass for that or the next day.

Whatever the reward, remember two things ... first, make it something that will be a targeted priority for everyone in the room and second, the prizes are based on daily performance rather than an accumulation. Thus, when class is over, we cleanse the palate. Everyone grabs their sticky notes and deposits them either in your awaiting arms, or into a pre-determined garbage can. You don't want them to "accidentally" find their way onto the black market to assist the students in your classes later that day.

6. Can this system be used class-wide rather than for individual students?

I think I already addressed this question somewhat in number 5 above, but I will make an effort to include a bit about this in the next answer, too. No need to fill valuable space with redundancy.

7. I have student who get very angry because they always feel outperformed by classmates. Is there either a way to deal with this situation, or perhaps a

different method to dole out rewards for Token Economy?

This situation is actually one that occurs with relative frequency, and can get some of the better-behaved kids pestered when you are not around. What happens is the students who have a hard time maintaining a consistent income (if you know what I mean) grow weary and jealous of the students who seem to always be at the top of good-behavior points. So, they act out against the weepy chess club kid named "Mickey" who *always* wrecks the curve.

In this case, rather than play the game straight, we can adjust the rules to maintain hope for those who may struggle against the rest of the class. They will never have the purchase power to get some of the larger ticket items if they feel frustrated and hopeless in the system. Instead of linear pricing for the rewards, juggle the system to resemble a raffle.

What I mean is that we make the tokens resemble something other than money. They will be chances dropped into the hat to be pulled out for the rewards. This way, even if you only get a couple of tokens in any given grading period, you still have a shot to hit the reward. Obviously, the better behaved, the more chances you will enter into the raffle, but here is a secret from me to you that will help distribute the wealth; *You are completely in control of who wins each round!* Unless there is a student peering over your shoulder when you pull the winning ticket out each afternoon (or whatever the time-frame happens to be), you can "miraculously" pull the ticket of some of the more poorly behaved students once in awhile.

This will keep them engaged, and reduce the level of tension. Everybody wins sometimes. You keep the well-behaved kids on the line, but also set the hook for some of the more troublesome students. And, in keeping with the spirit of this system, the better behaved they become, the more their chances of winning. Just have them do the math! Plus, you can use this as a wonderful tie-in to the algebra you are trying to teach. That way, Mickey and all of his *Dungeons and Dragons* pals can rue the day they went up against you for the behavior prizes. I wonder if *he's* a doctor today!

A second idea is to randomly draw a couple of student's names at the beginning of the class period or the day. Then, seal the names in an envelope and attach the envelope to the blackboard for all to behold. Then, set up a class-wide system whereby points are awarded to the class as a whole for their behavior. At the end of the day or the class period, open the envelope and allow everyone to see who will be credited with the points or the prize for the day.

In this system, the students are motivated to maintain good behavior, because, presumably, they each have an identically equal chance of being selected the "Student of the Day" or the "Mystery Student" or whatever clever name you wish to assign to the program. Plus, as an added bonus feature, you can play a role in making necessary "adjustments" to the students who win each day. So, if somebody has been snubbed, even simply due to dumb luck or random chance, you can delight in discovering his or her name the next day as the special student.

8. Do I also take away tokens for poor behavior?

This question often inspires some spirited debate. So I will defer initially to my statement form earlier in the book, which is: If you are doing something that works, keep doing it!

We always recommend that teachers or parents, who begin a Token Economy, *not* take away tokens for bad behavior. In other words, once the student earns a token, it is his or hers to keep.

The reason for this recommendation lies in some of the roughest kids to manage in your room. With these students, you know that for every token they earn, they are probably going to lose many more. So many, in fact, that by the end of the second week, they actually owe you *money* because there are not enough tokens to possibly cover the markers they have with you. Bang – gone is hope for success, and motivation along with it.

With hope goes the game. These students, to repeat, are good at losing, and don't expect they can win in the first place. So, particularly with them, it is important to use the Token Economy as a system of Positive Reinforcement. This way, you drive home the point that once they earn a token, it is theirs to keep. From there, they can spend it, they can keep it, they can sell it on EBay – it really doesn't matter to you except to say that it is theirs.

Having said that, I do understand that there are situations that require some sort of consequence system to be in place. I will speak more to this end in Chapter 16 where we discuss dealing with the *really* poorly behaved students. But, we can also preliminarily offer an alternative for now. We can shift focus from a Token Economy, which works solely as a system of positive reinforcement, to a system called Response Cost.

9. *What is "Response Cost?"*

Response Cost is the system we use with Token Economy to address the need for a consequence system. In this program, we use the same exact rules for Token Economy, but we come from the opposite perspective.

In Token Economy, everybody starts out with *nothing*, and then earns for good behavior. In Response Cost, everyone starts out with *something*, and then loses for poor behavior. At the end of whatever period of time you designate, we reset the clock and get everyone back up to the magic number – except that now, any tokens left over become Token Economy tokens, in that they are now that student's to keep. We will not take those away.

Let's try to put this into perspective by using an example. Let's say you teach a self-contained class of twelve students. You determine that everyone is going to start the day with twenty tokens, and that you reset the clock twice per day... after lunch and at the end of the day when the students are preparing to go home. Or, if the end of the day tends to be chaotic, maybe you should save the reset until the following morning.

Whichever the case, you still arrange your menu, but you add a third page dealing with transgressions. And obviously, not every rule violation costs the same amount – some are worse than others. Similar to how we pay different fines if we get caught doing fifteen or twenty-five miles per hour over a speed limit.

You can say that, maybe, talking out in class is worth 1 token, missing homework assignments is worth three tokens, maybe slugging someone on the playground is worth ten tokens, and you're off to the races. You get the drift.

Recall the discussion earlier about how often you reset the clock. You may begin doing it twice a day. Or, if you have a room full of students who are going to burn through those tokens fast, you may want to reset every hour. Reach a point of equilibrium, and then begin to pull back.

You can combine both programs *if* you have students who will not over-burn their cache. In other words, you can have the number of tokens a student has in his possession be somewhat fluid – giving for good, taking for bad – but only if you do not encounter a scenario whereby a deficit occurs, and the students begin to lose hope. Success is imperative, especially for those who have learned that they will not succeed.

10. Closing words of wisdom

I've addressed two of the three most common points of feedback I typically field when I present this information live, but there is a more interesting philosophic discussion that occasionally arises. This question usually comes from the educators who tend to be somewhat pensive in their approach to most matters, and their concern merits a bit of space in a chapter like this one.

The point they bring up has to do with intrinsic versus extrinsic motivation. In simpler words; are we merely training our children to respond solely to rewards provided by the environment and not to "do the right thing" just because it is the right thing to do? Shouldn't the drive to perform an appropriate action come from within?

That is a great question, and one that I do not have a rock-solid retort to. Any behavior management plan you will encounter in seminars, staff developments, or in-service trainings tend to rely exclusively upon external rewards for good behavior. In fact, in our business, rewards typically are, by definition, elements provided by the environment.

To dig further into this aspect, even a reward which triggers a sense of pride, like compliments or appreciation, is necessarily provided by external sources (i.e., in this case, the teacher). Can we foster that intrinsic motivation in a system which centers on external rewards?

My answer to this question lies in the origin of intrinsic motivation in any of us. Are we born with it? Is there a class or a TV show which teaches this to us? Does it come as the surprise in a box of over-sweetened breakfast cereal?

Here is my point. Intrinsic motivation is never something inscribed directly into our DNA. It is planted and nurtured by the adults in our lives who teach us to become the wonderful human beings we are today. These adults accomplish this task not only by building our sense of worth and esteem, but also by emphasizing and shaping (i.e., *teaching*) the interpretations we make to ourselves when we either engage in a nice or naughty behavior.

Let me try again: intrinsic motivation can be taught alongside of any current behavior modification plan if the instructors do a couple things (which, frankly, you may already be doing anyway): first, use praise and compliments to reward effort and positive behavior. Upon doing this, you should also underline for the student the intrinsic message of pro-social behavior. For example, "That was really cool, Taylor. You not only helped Melissa, but you also made her grateful for the helping hand. That feels good."

In this example, you gave an external re-enforcer (praise), but also handed Taylor a way for her brain to interpret that behavior as striving for an external reward. You essentially highlighted two other aspects; first, you helped develop empathy by making an interpretation of Melissa's behavior and, second, you put a name to a potential intrinsic motivator. Incidentally you also sent a message to Taylor that she can gain your approval or attention by conducting herself in an equally intrinsic manner in the future.

That is the first thing you can do. The second has already been touched upon earlier in this book when I spoke of pushing the wall back as the students gain mastery of self-monitoring/self-management. In this case, you require longer periods of time of positive behavior before the reward is doled out. During these extended periods of self management and pro-social behavior, you can continue to hammer home the point that, despite not being reinforced on the outside for the actively good behavior, they are still maintaining because they are learning to do things out of respect for themselves and those around them.

Sure, you will still have students who will want to take umbrage with this point, as they argue the fact that it remains the pot of gold at the end of the rainbow they are aiming at. Even with these students however, I think it remains important to emphasize how they may be doing, but parallel to this process, they are still potentially learning the "right thing to do."

It's a tough question. With some of the students in our classes, we really are like their mom or dad. In fact, you may find yourself playing that role more than you wish.

If kids are not getting these lessons at home, certainly they will need to be introduced to them in a safe and nurturing environment… as opposed to the justice system or by their equally problematic buddies! I think it is absolutely vital for educators to not only teach the basics, but to also teach other ways of thinking or interpreting life.

I know a lot of folks who think differently, that teachers are there to only provide the three "R's" and nothing else. They argue that life's lessons are learned in the home and that other points of view should be discouraged instead of encouraged... stating that they only serve to confuse the kids and, thereby, creating dissonance and rebellion.

I understand that position – and will *always* urge parents to take active roles in teaching kids how to fish rather than just giving the fish to them.

Mental and emotional flexibility are underpinnings of success far more often than rigidity and unwillingness to adapt. Thus, I think it absolutely imperative that teachers reinforce exploration, questioning, and responsibility for one's actions. Intrinsic motivation... You bet! But along the way, students can take part in extrinsic delights like Tootsie Rolls®, stickers, extended recess, and bonus points on the mid-term.

Chapter 16

Tips for Dealing with Maximally Problematic Students

Helpful Hints to Consider

What do we do with the students who make sure that nothing else works?

I'll address this question, as this is the main issue that brings educators into my seminars in the first place. I'll divide this chapter into sections based upon the type of student you are dealing with. Bear in mind, however, a few things; a) these students are truly the oil tankers. Nothing will work immediately, and progress will be measured slowly, b) the ideas I am about to recommend are not intended to be "magic wand" cure-alls, but rather further matters of thought to aid in turning said tankers, and c) these ideas should be used in *conjunction* with a structured behavior management plan, not *instead* of.

As you know, the best behavioral plans are meant to provide a choice (through warning and mentoring systems), focus on the present and the future (don't dwell or hold a grudge), and instruct and guide the students (in providing alternate behaviors, talking through and debriefing). When all of this begins to falter because of deeper issues or neurochemical problems brought to the classroom, we move into some alternative programming.

As I argued in a previous Chapter, this will not give you what you are looking for. All of you have a specific scenario in mind and you would like to know *exactly* what to do in said scenario. I can only suggest general recommendations with the caveat that you adapt them to your classroom, to your unique personality, and to your specific group of students.

Before I get real specific, let me set forth a few general thoughts for dealing with these students. And let me also say that *whatever* you decide to do behaviorally will work most of the time with about 80% of our students. Most of the students we teach are pretty good kids. They will grow up, get good jobs, have good families of their own, and pay their taxes. Unfortunately, we tend to lose sight of that sometimes when we have difficult students, because it is about 5% of the kids who consume 90% of our energy!

1. Drop the authoritarian techniques

If any part of your being leans toward the "authoritarian" end of the scale (refer back to the Teaching Style Questionnaire), you are going to have to back it down a notch. Remember the hunting dog (or tug toy) kids – they will *not* respond well to the rigidity or structure you are going to be demanding of them. We discussed this in Chapter 12, but it is worth repeating because there is no better set-up for failure than allowing a defiant student the opportunity to keep his horns locked with you.

Once again, one of you is going to blink, and *you* are the grown-up, so you are better equipped emotionally to pull off the maneuver. Give some slack, offer a choice, and allow the student the opportunity to choose compliance rather than have it thrust upon him.

2. Remain emotionally neutral

This is another re-hash, but an important one. Remember to take energy out of the situation rather than add energy to it. Your getting "amped" up is going to serve as jet fuel to the escalating situation and may actually make it worse. Plus, you are essentially taking your "clarity of thought" and "goodness of judgment" out of the equation, as you cannot think as well when you are in a state of escalation.

3. *Recognize the function of the behavior*

This is starting to feel like a re-cap of the rest of the book, but it will serve well to set up the rest of this chapter.

Go back to the discussion about diplomacy, as you are in the best position to diffuse bad behavior if you understand what is behind it, pushing it and energizing it. The better you are able to recognize the need being met by the behavior or the message that is intended to be communicated by it, the better you will be in determining how to help that student achieve the need or message in a way that is more appropriate in the classroom.

Sure, s/he has to go home every night and will un-learn most of what you had been trying to teach – after all, the behavior patterns they are exhibiting are remarkably well-suited for the environment within which they evolved. Work in baby steps!

4. *Focus on positives embedded in negative behavior*

Here again, I implore you to find those cool aspects of "The Bad Kids." These will not only help you connect, but they will provide a more effective compliment than a generic "try to find something good to say." In trying to change the rules of how these kids identify themselves, do your best to not throw their good qualities down the same garbage disposal because they are "Just the Bad Kids."

Leadership was one quality I referred to earlier, but there are a number of strengths your "Bad Kids" may exhibit. For example, class clowns may have really fast processors in their brains – they can turn a phrase quick or they are good at manipulating language, or they can tie together different aspects of a situation to make it funny. Those are strengths if they are re-applied.

Kids who shout insults back and forth may be fantastic at conjugating swear words in ways you never thought possible. Well, okay... that may not in itself be a very flattering characteristic, but it does belie an underlying intelligence, right?

This point was brought home to me a couple of years ago in Nashville. It must have been a slow news day, but the 5 o'clock newscast had a live breaking story about two teens that were being taken to jail for spray-painting graffiti on an office building. The news cameras were there, of course, and eventually panned over to show the graffiti.

I remember sitting there in my easy chair, staring idly for a minute at the office building being shown on my 32-inch, garage-sale TV, and then thinking to myself, "Hey... *that's pretty good!*"

Those kids had some real talent. But, I wondered if anybody else had noticed and if there was a teacher who took an interest in these guys because, despite their being "Bad Kids" who defaced private property, they actually had some talent. They were remarkably creative and artistic. If this strength was pointed in a positive direction, it could genuinely pay off for them.

But alas, who will be the teacher to step up and foster this evolution rather than wash it all out with "The Bad Kids?"

5. Respond with care

I'll give you something to think about. If a student gets you to react with anger and resentment, he has effectively made you into every other significant adult in his life. How can change happen if these kids are allowed to re-create their own warped world over and over? Change the rules!

It's easier said than done. Tuck away in the back of your mind that doing the same thing over and over while expecting different results is the definition of insanity – *or childhood*. It is up to grown-ups to help our kids learn a different means of meeting their needs.

6. *Remember the "Golden Rule"*

If you become frustrated, you may inadvertently treat the offending student harshly. Seriously, you'll get no judgment from me – you guys have a tough job! But occasionally take a step back and think about if you are acting in a manner to which you would also like to be treated. Turning yourself into a proactive rather than a reactive teacher can help diffuse tension, both in the classroom, and in your mind!

We have covered some general tips; now let's traverse into the minefield of dealing with some specific types of utterly resistant students. In no particular order, here are *The Big Three:*

a) Students whose self-image is threatened

These are the students who have a reputation to maintain or who are trying to save face in front of their buddies. A few ideas to consider:

Set them up for success

However you are able to achieve the core concept in adjusting your teaching style to meet the needs (or learning styles) of your students, the better behaved they will become. Not saying they will be angelic by any stretch – but, once again, the best you can do to make school less of a disaster for them, the more likely they perform for you.

Plus, think about it this way; if you feel constantly attacked, you will circle the wagons and start to shoot back. In the classroom, the students who are not the best academicians may feel school is a constant barrage of information and demands that they will never be able to comprehend. Thus, they are faced with the option of looking bad in front of their buddies, or looking *"bad."*

The bottom line of this recommendation is to have teachers be sensitive to the learning styles employed by their students. The less the students feel plowed under by your teaching, the less likely they are to act out – or, to punish you.

Also, bear in mind the advice I gave early on in the book when dealing with some of the angry students in your room. That was, temper your approach. The more you come on strong and let them know how wonderfully they have been performing, the more pressure they will feel, and the harder they will work to undo the compliment. I'll say more on this when we hit the third type of tough student.

Reminisce about past achievements

With students who self-handicap (i.e., those who would rather not try at all so as to not look as if they gave their best effort and then failed) or students who generally cut their own legs out from underneath them in order to protect themselves from looking bad , you really have no leverage at the outset.

If a student decides that he or she is not going to do an assignment, can you *force* them to do it? Can you hit them with a blow-dart loaded with sodium pentothal to give them a post-comatose suggestion to do their work? Is Wonder Woman's magic lasso available for mass consumption?

Probably not … if a student stubbornly refuses to do something, they have absolute power. Frankly, if they want to get kicked out of the classroom, or kicked out of school, they will also do just that. In fact, getting kicked out of school is relatively easy – not too much effort required if you really put your mind to it.

For the students who are on that track, we have to make hay while the sun shines. Work at relationship building when they are present or are participating. For the students who self-handicap, the same principle applies.

If a student decides to not do a homework assignment, let us help him understand that this is a choice he is making rather than whatever his excuse happens to be. In most cases, the excuses vary from, "I don't know how" to "I can't."

If you reflect a moment to a time when you know he or she *did* perform the operation, then suddenly the task in question moves from *externally controlled* to *internally controlled*. Put another way, the task moves from being something they have no control over, to something that they are *electing* to avoid. If they *can't*, there is no reason to try. If they are making a *choice*, there is at least the *possibility* of a different outcome.

It has a very different spin than if they are powerless to change the outcome. The student may still choose not to do the assignment, problem, or test, but now it is not because they are unable.

Avoid using positive labels

I know I touched on this point earlier in Chapter 4 when I introduced the Oppositional Defiant student. I elaborated a bit then, so I will truncate this section.

Remember again, a teacher's natural tendency, at times, is to want to "make up for" or "balance out" a rough home life or upbringing. You may make an approach that is so far weighted to the positive that the student has no idea how to incorporate the concept into the paradigm of how he sees himself.

Let me state this again – his self image is probably pretty negative. Plus, you add to that the fact that he has a well-established reputation to maintain with his buddies, and you have yourself a student who will not be able to handle you coming over and telling him he can be president some day.

Add to that, when you use a remarkably positive label, you put pressure on him to perform to the standards of that label.

I have been preaching that we need to raise standards to let students know they are indeed capable of adjusting their game, but the more you make that overt, the less likely the angry students are going to want to participate.

A better approach would be to temper your positive labels, and remain more data-focused. For example, saying, "Dexter, you got an 88 on the last quiz. That was among the highest grades in the class," is a better alternative than stating it as, "Dexter, what a great job! You are one of the brightest kids in here this year!"

One lets him save face *and* feel pride at the same time. The latter requires him to wriggle out of the positive label so he doesn't have to explain himself to his friends or carry the weight of the positive label.

Prepare them for positive feedback and then make a quick retreat

Obviously, giving compliments and positive feedback are a vital part of building relationships and raising self-image. The problem is the angry students are not going to be able to tolerate the compliment – particularly if you hang in their emotional space afterwards!

For example, if you walk over to Antonio, and say to him, "Antonio, that was really cool what you did" and then you hang around and maintain eye contact with him, his anxiety is going to spike. Because now, he feels like you are requiring him to say something nice back to you and that creates an untenable situation – particularly if his buddies are nearby. Because now, they are all looking to him to see how he handles this and they sure don't want to be put into a similar bind.

So, Antonio will invariably do one of two things; 1) he will punish you for putting him into that situation in the first place or 2) he will work double-time to undo the compliment so that you *never* put him in that position again.

The only shot your compliment has to soak into Antonio is if he has to sit with it … he will *not* do that if you hang there with him. So, when you compliment or praise a student, my advice is to hit it and then keep on walking. He may shout something at your back as you move away, but what you are essentially doing is taking the battle away from him.

There may also be times when you make an emotional interpretation of something your student goes through. For example, you may see Juan embarrass Carlton, so Carlton slugs him. On the way to the principal's office, you can drop into the conversation, "Whew… that had to be embarrassing, brother. Sorry about that."

This interpretation is important for Carlton, because it will help him to open up other internal emotional possibilities. Carlton is good at being angry – he spends most of his life being angry. What he lacks is the awareness to help him interpret his experience any other way – you can help develop some further differentiation and identification of feelings in him, but he will (once again) fight you on it if you hang there with him.

To think of this pragmatically, think about how boys and men interact. There is not a lot of emotional "sharing" that goes on, right? Monosyllabic grunts maybe, but usually very little in the arena of emotional dissection. Similarly, when you make the interpretation, just hit it and move on. Let it soak in by not forcing it to soak in.

b) If there is open conflict between student and teacher

What follows is a brief section of things to keep in mind when you encounter a situation with a student whereby the two of you end up like a couple of mountain goats with your horns stuck together. In other words, occasionally there arises a relationship with a student that is founded solely on negative interactions – you two cannot escape each other's orbit, and it creates a negative synergy.

At face value, most teachers would read the preceding paragraph and chuckle to themselves. Essentially, that chuckle would indicate about 5% sympathy, 10% familiarity, and about 85% outrage. "I cannot believe the temerity of such teachers!" some of you are shouting at the open pages of your book. True, we cast aspersions on teachers who tend to give a bad name to the rest of us, but I want to at least remind you that most of these teachers began their career with the best of intentions. It was only over time that they eventually found themselves in this predicament.

And really, it is sort of human nature to keep searching for a bigger and bigger stick to hit the student with until we finally figure out how big stick it's going to take for him or her to actually listen to us. Unfortunately, you paint yourself into a corner, and there seems to be no way out for either of you!

Here are a few pointers to file in the back of your mind.

Recognize that the student has been hurt, does not trust, and is trying to prevent future hurt

This was discussed in chapter 4 under the general heading of Oppositional Defiant Disorder, but it is worth repeating here to keep your hope alive.

The simple truth of the genesis of the ODD child is extraordinarily difficult to focus on when you are locked in battle with the student. Still, recall that Positive Behavior Supports is founded not only on the positive reinforcement, but also the relationship you forge with the student. With the ODD students fighting you every step of the way, you fall into their trap of making sure that they don't have to like anybody – particularly you.

Changing the rules involves your understanding the wheels that are turning behind the eyes of the children you teach. Remember, that once you are in the locked-horn position with a student, he or she has got you. Now, they have put you into the same role as every other grown up in their life, plus they have you off balance and at the mercy of their manipulation of your emotions.

Avoid coercive statements and directions

Again, human nature has us acting and reacting differently when we are royally frustrated and angry. I know none of you wake up in the morning with a sinister plot to tear down the esteem of a student in your room, but those sorts of ideologies can eek into your interactions as you get more hopeless in your role as mentor.

This frustration leads to toxic interactions, and while it may make you feel some guilty pleasure if you are constantly struggling to get a toe-hold with this student, you will erode the relationship. Trust cannot build in an atmosphere poisoned by negative complicity – these students are skittish enough the way it is. As you grow more coercive, you are adding credence to the students' notion that relationships cannot build and that trust cannot be obtained.

This is particularly true if sarcasm is a part of your interactive style. I know this was covered previously as well, but I'll tell you this: if you use sarcasm as a regular part of your interactions with the students, you *will b*e drawn into using the sarcasm in negative ways when you get frustrated. Once again, as your stress and anger builds, back off the sarcasm or you will cross the line between tasteful jocularity and egregious coercion.

Finally, remember the tug toy and hunting dog students. These are the ones who will push back twice as hard when they bump up against a coercive statement or direction. The more you say, "Oh yes you will," they will be shouting back,

"Oh no I won't!" And then where will you both be? Relax, breathe, and re-approach in a manner that will allow for your message to penetrate.

Avoid toxic or overbearing penalties

Probably the most common question I used to receive when I began putting on seminars was some version of... "Dr. Steve... can you please give me a consequence I can lay on the students that will actually work?"

Behind that question is a story of frustration and of two mountain goats that started to actually tumble off the side of the cliff because they could not disengage from each other. Teachers will punish, then up the ante, and then ratchet the intensity up even more; all in an effort again to find a big stick that will work. In the end, you use up the biggest board in the shed, and they are still not compliant.

Unfortunately, a couple things begin to happen when you are stuck in the cycle of consequence-avoidance as a means of behavior management: first, the student in question now has control. He is not going to let you know if your consequences have any impact because either they really don't, or even if they do, his lack of emotional response frustrates you, and that is fun to him.

Remember too, that to some of the kids wearing "The Bad Kid" label are good at being punished. For some of these kids, your consequences really *do not matter*. Frankly, in this situation, nothing you can do to them is going to faze them one way or another, particularly those kids who come from a disastrous home life. Consequence at school pales in comparison to the world they have to survive when they go home at night.

Plus, there really are some kids who are saturated with punishment, and truly do not care what else you do to them. To illustrate this point, I am reminded of Judd Nelson in the movie *The Breakfast Club*. I believe in this film, Judd's character had Saturday detention until he was forty-one years old. Does he really care if you add another three Saturdays? No! He is maxed out with penalty, and really could care less if anything more gets heaped onto the pile.

For these students, hope is not only fading, but it has been obliterated. A lack of hope will always inspire bad behavior because consequence becomes irrelevant to the decision-making process. If you don't get hurt by blows to the head, are you really afraid to join in a fistfight?

In these situations, I can almost guarantee you that there is a notable absence of positive interactions between you and the other mountain goat. Those horns have been locked for far too long, and you two have not had enough distance between you to see the light of day. A breath and a step back are vital, but so will be a first step to building positive reinforcement – remember PBS?

I'll also say this; it is sometimes hard to help teachers change their mindset away from behavior management via consequence avoidance, and toward a mindset of behavior management via goal attainment.

In other words, kids will wear you out trying to find the "Ultimate Consequence" of compliance – a fair amount of you will no doubt follow. But, especially for kids who are accustomed to losing, good at being punished and starkly devoid of hope. Their academic lives are lived from a consequence-avoidance point of view. They have power in not caring.

Change the rules, and offer the gift of hope. It sounds a bit rah-rah and a little like empty rhetoric. It is difficult to wrangle with students day after day. You can fall into the trap of allowing the students to make you feel ultimately hopeless. And ultimate frustration leads to nowhere.

Use "Symptom Estrangement"

I'll add just a quick paragraph here to address hope one more time. Remember the analogy of "bad kid... or bad behavior" with the shirt and the ketchup stain? Same deal! If you feel hopeless (i.e., that this is a bad kid), then your approach will be more negative, more consequence based, and will feed the cycle of hopelessness.

As best you can, try to see these students as harboring bad behavior in an effort to keep hope alive. At the end of the frustration chain is burnout for *you*, and that is not a fun place for you to be.

Don't take it personally

This is another idiom you hear repeated as part of the rhetoric in every seminar on behavior management, and every book you pick up on the topic. This is one of the mantras we tell you to repeat to yourself like a mini-version of Alcoholic Anonymous' Serenity Prayer – leading to some cynicism on your part, because it is easier to make statements like these when we, as authors, are not stepping into the line of fire like you are every day in your classroom.

Remember that this "anger defiance attitude" is not about *you*. The student is reacting toward you in a venomous manner because you fill the stencil in his or her mind. You have stepped into the role of authority figure or grown-up and these are roles that have traditionally driven the kid nuts.

It is doubly hard to keep this point in mind; because these are the students who will work double-time to make it as personal as they possibly can. They are trying to push buttons and keep you emotionally off-balance.

Never give up on a student

This is more than just a little bit of a true rah-rah, but remember too that sometimes the change you effect in these students may not become apparent until years later. Sometimes these students will return to your room and tell you about an event from the eleventh grade when you did something they never forgot – something you could have never predicted would have an impact. Maybe it was even something you had no recollection of ever doing, because it wasn't intended to be profound! I guess I want to warn you to not underestimate the power you have in the lives of most of your students.

Think about some of the angry students who do have a rep to keep – they will never let you know if you get to them! That makes them too vulnerable, and they cannot tolerate this position. Plug away at the issues and change the rules. Be the change you wish to see in your students!

c) If there is fear of failure on the part of the student

These are the students who share features in common with those in *paragraph a)* previously discussed. They have probably grown into sharing space on your radar screen with those in *paragraph b)*. The facet that sets these students apart is the shame they are feeling due to a sense of inadequacy – perhaps due to an undiagnosed learning disability or some other problem with learning. For example; perhaps they were passed through earlier grades without clearing the academic hurdles necessary to provide a foundation for future learning, thus setting them up for continued failure and frustration. When this happens, the students create diversions, or smoke screens, to cover their tracks and not let others into their 'secret.'

Discreet note writing

Actually, I usually save this suggestion for the end of my live shows, as this can be one of the most powerful interventions you can initiate with a student who has a profound fear of failure. And, whether s/he is a behavior problem or not, they still harbor 'the secret.'

In this case, I recommend dropping a little note to the student. For example, let's say you have a fifth or sixth grade boy in your class, and he is struggling to read. Now, you are currently doing one of those exercises in your class whereby everyone reads a little bit out loud and then passes off to another classmate to carry the torch.

You, being an astute student of human behavior, notice that Connor is starting to crouch like a puma because something has got to give. He is going to perpetrate some reign of disruption upon the room so he does not have to feel stupid in front of the room.

When you see this tension begin to rise, stroll by and – as subtly as you can possibly muster – drop Connor a quick note that says something to the order of: *"Do you want some help?"* and then just keep on walking.

By the way, never write "Do you *need* help," as the word 'need' infers a very different spin in Connor's already-defensive mind. It will basically mean to Connor that you think he really is as 'stupid' as he already thinks he is.

Stick with allowing him the grace and dignity to dictate what happens next. After a minute or two, catch his eye, and if he gives you a look that seems to indicate the door may be open slightly to the idea, or if his eyes or face seems to cautiously say, "I don't know... what do you have" then pass by and drop him another note as surreptitiously as humanly possible. This note can say something like, *"Do you want it to be from me or one of your classmates?"*

Once again, the point is to doll out the rope. Put Connor in command of the pace and the direction that this exchange is about to sail in. If he decides not to pursue, don't push it; he has spoken for now. Still, the door is open in as non-threatening a way as possible under the circumstances.

On a deeper level, though, your note is extraordinarily important to Connor because it essentially says two things. First, it tells him that you get it – there is an elephant in the room, and his name is "you don't read so well." You are not going to ignore the elephant any longer, nor are you going to judge or ridicule Connor despite having this information.

Most importantly, though, your note says something that speaks to Connor exactly in his language. Your note also conveys that you will protect him from the rest of the class if he wants you to. Despite calling out the elephant, you are not going to embarrass Connor in front of his buddies or his girlfriend or the rest of the room. This secret is between exactly two people – you and he. Plus, if he wants some help, you can make sure to provide that free from shame or judgment.

Private notes can have a completely different spin to them as well. For example, you could also write one that says, *"Dear Nolan: It's lonely in here without your homework. Signed; Your Folder."*

A note like this one can take some of the punch out of what has probably been a series of tense exchanges between Nolan and every other teacher he has experienced. Leave him with the dignity of knowing that you are certainly not ignorant of what is going on with him, but that you also understand the circumstances that may exist in his life that distract him from being able to keep his eyes on the finish line. Take the punch out, and he will be more likely to discuss options with you than if you come straight at him from a consequence-based viewpoint.

There are probably some students in your room who are wound tighter than a Swiss watch, and will freak out if they miss a homework assignment. For them, taking the seriousness out of an occasional misstep can be a powerful intervention, as it also conveys to him or her that life will not come down to a specific assignment. Relax, and let your natural ability flow.

Finally, I am certain many of you also send good notes home to mom and dad. This can also be a powerful intervention, because parents who have had "The Bad Kid" for several years get tracked in when they deal with the school system. Even to the point that they immediately jump to the defensive if the phone rings, and the Caller ID reads, "School." They avoid answering all together. Either way, they start asking themselves what their child did now.

Before I continue, I want to let you know that I understand the parenting issue with sending good notes home regularly. In a nutshell, I know that the parents who are most likely to show up for parent/teacher conferences are the parents who want their kids to do well in the first place. They are the parents of the "Good Kids," those who *want* their children to read and write and behave.

Every once in awhile, you will have a situation whereby little Ethan is acting out and you have no idea what's going on with him; and then mom and dad walk in, and it's all suddenly abundantly clear.

But that is far more the exception than the rule. For the most part, if you have a "Bad Kid," you will probably have a difficult time maintaining contact with mom and/or dad. If you line up a hundred "Bad Kids" and give each of them a note to give to their mom or dad, maybe fifteen or twenty notes will actually find their way in front of a parent's eyes?

Still, that fifteen or twenty is an important group to help, because good notes going home can do a couple of positive advantages. First, it can begin to change the rules at home for these students. If a parent has had a "Bad Kid" for six or seven years, it is probably difficult for them to conceive of their child doing anything other than acting out and getting into trouble. Cracking the door in that parent's mind just a smidge to let some light in could help the student.

Secondly, it gives you a little credibility in the mind of the parent, because you are not immediately set up as the antagonist in the drama that the parent anticipates is certain to unfold between August and June. If you can show you will offer a balanced view of their child, you may diffuse some of the parent's defensiveness.

Scaffolding

Scaffolding implies that you get students started with help and support, or help them to break an assignment down into smaller, digestible bits, but you then allow them the opportunity to complete the task by themselves. In other words, you provide just enough support to ensure success, but you pull back to short of basically doing the task for them. Allowing a certain level of struggle or frustration can help the student to learn if the struggles and/or frustrations do not reach too high a level, and don't exceed the student's ability to manage or cope.

It's like teaching a youngster to tie her own shoes. If you keep tying her shoes for her, she'll never learn. Left completely to her own devices, she'll never learn it either, as shoe tying is a very complicated operation. A good parent will guide and support – while the whole time having the child go through the motions on her own. Teach her to fish, you feed her for life!

Be prepared to modify teaching style, or work requirements

In this case, I don't mean to hold teachers up and suggest the entire class be held hostage by the learning style of one or two students. Rather, modifications can be made on a person-by-person basis for those students who may have a learning style not reflected by traditional classroom techniques or may need to have the system focus on effort *baby steps* rather than huge strides toward the finish line.

An example would be if one of your students needs to use a MP3 recorder or a laptop computer to help with "getting" all of the information either from you or getting work back to you. Having a processing deficit or a problem with reading or writing may necessitate this step. It also works to help scaffold the student enough that he or she is able to keep up, and not feel snowed under by the pace set by the rest of the room.

Occasionally, a teacher will ask how to handle the classroom dynamic that may arise if one student is different in the way he or she is handled by you, or even if the rules are slightly different for one student.

When this happens – and remember, students have a very quantitative sense of justice – you will have to hit it head-on to avoid disgruntlement among the masses.

My first piece of advice is to take the emotional valence out of the circumstances. Model a sense of normalcy for the rest of the room. If the students get the sense that you are also feeling a little guilty or unsure about what is happening, they will smell blood in the water and begin to circle like piranhas. They need to be assured, at some level, that this is *normal*. So, state the situation (whatever it happens to be) with this particular student in as matter-of-fact a tone as you can. Say it just like you are ordering lunch – no emotional spin whatsoever. Yes, there are special rules for one of the students, but you are not put off at all by that.

Plus, you can point out that the class makes special accommodations for students who have specific needs all the time. Remind them of when Carly broke her leg, and she was allowed to pull up an extra desk to rest her cast upon. Or, remind them of when Joanna's grandpa died, and you let her make up the work in time after the funeral and a little respite to mourn. Fair does not mean everyone is treated the same – rather, it means that everyone gets what they need.

Whatever the circumstances, your job is to make sure the class helps out their classmates. This also works if the students may start to harass the one kid who may need a special accommodation. That type of behavior has to be nipped immediately to avoid fostering the shame already present in the heart of the struggling student.

A Town Hall Meeting is the perfect venue in which to inform everyone of the new set of rules and that they are not going to affect the way you continue to deal with your students.

Implement cooperative learning

Set students up for success by creating group projects. Include lower, middle, and higher academic students and let students help each other. Or create a project where students can contribute from a point of strength rather than weakness.

The bottom line for any plan with students who are hiding their struggles is to let them know that you will do your best to ensure better experiences. Ultimately, the student can decide not to do the work or not to learn. Relationship building is your only chance with them from here. The consequence of failure weighs much more heavily on them than any consequence you can conceive.

Show them that the academic experience does not have to lead to failure, even if you are just one life raft in a flood of bad experiences.

Epilogue

Well, here we are. I have followed the basic flight plan of Positive Behavior Supports, and have led you down paths related to the understanding and behavioral management of problematic students in the classroom. Hopefully, I have made a case for changing your perception of "Bad Kids" to Badly Behaved Kids." Somewhere along the way, I also tried to cover a little bit about stress management and leadership style to help you become the best you can be in the front of the room.

At times, teachers have wondered aloud why I go into such effort to help the seminar participants get a better grip on where the students are coming from. Often, these are the folks who want more nuts and bolts of strict behaviorism. My answer to that thought, and a good line to end this summation on, is this: Through knowledge, we build understanding; through understanding, we build relationships; through relationships, we change the world one child at a time.

Plus, if you don't understand *why* you are doing something, you will have difficulties making adjustments. You learn only one way and have nowhere to go if you begin to falter.

I want to thank you for reading this book and I hope you have found the content constructive and a "fun read." I will close by offering you an Email address where you can contact me if you have thoughts, comments, questions, additions, deletions, or "over-the-top" raves about the book.

Email: dr.steve.o@hotmail.com

Try to reserve my inbox for thoughtful comments only. I don't want to sift through the wreckage I may receive if you fall into one of the following categories:

Someone who hated the book

Someone who hated me

A St. Louis Cardinals fan

Anyone who has ever dated Heather Locklear

A person with no detectable sense of humor

Die hard Trekkies

Anyone who has ever attended an opera... and understood it

A parolee who has homicidal impulses toward good-looking authors

Cat people

Psychotic ex-girlfriends (you know who you are...)

Folks who don't love Bon Jovi

Acura NSX owners (lucky dogs...)

Anyone who has ever served Hummus to guests without issuing a strong warning first

Extremist whackos on EITHER side of an issue

Competitors who masquerade as interested fans

Bankers

The morally intrusive

Administrators at Marquette University

Anyone who has broken my nose (there are two of you out there...)

People who aren't home during trick-or-treat

*Critics who have never risked getting into the
ring themselves*

Whiners

People who pretend to like vegetarian hot dogs

Low talkers

Blow-hard know-it-alls

*Anyone who has heard of Tony Stewart, and won't cheer
against him*

Those who expect the world to be handed to them

*Weirdoes (scratch that – some of us are actually
pretty cool...)*

The guy who stole the stereo out of my car in 1987

The easily offended

Men who use the word "galoshes"

People who can't sing, but still love to Karaoke

Anyone who bowls worse than I do

Every girl who has ever broken my heart

*Those who've never felt the freedom or the ability to have an
original thought of their own...*

Merry teaching to all, and to all a good night! Be well,

Dr. Steve

References

Allen, J.S., Damasio, H., Grabowskia, T.J., Brussa, J. and Zhang, W. (2003). Sexual dimorphism and asymmetries in the gray–white composition of the human cerebrum, NeuroImage, 18: 880-894.

Allyon, T. & Azrin, N. (1968). The Token Economy. Appleton-Century-Crofts: New York, NY.

American Academy of Child & Adolescent Psychiatry Online (December, 1999).

72.http://www.aacap.org/cs/root/facts_for_families/children_with_o ppositional_defiant_disorder.

American Psychiatric Association. (2002). Diagnostic and Statistical Manual of Mental Disorders (4th ed., Text Revision). Washington, DC: Author.

Aristotle (2001). "The Nichomachian Ethics" Classics of Moral and Political Theory. Third edition. Ed. Michael L. Morgan. Hackett Publishing Company.

Barkley, R. (1997) Attention-Deficit Hyperactivity Disorder: A Handbook for Diagnosis and Treatment, Second Edition. Guilford Press: New York, NY.

Barrish, H.H., Saunders, M, & Wold, M.M. (1969). Good behavior game: Effects of individual contingencies for group consequences on disruptive behavior in a classroom. Journal of Applied Behavior Analysis, 2, 119-124.

Batsche, G. M., & Knoff, H. M. (1994). Bullies and their victims: Understanding a pervasive problem in the schools. School Psychology Review, 23 (2), 165-174.

Beck, A.T. (1979). Cognitive Therapy and the Emotional Disorders. Plume Publishers: New York, NY.

Benson, H. & Klipper, M.Z. (1976). The Relaxation Response. HarperTorch/ HarperCollins: New York, NY.

Brown, R., & Gerbarg, P. (2005). Sudarshan Kriya yogic breathing in the treatment of stress, anxiety, and depression: Part I — Neurophysiologic model. Journal of Alternative and Complimentary Medicine, 11 *(1)*, 189–201.

Burns, J. M. (1978). Leadership. Harper and Row Publishers Inc., New York, NY.

Cahill, L. (2005). His Brain, Her Brain. Scientific American, May, 2005.

CBS News (2007). The Plague of Sexual Misconduct In Schools. Reported October 20, 2007. Web link: http://www.cbsnews.com/stories/2007/10/20/national/main3388380.shtml

Cherry, E. C. (1953) Some experiments on the recognition of speech, with one and with two ears. Journal of Acoustical Society of America 25(5), 975—979.

Chess S, Thomas A, Birch HG, Hertzig M (1960). Implications of a longitudinal study of child development for child psychiatry. American Journal of Psychiatry, 117: 434–441

Cohen, S.; Kessler, R.C.; & Gordon, L.U. (1995). Strategies for measuring stress in studies of psychiatric and physical disorders. *In* Cohen, S.; Kessler, R.C.; & Gorden, L.U. (Eds). Measuring Stress. A Guide for Health and Social Scientists. Oxford: Oxford University Press.

Dekaban, A.S. and Sadowsky, D. (1978). Changes in brain weights during the span of human life: relation of brain weights to body heights and body weights. Annals of Neurology, 4: 345-356.

Descartes, R. (translated by John Cottingham; 1984) *Meditations on First Philosophy*, in The Philosophical Writings of Descartes Vol. II (Cottingham, Stoothoff, and Murdoch, Eds.). Cambridge University Press: London.

Disability Online (2004). Link at:
www.disability.vic.gov.au/dsonline/dsarticles.nsf/pages/Recepti
ve_language_disorder?OpenDocument

Dworkin, S. (1939). Conditioning Neuroses in dog and cat.
Psychosomatic Medicine, 1(3), pp 1-9.

Freud, Sigmund (1949). The Ego and the Id. The Hogarth Press Ltd.
London.

Gardner, H. (1983). Frames of Mind: The Theory of Multiple
Intelligences. Basic Books: New York, NY.

Geller, B. (2003) Neurochemistry of ADHD and its medications.
Journal Watch Psychiatry, April 9, 2003.

Greenberg, J. S. (1999). Comprehensive Stress Management (6th
ed.). Boston: McGraw-Hill.

Haley, J. (1993). Uncommon Therapy: The Psychiatric Techniques of
Milton H. Erickson, M.D. W.W. Norton & Company, New
York, NY.

Hargreaves, D. & Colley, A. (1986). The Psychology of Sex Roles.
Harper & Row, Publishers: London.

Herzog, D.B.; Greenwood, D.N.; Dorer, D.J.; Flores, A.T.; Ekeblad,
E.R.; Richards, A.; Blais, M.A. & Keller, M.B. (2000). Mortality
in eating disorders: A descriptive study. International Journal of
Eating Disorders 28 (1): 20-26.

Holland, J.G., Skinner, B.F. (1961). Analysis of Behavior. McGraw-
Hill.

House, R. J. (2004) Culture, Leadership, and Organizations: The
GLOBE Study of 62 Societies. SAGE Publications: Thousand
Oaks, CA.

Ingersoll, G.M. & Benson, K. (1996). What is your classroom
management profile? Teacher Talk 12(1).

Johnson, F.J. (2006). Proactive Discipline for Reactive Students: A
Guide for Practicing. Butler Books: Louisville, KY.

Johnson, F.J. (2006). Effective Classroom Behavior Management. Butler Books: Louisville, KY.

Kaplan, R. M., & Saccuzzo, D. P. (2005). Psychological testing: Principles, applications, and issues. Thomson Wadsworth, New York, NY.

Kindlon, D. & Thompson, M. (2000). Raising Cain: Protecting the Emotional Life of Boys. Ballantine Books: New York, NY.

Kolb. D. A. and Fry, R. (1975) Toward an applied theory of experiential learning. in C. Cooper (ed.) Theories of Group Process, London: John Wiley.

Kotler, Lisa A., Cohen, P. & Davies, M. (2001). Longitudinal Relationships Between Childhood, Adolescent, and Adult Eating Disorders. Journal of the American Academy of Child and Adolescent Psychiatry 40 (December): 1434-1440.

Lahey, B., & Loeber, R. (1994), Framework for a developmental model of oppositional defiant disorder and conduct disorder. In D.K. Routh (Ed.) Disruptive Behavior Disorders in Childhood (pp. 139-180). Plenum Press: New York, NY.

Maccoby. E.E, Jacklin. C.N, (1974) The Psychology of Sex Differences, Stanford: Stanford University Press: Palo Alto, CA.

Maslow, A.H. (1943). A Theory of Human Motivation. Psychological Review, 50: 370-96.

McFarland, K.L. (2000). Specific Classroom Management Strategies for the Middle/Secondary Education Classroom. ERIC Document #ED437340. Posted 1/12/2000.

McPartland J, Klin A (2006). Asperger's syndrome. Archives of Pediatrics & Adolescent Medicine, 17 (3): 771–88.

National Health Interview Survey, 2003. Available at http://www.cdc.gov/nchs/nhis.html.

National Institutes of Mental Health Fact sheet (2000). Child and Adolescent Bipolar Disorder: An Update from the National Institute of Mental Health. Full Text:

http://www.nimh.nih.gov/health/publications/child-and-adolescent-bipolar-disorder/summary.shtml.

Pavlov, I. P. (1927). Conditioned Reflexes: An Investigation of the Physiological Activityof the Cerebral Cortex. *Translated and Edited by G. V. Anrep.* Oxford University Press: London.

Peterson, G. B. (2004). A day of great illumination: B. F. Skinner's discovery of shaping. Journal of the Experimental Analysis of Behavior, 82: 317–328.

Premack, D. (1959). Toward empirical behavioral laws: I. Positive reinforcement. Psychological Review, 66, 219-233.

Redl, F. (1972). When We Deal with Children: Selected Writings. MacMillam Publishing Company: New York, NY.

Roth, T. & Roehrs, T. (2004). Insomnia: Epidemiology, characteristics, and consequences. Clinical Cornerstone 5 (3): 5-15.

Ruble, D. N. (1988). Sex role development. In M. H. Barnstein & M. E. Lamb (eds.) Developmental Psychology: An Advanced Textbook, 2nd ed. Erlbaum: Hillsdale, NJ.

Shaffer, D., Fisher, P., Dulcan, M. K., Davies, M., Piacentini, J., Schwab-Stone, M. E., Lahey, B. B., Bourdon, K., Jensen, P. S., Bird, H. R., Canino, G., & Regier, D. A. (1996). The NIMH Diagnostic Interview Schedule for Children Version 2.3 (DISC-2.3): Description, acceptability, prevalence rates, and performance in the MECA Study. Methods for the Epidemiology of Child and Adolescent Mental Disorders Study. Journal of the American Academy of Child and Adolescent Psychiatry, 35: 865–877.

Simmons, R. (2002) Odd Girl Out: The Hidden Culture of Aggression in Girls. Harcourt Press: New York, NY.

Simpson, Katherine (2001). The Role of Testosterone in Aggression. McGill Journal of Medicine, 6: 32-40.

Staats, A.W. (1970). Learning , Language and Cognition. Holt, Rinehart & Winston: London

Stein, M.A., & Weiss, R.E. (2003). Thyroid function tests and neurocognitive functioning in children referred for attention deficit/hyperactivity disorder. Psychoneuroendocrinology, 28(3): 304-316.

Stossel, J. (1998). "Boys & Girls Are Different: Men, Women, and the Sex Difference," ABC News Special, January 17, 1998, transcript from the Internet, The Electric Library.

The Miracle Worker (1962) at the Internet Movie Database

Thomas, A., & Chess, S. (1977). Temperament and Development. Brunner/ Mazel: New York, NY.

Thorndike, E. L. (1898). Animal intelligence: An experimental study of the associative processes in animals. *Psychological Review Mdddh Supplement*, 2 (no. 4), 1-109.

Treffert, D.A. & Christensen, D.D. (2005). Inside the Mind of a Savant. Scientific American, 293(6).

Viadero, Debra. (1998). AAUW Study Finds Girls Making Some Progress, But Gaps Remain. Education Week; October 14.

Viorst, J., & Cruz, R. (1987). Alexander and the Terrible, Horrible, No Good, Very Bad Day. Aladdin Paperbacks: New York, NY.

Walsh, B T; Roose, S P; Glassman, A H; Gladis, M & Sadik, C (1985), Bulimia and depression. Psychosomatic Medicine 47 (2): 123-131.

Wood, T., & McCarthy, C. (2002). Understanding and Preventing Teacher Burnout. ERIC Clearinghouse on Teaching and Teacher Education Washington DC, ED477726.

Yapko, D. (2003). Understanding Autism Spectrum Disorders: Frequently Asked Questions. Jessica Kingsley Publishers, New York, NY.

About Dr. Steve

As a psychologist in Private Practice, Dr. Steve has worked with children, teenagers, and their families since 1991. He truly enjoys the spontaneity, creativity, and honesty of this population. Through this work, he has developed an extensive practice helping teachers, schools and school districts; both to help manage individual clients and to conduct staff development and trainings.

Dr. Steve earned a B.S. and M.A. from The University of Wisconsin (Whitewater Campus), and culminated with a PhD in Counseling Psychology from The University of Oklahoma.

All of that after a somewhat auspicious start to his academic career, during which time he earned several infamous distinctions at St. James Elementary, Mukwonago High School, and a brief stint at Marquette University. He has tried his hand at Improvisational Comedy, has written a weekly column in Nashville's local newspaper, and has co-hosted a popular radio show. Currently, he is lamenting the death of his dream to play for the Chicago Cubs... but remains hopeful that Heather Locklear will someday call.

Dr. Steve currently lives in Tennessee with his wife, Heather (not Locklear... but close). He also has two children who, with any luck, will someday have nutty kids of their own.